DREAMS

OF A

BILLION

Also by the same authors

Sellotape Legacy: Delhi and the Commonwealth Games, 2010

By Boria Majumdar

Corridors of Uncertainty: World Cup 2007 & Beyond, 2007

Cooking On The Run: An Average Indian Man's Encounters With Food, 2012

Feluda @ 50, 2016

A History of Indian Sport Through 100 Artefacts, 2017

By Nalin Mehta

India on Television: How Satellite News Channels Changed the Way We Think and Act, 2008

Behind a Billion Screens: What Television Tells Us About Modern India, 2015

DREAMS

OF A

BILLION

INDIA AND THE OLYMPIC GAMES

BORIA MAJUMDAR

NALIN MEHTA

Harper
Sport

An Imprint of HarperCollins *Publishers*

First published in India in 2020 by Harper Sport
An imprint of HarperCollins *Publishers*
A-75, Sector 57, Noida, Uttar Pradesh 201301, India
www.harpercollins.co.in

2 4 6 8 10 9 7 5 3 1

Copyright © Boria Majumdar and Nalin Mehta 2020

P-ISBN: 978-93-5357-600-4
E-ISBN: 978-93-5357-601-1

Boria Majumdar and Nalin Mehta assert the moral right
to be identified as the authors of this work.

Typeset in 10.5/13 American Garamond at
Manipal Technology Limited, Manipal

Printed and bound at
Thomson Press (India) Ltd

FSC   MIX
Paper
FSC   FSC® C010615

This book is produced from independently certified FSC® paper to ensure
responsible forest management.

For my sister, Rochona, who battled cancer and is a real superstar to me
—Boria Majumdar

For my father, Rakesh Mehta, who remains a guiding lodestar in our lives
—Nalin Mehta

Contents

Introduction

'Her career is over,' whispered the stretcher-bearer. Just minutes before, India's star wrestler, Vinesh Phogat, had been leading in her Olympic quarter-final match against her Chinese opponent, Sun Yanan, in the 48 kilogram category. Now, she was screaming while being carried away from the ring on a stretcher.

It was around 11 am in Rio on 16 August 2016. Vinesh had started the match well, having won her pre-quarter-final earlier in the day fairly convincingly. Many had tipped her to break India's medal jinx at the 2016 Olympics and it was no surprise that the entire Indian media contingent was there to cheer for her. We had just found our voice when Sun attempted a leg takedown. It is a common wrestling move and none of us were concerned till two journalists sitting with us pointed out that something was wrong. '*Voh ro rahi hai*,' said a colleague. (She is crying.) Vinesh was in serious pain and the Indian coach rushed to comfort her. The referee had stopped the contest and within seconds a stretcher was brought in to carry her to the medical room. As we rushed down the courtside to find out what had happened, the words of the volunteer carrying her stretcher made us stop in our tracks. 'This can be career-ending,' he was telling the ringside organizer. 'Clearly, it is a dislocation and who knows if she can ever make a comeback,' we heard him say. When we saw Vinesh again, she was being carried away for urgent medical attention, still screaming in pain. Not only

1

had her Olympic medal dream come to an abrupt end, but it was also clear that her career had taken a merciless blow. For four years she had trained for Rio, and here she finally was – her Olympic dream crashing to ill fate.

That very evening, it was the relatively inexperienced Sakshi Malik who broke the medal jinx, becoming India's first female wrestler to win an Olympic medal. As all of us shifted our attention to documenting Sakshi's journey to stardom, Vinesh Phogat and her suffering slowly receded in importance in the day's news cycle. While Sakshi was feted and celebrated across India, Vinesh was left all alone struggling with an injury and an uncertain future. It was a stunning shift because Vinesh was supposed to be the star, whereas Sakshi was the underdog at best. Now the roles had been reversed. While Sakshi's Olympic bronze medal catapulted her smiling visage to billboards all over India and companies vied to piggyback on her extraordinary achievement on the Olympic stage, Vinesh faded from people's memories, left to undergo a painful rehabilitation and attempt a comeback.

For us, however, Vinesh and Sakshi were both of equal importance. They represented the two sides of India's Olympic story. While it was important to celebrate a champion, it was equally necessary to stand by the talented but injured Vinesh Phogat. She reminded us of Henry Rebello in 1948. Fancied to win a medal in the triple jump event, he had to pull out due to a torn hamstring. He passed away in 2013, never having competed again. Vinesh, however, is back in the national consciousness, having won a bronze medal at the World Wrestling Championships in Nur Sultan in September 2019. She is now a favourite to win a medal in Tokyo, and if she does, the story of her redemption will be complete. And of course, we will be there to document her exploits in July of 2020.

Frankly, it doesn't matter whether or not you follow sports. When the Olympics arrive every four years, they bring with them a familiar feeling of anxiety for most Indians. With a population of over a billion, where are the medals? Why does a country of our size not win enough? At one point or another, most of us have asked ourselves this. It is a question that bothers a lot of us and tugs at our heartstrings.

It is why those who may have never cared for badminton cheered for P.V. Sindhu each time she screamed on the court against Spain's Carolina Marin in Rio; or when the national anthem was played and the tricolour went up in Basel after she demolished Japan's Nozomi Okuhara to become the badminton world champion in 2019. It is why so many who would have never even thought about gymnastics before found their hearts in their mouths when Dipa Karmakar took off for her 'vault of death' – the Produnova – on 15 August 2016.; or why so many Indians started googling the previously unheard-of term 'repechage' – a wrestling rule which enabled Sushil Kumar in 2008 and Sakshi Malik in 2016 to make a comeback and win Olympics bronze medals despite their previous losses.

Besides the sheer beauty and the supreme physicality of the athletic contests, the Olympic Games are also a crucible of symbolic force. A stage where, as historian John J. MacAloon says, nations play out their 'hopes and terrors'. For India, the Olympics serve as a reality check every four years on where our athletes measure up globally. India has overcome its old shortcomings on several counts and become a rising global power. It currently dominates the world of cricket, both financially as well as on the pitch. It has left behind many older narratives of failure. Yet, we have remained an inexplicable minnow in the realm of global sports.

In its first eighty-four years of participating at the Olympics between 1920 and 2004, India won a total of fifteen medals. This is not counting the two medals won by Norman Pritchard at the Paris Games in 1900.[1] Gulu Ezekiel has persuasively argued for the inclusion of his medals in the Indian count, in which case the number would go up to seventeen. Eleven of these (almost two-thirds) came from hockey back when India was a hockey superpower. Our sporting legends have been built on heartbreak surrounding what-could-have-been scenarios: if only P.T. Usha had lunged her chest forward in 1984; if only Milka Singh was faster by a hundredth of a second in 1960.

From the 1990s onwards, India started seeing individual medal-winning strokes of brilliance, which served as partial face-savers while also helping the country overcome a dispiriting state of hand-wringing: the adrenaline-fueled, tricolour-waving Leander Paes in 1996, the underrated superstar weightlifter Karnam Malleswari in 2000 and Rajyavardhan Singh Rathore who came out of the Army's training programme to win a silver medal in Athens in 2004. Yet, their triumphs were blips of hope on a barren landscape, not a systemic shift.

India entered the second stage of its sporting evolution in 2008 – the year Abhinav Bindra shattered the narrative of grand failure with India's first (and so far its only) individual Olympic gold medal. Between Beijing

2008 and Rio 2016, Indian athletes won eleven Olympic medals (two-thirds of what the country's athletes had won in the last eight decades put together).

For China, Beijing 2008 was its coming-out party as a global superpower. For India, it symbolized the promise of a new sporting resurgence. The fact that India won three medals at the Beijing Games in its traditional disciplines – shooting, boxing and wrestling – suggested that a real sporting turnaround was beginning to look possible for the nation. Since then, the trajectory of Indian sports has been going upwards though progress has been uneven.

Initially, things seemed to be on track when India doubled its Beijing medal tally from three medals to six (two silver and four bronze medals) at the London Olympics in 2012. London was India's best-ever Olympics performance. We followed the travails of Team India in London: a team of eighty-three athletes, which made our single biggest Olympics contingent ever until that point. The sense of hope surrounding progress in Indian sport back then was palpable.

Then came the fall in Rio. More Indian athletes – 122 in all – went to Brazil than any other Olympics before it. The mood was optimistic. So much so that the Mission Olympic cell of the Sports Authority of India (SAI) submitted an official report ahead of the games predicting between twelve and nineteen medals. The SAI's detailed assessment report analyzed each of India's athletes in detail, benchmarking them with their global competition with progress charts and estimated predictions.

That rosy prediction was a measure of the optimism among those who ran Indian sports preceding Rio. Indian athletes came back with two medals, standing sixty-seventh on the overall medals tally. One of us followed the athletes in Brazil, documenting the heartbreaks, the drama and the occasional mood-lifters. With the shooters, archers and fancied wrestlers wilting in Brazil, Sindhu and Sakshi were left with the responsibility of salvaging the tricolour at the Games along with the Paralympians – Mariyappan Thangavelu (high jump gold), Devendra Jhajharia (gold in javelin), Deepa Malik (silver in shot put) and Varun Singh Bhati (bronze in high jump).

There is no question that Rio was a real disappointment; a serious setback just when we seemed to be at a turning point. It was also a reminder of the sheer uncertainty of sports. You can do all the training in the world, prepare for every eventuality and still trip at the last second. If there was a medal for preparation, Abhinav Bindra would have surely won it. That is why we watch sports after all – for its sheer drama and unpredictability.

Despite the setbacks, as we look ahead at the Tokyo Olympics in 2020, it is clear that several key building blocks are in place.

First, on the positive side of the ledger, the funding for sports in India has increased. In early 2016, India was spending about Rs 11.5 per Indian on sports (with about Rs 1,541 crore in the union sports budget). By 2019, this spending had increased to Rs 16.5 per Indian (with an overall sports budget of Rs 2,216.92 crore).[2]

What does this mean in real terms? The National Sports Development Fund (NSDF) was set up by the government in 1998–99 with just Rs 2 crore in its corpus. In the two decades since, it has raised over Rs 240 crore (with roughly 38 per cent coming in from private sources, 35 per cent from government-owned companies and the rest from the government itself). Overall, as the sports ministry reported to Parliament, funding for the training and participation of elite athletes in international events through support given to sporting federations went up almost fourfold between 2014–15 (Rs 130 crore) and 2019–20 (Rs 482.5 crore budget ceiling).[3]

For Tokyo 2020 in particular, the SAI announced in December 2018 that Rs 100 crore had been earmarked for the government's Target Olympic Podium Scheme (TOPS), which identifies elite athletes and supports their training. The TOPS itself was set up in September 2014 and became operational by mid-2015. Abhinav Bindra headed its selection committee through all of 2017 when 220 athletes were funded by the scheme. In 2016, the TOPS spent Rs 19.9 crore on athletes in seventeen sports. This spending increased to Rs 28.17 crore across nineteen sports in 2017–18. By September 2019, eighty-nine sportspeople, including several para-athletes, were being funded in twelve sports.

What do these numbers mean at the ground level? Let's take the example of badminton national coach Pullela Gopichand and his academy in Hyderabad. 'The total players in the academy', he told us, 'are not much actually. It's about 160 odd. But overall the number of players who are playing badminton in the country has grown drastically. The government has been supportive. For the SAI Gopichand National Academy, they gave about Rs 5 crores in funding from the NSDF, which was very good. Also for the Gopichand Academy, we have about fifty players supported by the government in terms of food and accommodation. So overall, food, accommodation plus tournament exposure for these fifty kids is a huge support from the government of India. In the last few years, whether it is elite players or the Academy, I definitely would say that the top players should be very thankful for the tremendous support we have got from government.'

Second, there is a lesson to draw from cricket, which grew as a business because of the money that television brought into the game. Cricket reigns supreme in India, but in the last few years, the country's market size for sports has also grown significantly. The industry's size expanded from $1.7 billion in 2013 to about $2.7 billion in 2018. This is important because sporting infrastructure requires money.

In 2018, the managing director of Star India at the time, Sanjay Gupta, told the Confederation of Indian Industry's (CII) Scorecard forum that the sports industry's size can expand to about $10 billion by 2023–24. 'Over the last few years, the kind of activity around the business of sports has been tremendous,' he pointed out. 'There are now over fifteen domestic leagues in the country – across kabaddi, football, wrestling, boxing, badminton – from just two, five years back.'

When television starts focusing on sports and creating stars, it has a knock-on effect in terms of aspiration. In the case of badminton, as Gopichand points out, the catchment area has increased: 'I think what used to be about thirty or forty players in numbers has actually gone up to around 2,000–2,500. So, the number of people playing the game seriously has increased drastically by maybe 100–200 per cent every year in the last few years, especially in the thirteen- to fifteen-year sub-junior categories. These are amazing numbers and the quality of players who are playing at a certain level has gone up as well. Earlier, ten years ago, there were maybe ten kids who could actually play a serious rally. That number has gone to a thousand now. So, I think, the overall standard of grassroots-level badminton has grown drastically.'

At the same time, serious negatives continue to haunt Indian sports. The first among these is the terrible politics that underpin many sporting federations. Take the case of gymnastics. Dipa Karmakar's exploits in Rio should have been the bedrock of a gymnastics renaissance. Yet, uncertainty has ruled the sport ever since the sports ministry derecognized the gymnastics federation because of factionalism in 2011.

This has meant that two federations continue to exist, one affiliated with the International Gymnastics Federation (FIG) and the other recognized by the Indian Olympic Association (IOA). In practice, this duality often means confusion.

In September 2019, as officials scrambled to decide on who was entitled to hold Team India trials, the gymnastics trial dates were changed at the last minute on the road to Tokyo, reportedly due to conflict over jurisdiction. Hence, when young Ruthuja Nataraj, a sixteen-year-old gymnast, flew in with her family from the US for trials initially announced for 2–3 September, they were suddenly told that the trials had been cancelled. A fresh date was eventually announced, but by then, as the Hindustan Times reported, young Rujutha had 'had enough of the experience' and returned to the US. 'It wasn't a good experience,' her father told the newspaper.

The issue of mismanagement spans several sporting bodies. For example, in September 2019, the sports ministry derecognized the Paralympic Committee of India for not following the government sports code. Four years earlier, in 2015, the Indian body had been suspended by the International Paralympic Committee for 'individual conflicts at the national level between different groups and persons.'

Secondly, though very few governments fund sports as India does and we currently have more government funding than ever before, in real terms, we are still falling short by a great deal considering how much is actually required. 'This is peanuts', said Sports and Youth Affairs Minister Kiren Rijiju in October 2019 on the subject of funding. With coaching costs going up to Rs 10–15 lakh per month for foreign coaches, the sports minister said he is a 'worried man' because the NSDF was 'drying up', as he appealed to corporates to come forward. Simply put, Indian sports have more money now but they need much 'deeper pockets.'

The third big problem is that of how government funding is spent. While funding has currently increased for those at the top of the heap or in select circles, it hasn't seeped through to the grassroots. 'On the Target Olympics Podium Scheme, I do not agree with it as a model,' said Pullela Gopichand, a member of the Olympic Task Force (created by Prime Minister Narendra Modi to chart out a blueprint for Indian sports), on the funding mechanism where leading athletes identified as Olympics medal prospects are financed by the government. 'The model was born out of people like Rajyavardhan Rathore, maybe also Abhinav Bindra. It was created to fund elite athletes by looking at a few examples. The people associated with it, especially now with Commander Raj Gopal, are fantastic. They are doing a fantastic job. But as a model, it is not a great sustainable model.'

Why does he think so? 'This is because they pick individual athletes and then fund them enormously, end-to-end. They don't invest in the system or look at it in the long term. So, it being part of a strategy which actually looks at all other pillars or all other structures is great. But individually, just to pick one player and support him or her and leave even the second and third out of the system, in the long run, is not a good model to follow.'

Gopi's critique is thoughtful and profound. 'The simple reason is that if you pick someone who is already good – say if you pick Mary Kom and don't fund number two and number three – then the difference between her and the rest will grow. It's the same case with wrestling or shooting.'

As Gopi puts it, an alternative way could be to pick up certain sports and fund them together. 'My view is that you have to pick five or six players in a sport and then fund them as a group so that you actually have bench strength and you invest in models which are sustainable. Our current approach is what helped Rajyavardhan win an Olympic medal in Athens because of the crore rupees provided by the Army as well as some money from the government, or the very individualist approach by Abhinav which won him a gold in 2008. These were fantastic, but I think to just go by those models alone is not enough. That is exactly where everybody has jumped on the bandwagon. Mittal Champions Trust started it off, then Olympics Gold Quest, then GoSports, then the TOPS scheme. I think everybody is looking at the same model: to pick individual athletes, fund them and claim credit for them.'

Gopi makes a fundamentally sound point. It is one we must ponder over if we are really to produce a deeper and more sustainable sporting culture and make a serious dent in Olympic sports.

DORABJI TATA AND THE NEW ORIGINS OF INDIA'S OLYMPIC ENCOUNTER

When the Mumbai industrialist Sir Dorabji Tata organized the first modern meet of Indian athletes with his eyes on the 1920 Antwerp Olympic Games, he found that despite running barefoot, the performers compared 'well with the times done in Europe or elsewhere.' Suitably impressed, Tata personally financed three of the best runners for Antwerp, a move that, in his own words, 'fired the ambition of the nationalist element in the city'.

Existing accounts of India's Olympic history trace back to 1920. It was at Antwerp, Belgium, that India first participated in the Olympic Games. For years now, this is what has been accepted as the start of the Olympic movement in India.

Interestingly, however, recently discovered documents at the Public Record Office in Kew Gardens, London trace India's Olympic story further back to 1912. This was almost a decade before India sent its first team to Antwerp. These documents, a couple of which have been reprinted for this book, demonstrate that a series of letters were exchanged between the British Olympic Association, the International Olympic Committee and the India Office discussing the prospects of Indian participation at the 1912 Stockholm Olympics.

Had such participation taken place, India would have become the first Asian country to embrace Olympism alongside Japan, which established a national Olympic Committee in 1911 before participating in the 1912 competition as the first Asian country to do so.

Furthermore, the exchange of letters did not abate after the 1912 Games. Rather, their frequency only increased as all sides were focused on the prospects of India's participation at the planned 1916 Olympic Games in Berlin. That these Games did not eventually take place because of the outbreak of the First World War is a different matter altogether.

Yet, as the trail of newly unearthed documents demonstrates, India would surely have sent a team to the 1916 Games had they not been cancelled. This is clear from India's request to have advance intimation about the dates of the 1916 Olympics to ensure that requisite funding to send a team was in place.

The standout feature of these letters is the debate on what the Indian team, at a time when India was still a British colony, would be called. Would the athletes participate under the India banner or would they represent Britain? If they represented British India, what would that mean for the Olympic Games in general? Chances are the success of the all-India cricket team's tour to Britain in 1911, a tour organized by the Maharaja of Patiala, the leading patron of Indian sports, acted as a catalyst for India's Olympic participation. This tour received widespread support among the sporting communities both in India as well as the UK, and is considered a turning point in the history of Indian sports.

Among the many dispatches discussing India's participation, it is evident that funding was a key issue. Who would fund the team and how many of the athletes were entitled to receiving support from the host city was a constant thread of discussion. That nothing came out of this effort doesn't jeopardize the significance of the exchange because an ideational foundation had already been laid.

It was on this base that the superstructure to send an Indian team to the 1920 Olympic Games was built. The discovery of these documents adds a new chapter to the story of India's Olympic encounter. It helps date the story back more than a century to 1911-1912.

THE TRICOLOUR AND THE AGE OF BINDRA

When K.D. Jadhav won India's first individual medal for wrestling at the Helsinki Olympics in 1952, the celebrations at home were extremely muted; they were restricted to the sports pages of newspapers. This was very different from the extensive media coverage in September 2019 for wrestlers like Bajrang Punia, Deepak Punia, Ravi Dahiya or Vinesh Phogat when they won silver and bronze medals at the World Wrestling Championships in Nur Sultan, Kazakhastan to qualify for the Tokyo Olympics.

India was a different country seven decades ago. To compound Jadhav's snub, the political class gave the victorious hockey team of 1952 a tumultuous welcome in ceremonies across the country. The medal-winning wrestler, on the other hand, had to make do with a localized cavalcade of a hundred bullock carts from his native village.

In 1952, hockey was a potent symbol of Indian nationalism. Jadhav, despite winning independent India's first individual Olympic medal, was left to ultimately die in poverty. He was forced to sell off his wife's jewellery to build a modest cottage and was honoured with a posthumous Arjuna Award only in 2001.

In sharp contrast, by Rio 2016, while India still made up the bottom of the Olympic medals table, when measured by GDP or by population percentage, it did quite well when it came to bonus payments for medallists.

As a writer for the *Wall Street Journal* pointed out soon after the Rio Games, the government's official reward of Rs 30 lakh ($42,000 approximately) for bronze medallist Sakshi Malik or Rs 50 lakh ($70,000 approximately) for silver medallist P.V. Sindhu or Rs 75 lakh ($106,000 approximately) for Mariyappan Thangavelu's gold was more than what most rich countries such as the US or France give as official rewards to their Olympic medallists.[4]

Sure, some countries like Singapore ($1 million) or Indonesia ($746,000) reward their medal winners with greater bonuses. Yet, the fact that India rewards its athletes more than many richer sporting superpowers is telling.

The rewards are higher in India *after* you have won, precisely because of the linkage of sports with the nationalist register. Just think of Prime Minister Narendra Modi's tweets calling Sindhu 'India's pride' or the instant photo-op of the two meeting on the very day she flew back to Delhi after winning the world badminton title in Basel in August 2019.

This welding of sports with patriotism changed gears after Abhinav Bindra finally found the Holy Grail in the 2008 Beijing Games. As the Indian tricolour was hoisted in Beijing, the poise and pride on the bespectacled shooter's visage spoke to a billion Indians, becoming a leitmotif of gung-ho chest-thumping in media commentaries and nationalist iconography.

The Beijing victory created an unprecedented national frenzy. In a country of a billion people and a competitive media industry looking for new heroes and new stories, the lone gold medal was a good enough justification to spark off celebrations worthy of topping the medals tally. Governmental coffers opened up for medal winners after 2008. In a nation starved of sporting glory, medal winners turned into nationalist heroes. The registers of iconicity had changed in the intervening years, with individual success becoming an important barometer of nationalist triumph.

The big difference in the age of Bindra (after Beijing) was that India's medal-winning athletes finally proved that it was possible to succeed in spite of the system. Here, at last, was India's answer to those that pointed to the success of the Jamaicans, Cubans or the Kenyans, for that matter. The BJP's late general secretary and former cabinet minister Pramod Mahajan once said only half-jokingly that the Indian IT and beauty industries rose to great heights only because the government did not realize their presence until they had already made a mark.

Abhinav Bindra and many of our medal-winning athletes followed a similar template, at least with respect to the national sporting superstructure. They could as easily have given up, blamed the system and have been content with Asian or Commonwealth Games medals. But they persevered. Their victories were born out of the pain of loss and an iron will to succeed. It indeed became possible to succeed without access to government-sponsored sporting facilities.

This is not to argue against creating efficient systems – that would be a terrible folly – but in sports there are moments when all it boils down to is self-belief.

In early 2018, when then-sports minister Rajyavardhan Rathore, himself an Olympic silver medallist, was asked a series of questions in Parliament about the reasons for India's poor performance at Rio 2016, he answered with a long list of reasons. The first was a 'lack of professionalism and factionalism/infight [sic] in the sports bodies and long term strategies by the National Sports Federations (NSF)'. This was followed by 'poor governance in sports by NSFs', 'absence of strong domestic competition structure', 'lack of strong talent identification and long term athlete development system', 'non-integration of sports with education at school, college and university level', 'inadequate support in terms of high performance coaches and other support staff, sports sciences and medicine etc.'

Have we fixed these problems? India's aspirations for the Olympics may have changed but has its sporting systems fundamentally changed? Have we really managed to create a new overarching sporting culture? We have got new enhancements and new energy for sure, but no one who follows Indian sports will answer in the affirmative to these questions.

In January 2017, for example, the government appointed an Olympic Task Force studded with former Olympians to create a road map for the Olympic Games in 2020, 2024 and 2028. Among the task force's recommendations was the creation of an empowered steering committee to drive all decision-making on Indian sports, the appointment of an internationally acclaimed high-performance director like Rod Karr, UK Sport Chair, or sports leader Stephen Norris and the removal of salary caps on Indian coaches.

Four months after the task force submitted its report in December 2018, the ministry of sports even approved the creation of such an empowered steering committee. Yet, by September 2019, this committee was still not in existence. The ministry's Mission Olympic cell, controlled by the SAI, continued to supervise the TOPS scheme for elite athletes. A high-performance director had still not been appointed and salary caps for Indian coaches had not been removed. Despite the best intentions, when it comes to sports, no one wants to give up control.

India's successes in Beijing and London along with the face-savers in Rio were certainly catalysts that helped correct years of frustration at India's poor sporting performances. As our athletes prepare for Tokyo 2020, parts of the underlying system, like the ballast from Hyderabad in badminton or the new juniors structure put in place for shooting after Rio, have significantly improved. Yet, the fundamental DNA of the overall structure remains the same.

What has changed is the skyrocketing expectations from this structure; the system itself remains imperfect. It has many flaws and can be significantly augmented. But it is also true that Indian sport has, in the past decade, strengthened its base. With the creation of supporting ancillary groups like Olympics Gold Quest, Gagan Narang Sports Promotion Foundation or GoSports Foundation, we now have a base that is better than it has ever been before.

What of the future? Many in India look longingly across the border at China's awe-inspiring sporting machine. The Chinese too built their success by initially focusing on key sports — gymnastics, table tennis, badminton and athletics. India, however, cannot hope to replicate the Chinese model blindly. The organization of Indian sports is far too complicated and far too political to allow a unilinear approach like the Chinese or the East Europeans before them.

Like Indian democracy, Indian sports too have evolved their unique model, distinct from everyone else. When Kapil Dev's unfancied team won the Cricket World Cup in 1983, no one could have predicted that the surprise victory, coinciding with the television revolution, would ignite deeper processes that would ultimately turn India into the spiritual and financial heart of the game. Tokyo 2020 offers opportunities that if harnessed well could very well usher in a new era in Indian sports.

What explains the change? Let us be clear: this is not necessarily about some newly found love or understanding of sports. There is a marked disconnect between the hype about a resurgent India that the badminton players or the wrestlers or the boxers going to Tokyo supposedly represent and the reality.

We all like appropriating champions once they become champions. If only we focused on them when they really need our support; before they become stars.

The first part of this book is the inside story of how some of our sporting stars became national icons. When we first attempted a history of India's

Olympics encounters in 2008, we were documenting the story by looking at the archives as historians. To be candid, we did not have an adequate understanding of the backstage. Our lack of access meant the story was incomplete. Over the last twelve years, our access to the backstage of Indian sports has placed us at ringside. We have seen the story unfold in front of us, firsthand. We have seen the suffering, the pain, the agony and finally, the ecstasy of our athletes. In the past decade, we have had the privilege of studying the innards of Indian sports as closely as is perhaps possible. On- and off-the-record conversations with athletes and administrators have helped us understand the backstory. These have contributed to making this book the first real on- and off-the-field account of Indian Olympic sports. In the next few hundred pages, we have tried our best to bring out some of the magic of these untold stories.

They are hair-raising tales of triumph and indomitable will fighting against the odds. We thought we were hard-bitten journalists who had seen it all. Yet, we were totally smitten by many of these sometimes-unbelievable tales of raw courage and unbending grit. Some of them – such as how Gopi built his champions factory in Hyderabad or how Deepa Malik bought microwaves for her two little kids when she was told she only had seven days left to walk or how Devendra Jhajharia cut firewood with an axe for days on end because he didn't have muscle-strengthening equipment – brought tears to our eyes. These are uniquely Indian stories and all we hope is that they strike a chord with you too.

In the second part of this book, we have documented the early story of Indian Olympic sports to tell you where we came from, the paths we have travelled as a sporting nation and the many possibilities that now lie ahead of us. Combining the nostalgia of the past with the excitement of the present, ours is perhaps the most comprehensive account of Indian sports.

This book is not just the story of Indian sports – it is the story of us as a nation; of our dreams and aspirations and how they play out for the few who represent a billion. It is the story of India and its journey told through the prism of sports.

We hope you enjoy it as much as we did writing it.

THE RINGSIDE

1

Three Wonder Women and the Yearnings of a Billion

Ringside at Rio with Sindhu, Dipa and Sakshi

The Olympics don't come every four years, they come every day

—Abhinav Bindra

On 15 August 2016, Independence Day, at 2 pm Rio time, every Indian journalist had the same question on their minds and lips: Where is an Olympic medal going to come from? Abhinav Bindra, still the only Indian to win gold in an individual Olympics event, had fallen, literally, a fraction short. Sania Mirza and Rohan Bopanna won the first set in the mixed doubles semi-final against Venus Williams and Rajeev Ram only to lose to Williams as she raised her game ten notches in the deciding set. They then dropped the bronze medal playoff to a handy Czech team. The shooters and, as usual, the archers flattered to deceive.

Three young girls, all between the ages of twenty-one and twenty-three at the time, salvaged India's 2016 Olympic campaign. Each of them also happened to be partial to a scoop (or two, or three) of ice cream. After their displays of grit, courage under pressure and, above all, explosive power, P.V. Sindhu, Sakshi Malik and Dipa Karmakar deserved to eat as much ice cream as they wanted (for a few days, at any rate), before they resumed their spartan regimens necessary to succeed as world-class athletes.

Karmakar turned twenty-three at the Olympics on 9 August. The very next day she became the first female gymnast from India to qualify for the final of the vault event with a score of 14.833. We bought her a cake to celebrate, but still in the throes of competition, she allowed herself only a microscopic piece. This is a small example of the sacrifice required. Denying yourself cake is an apt image; a metaphor for what an athlete goes through eschewing temporary comforts to achieve glory, both personal and national.

It was quite funny. The idea was to get Dipa and Vishweshwar Nandi, her coach and mentor, together to celebrate her birthday right outside the Olympic Village. Nandi, reluctantly perhaps, had agreed. What we hadn't anticipated was the struggle to find a cake shop around the Village. It was practically in the middle of nowhere. The closest thing we could find inside was dessert at McDonald's. In the end, a cake was arranged from the western Rio suburb of Barra. But we had forgotten the candles!

It was eventually left to Nandi to go back to his room in the Village to get candles before we cut the cake with Zeeshan Ali, the former Davis Cup star, who was joining us for a bite. As we were singing 'Happy Birthday Dipa' in the most uncoordinated manner, a lot of athletes who were walking past joined in to wish Karmakar a very happy twenty-third birthday. In a sense, this is what the Olympic Games are all about. While it is and will forever remain the highest benchmark for sporting excellence, it is also a melting pot of cultures from around the world and a celebration of sports like no other. It is the only space where a Roger Federer would stand in the same queue as a Dipa Karmakar in the food hall or a Rafael Nadal would wish a Sakshi Malik happy birthday. With 10,500 athletes and 30,000 media outlets covering the games, a number that is certain to grow by Tokyo 2020, the Olympics are a sporting spectacle like no other.

It is only natural that Olympic medals have become a marker for a certain kind of Indianness; a marker of global success, of prestige. It's a short-sighted and crude attitude. Athletes are essentially ignored and left to fend for themselves in their years of preparation until an opportunity presents itself for politicians, celebrities and the media to bask in second-hand glory every four years. If only jumping on the bandwagon was an Olympic sport!

The onus is still on individuals to succeed despite the system, rather than the system providing adequate structural support. This is precisely why Abhinav Bindra has the following words embossed on the walls of his state-of-the-art fitness centre in Chandigarh: 'The Olympics don't come every four years, they come everyday.'

P.V. Sindhu, badminton silver medallist at Rio and the first Indian to win a gold in the badminton World Championships, who has thrilled the country with her athletic jumping smashes and her vigorous attacking style, has had a relatively conventional rise to sporting superstardom. Growing up in an athletes' family, her story is one that people from more successful Olympic countries will recognize. She has athletic genes. Her parents, P.V. Ramana and P. Vijaya, are both former volleyball players. She began training at an early age, at an academy with first-rate facilities and expert coaching. Her coach, the legendary Pullela Gopichand, is himself an All England champion. A winner at the highest levels of the game, he is widely acknowledged as a master coach. In his hands, Indian badminton is clearly in good health. On the other hand, Sakshi Malik and Dipa Karmakar are pioneers. Sakshi became the first Indian woman to win an Olympic wrestling medal at Rio 2016 and Dipa the first Indian woman gymnast to qualify for the Olympics.

There were other prominent Indian women athletes at Rio as well such as Vinesh Phogat, who was also fancied to bring home a wrestling medal, but Karmakar was an outlier. And not just in India. She is among a handful of female vaulters in the entire world with the ability and sheer guts to attempt and land the so-called Produnova. This vault, named after Russian gymnast Yelena Produnova, the first person to successfully land it in 1999, is a move of great difficulty and is performed at such speed that severe injury is likelier than success, even for accomplished gymnasts. Nicknamed the 'vault of death', the Produnova involves a handspring off the vault and a double front-somersault in a tucked position before the feet touch the mat. Only five gymnasts have ever managed to land this vault. Karmakar is one of them.

Karmakar's audacious leap brought her within a whisker of a medal. Her fourth-place finish in the final with a score of 15.066 has forever inscribed her name on the pages of Olympic history. Still, Karmakar refused to be wowed even as she made the country swoon. 'Medal, medal *hota hai*', she said on the evening of her fourth-place finish at the Olympic Village, '*aur* fourth, fourth. *Hum jab* room *waapas gaye aur dekha ki* 0.15 *ka farak hai*, sir *aur main khoob roye.* Medal *ke bahut paas thi main.'* (A medal is a medal, and fourth place is fourth place. When we returned to our rooms and saw that there was only a 0.15 point difference between third and fourth place, both my coach and I cried a lot. I was very close to winning a medal.)

She would tear up while talking about it: 'Tokyo *mein main* medal *zaroor laoongi.* It is a promise.' (At the Tokyo Olympics, I will definitely win a medal.) Her Tokyo dreams have since been laid low with an injury. The greater tragedy is that despite the possibilities of Dipa's promise, Indian gymnastics remains stuck in a haze of uncertainty due to internal factionalism.

For all of Karmakar's bounce and the pep she put in our step, India's medal tally remained stagnant until Sakshi Malik took to the mat on 18 August 2016. Having lost to a finalist (a contender for gold or silver), Malik had a second chance through wrestling's repechage rule. It was an opportunity she would not squander, overcoming a 5–0 deficit with seconds left on the clock. All the pressure was on her after the highly touted Phogat was injured during her bout. *'Jab* Vinesh *ko lag gaya'*, Malik said, *'mujhe bahut bura laga. Voh* medal *zaroor jeetti. Aur mere pe bahut* pressure *aa gaya tha. Par main haar nahi maani. Main ladti rahi aur ant ke dus* seconds *mein maine* fight *poora badal diya. Voh dus* seconds *mere life ka sabse keemti dus* seconds *tha.'* (When Vinesh got injured, I felt very bad for her. She would've surely won a medal. And then there was a lot of pressure on me. But I didn't give up. I kept fighting, and in the last ten seconds, I changed the bout completely. Those ten seconds were the most valuable ten seconds of my life.)

It was the culmination, as Olympic medals are for so many athletes, of a childhood dream. Malik took to wrestling because she wanted an opportunity to travel the world. Sports at the highest level meant that *'sarkar mujhe* plane *mein chadhne ke liye* help *karegi, main desh–videsh ja paoongi'.* (The government would help me get on an airplane, and I would be able to travel the world.) With reporters from Mexico and the worldwide Olympic Broadcasting Service waiting to interview her, it was confirmation, if any were needed, that Rio was a long way from Rohtak, Haryana.

Malik was born in 1992, a few weeks after the Barcelona Olympics. 'Lakshmi finally came to our poor home that day,' said her mother, Sudha, forty-eight years old. While she was still in the maternity ward, Sudha said she received the appointment letter for her first job as an Anganwadi worker. Sukhbir Malik, Sakshi's father, was a bus conductor and was finding it hard to support his growing family with meagre earnings. Occasionally, those earnings were supplemented by produce from the family's landholding in Mokhra, their home village in the Rohtak district.

Badlu Ram, Malik's paternal grandfather, was something of a legend in Mokhra. His fame as 'Badlu Pehalwan' spread across Haryana and through parts of western Uttar Pradesh. Among Malik's earliest memories, she says, is the awe and respect her grandfather was greeted with when they would be out and about in Mokhra.

It left so much of an impression on twelve-year-old Malik that she would nag her mother to take her to wrestling classes. She went to the Chotu Ram Stadium in Rohtak where she was taken under the wing of wrestling coach Ishwar Dahiya. Malik would rise before dawn to make her 5.30 am training session, while Sudha would make sure her daughter had a glass of fresh almond milk waiting for her at the end of practice.

Brutally early training sessions in the morning are a consistent theme in the stories of all three athletes, perhaps the most with Sindhu, who would start her day at 4.30 am in the lead up to Rio. Her father, a tall, broad-shouldered former national volleyball player, used to drive her forty kilometres from their home in Secunderabad to Gopichand's academy – which Sindhu joined when she was only seven years old – every morning and back until she began to stay at the academy hostel. Now, they have a house nearby; a result of her earnings after Rio.

Hyderabad was a hotbed of competitive players, with Saina Nehwal being the standout star. But even in that company, it was clear to Gopichand that Sindhu was a champion in the making. In 2010, when Sindhu was just fifteen, Gopichand told *India Today* that she was one to watch. 'A lithe and lanky person', he said, 'is sure to go places in badminton.' A defeat in the Olympics final to the world number one, Carolina Marin, in a tense, draining match appears only to have whetted Sindhu's appetite. 'I want gold next time,' she said after the match.

Gopichand, who knows better than most how difficult winning can be and how much luck you need along the way, is more circumspect. But he is certain about Sindhu's potential. 'The world', he asserts, 'still hasn't seen the best of Sindhu. When she fully becomes what I see glimpses of in her right now, she will be head and shoulders above the rest.'

By the time the duo reached Rio, Sindhu was in top physical shape. But this was the Olympics – the biggest sports spectacle of all – and it was not simply about being in good physical condition. Dealing with pressure, nervousness and being in control of the mind were the key ingredients to success. Sindhu, understandably, was nervous. This was her first Olympics and in her final must-win group match she started poorly against Michelle Li of Canada, losing the first game. Years of hard work was now riding on the second game and Gopi, sitting in her corner, kept trying to free her mind. She did play a good second game, but at the start of the third was down 1–4. Her Olympic dream was in the balance and Gopi was staring at barrenness once again. Victory had previously eluded him in 2000 when he was in the prime of his career. 'I was perhaps the only Indian who went to Malleswari's room the next morning after she won the medal in Sydney. I wanted to own an Olympic medal and this was my way of doing it. It was essential to who I was,' mentioned Gopi.

Down in the third game, Sindhu had to dig deep. For months she had been told to play one particular shot and for months she had refused to oblige. It worked during practice but she just wasn't able to get it going in her matches. For some reason, it didn't happen. But all of a sudden, in what was 'the moment it all changed' in Sindhu's own words, the backhand cross-court defensive block came out. Balance, poise, positioning – it was a perfect stroke; as perfect as one could hit it. Even Gopi was surprised. Something had indeed shifted and Michelle Li was soon shown the door 21–17 in the third game. For Gopi and Sindhu, the quest for a medal was underway.

'That's the stroke we had kept practising for months ahead of the Olympics. It was the one weakness I was determined to overcome and pushed Sindhu to play it for hours and hours. It would take opponents by surprise and if they did not attack knowing she would play the defensive block, I was confident Sindhu would be in control. If you watch the semi-final in Rio, Okuhara tried it and bang! Sindhu played the stroke for a winner. Not once more did Okuhara attack her backhand and Sindhu dominated the match. That's what we had trained for,' Gopi said with a smile of contentment.

Ahead of Sindhu's semi-final, Gopi hardly slept. Rather, he paced the room and kept thinking. In his words: 'I couldn't let the medal slip away.'

'When I got up in the morning, Gopi sir was all ready to go out and train. He had showered and was waiting. I had this feeling he hadn't slept. While he never said that to me, I could sense he was not his usual self,' recollected Sindhu while smiling at Gopi, who by then was starting to look a little sheepish. 'And when I won the semi-final, I turned to Gopi sir and saw tears rolling down his cheeks. While I was delighted at making the final, to see Gopi sir cry made me understand the enormity of the achievement.'

And for Gopi, this was his moment of reckoning. Sydney, or rather the pain of Sydney was finally behind him. India had an Olympic finalist for the first time and Gopi had finally achieved his dream. 'Yes, the job wasn't done yet. But at one level for me, it was done. Maybe I was wrong because I did feel satisfied. Maybe if I hadn't, we could have planned the final differently. God willing that will also happen,' said Gopi.

'The tears were genuine. Sindhu could now leave the sport a decade later with an Olympic silver medal. It was hers forever and there was nothing left to chance anymore. All those months of effort had paid off and I was seriously happy,' he said.

The duo did all sorts of things in Rio. Using towels, they constructed a net in their room in the Olympic Village for practice. They practised in the morning and again late at night. They had simply given it their all. They had left nothing to chance – while still in Hyderabad, Gopi had taken away Sindhu's phone and banned her from eating ice cream and biryani.

Gopi was the guru, Sindhu his protégé and the Olympic medal their moksha.

Only once it was all over and she had ended her startling debut campaign with a silver medal did Sindhu did turn into the twenty-one-year-old youngster that she was. She had chocolates and ice cream at McDonald's in the Olympic Village, and the manner in which she spent her night unwinding forced Gopi, a reticent and calm person, to burst out laughing.

'When we went back to the room at night, I was surprised to see Wang Yihan waiting for us. Here was a former Olympic and world champion who had lost a close quarter-final to Sindhu, waiting for her to celebrate her medal. She was genuinely happy for her and they started running around the room like kids. At 10 pm or so I said, "Good night, girls," and went off to sleep. And when I woke up at 5.30 am the following morning and was going in for a shower, I was extremely surprised to see Wang Yihan sneaking out of Sindhu's room. It was as if she had been caught doing something wrong because she just ran away after giving me an awkward smile. I just couldn't believe what I was seeing and couldn't stop laughing. Here was a Chinese girl who did not understand English, and yet, it was no barrier. They could connect most easily and this will always be one of Sindhu's most endearing qualities, in my eyes,' concluded Gopi.

Sindhu was visibly embarrassed with Gopi telling this story. And yes, thrilled as well. It was a night like no other and she had done things her way to immortalise it – lived and celebrated it to the fullest; enjoyed dollops of ice cream and Chinese companionship, notwithstanding the language barrier.

It was indeed a memorable campaign. A journey that made P.V. Sindhu a household star in India and elevated her to cult status as a symbol of women's empowerment and an aspirational story of fulfilment. Sindhu, to her credit, has added to the legend. A World Championship silver in Glasgow in 2017 after playing a marathon final was proof of her endurance and stamina. The year-end crown in Dubai in 2018, in which she beat both Tai Tzu and Akane Yamaguchi, helped break the finals jinx as well. And finally, she made history by winning gold at the World Championships in Basel in August 2019, becoming the first Indian woman to do so.

Exactly twenty-four hours ahead of the Basel final, Pullela Gopichand was quietly confident. 'The courts are on the slower side and in conditions like these, Sindhu will always do well because of her physical agility. Players have to play every day, and by the time we get to the final, the body starts to give up on you. Sindhu is different for she can keep going for days and weeks,' said Gopi. 'Courts in Tokyo should suit her', he added, 'and there is no question she will have a major chance at the Olympics in 2020.'

But Sindhu's story isn't finished yet. 'I must say, I enjoyed seeing the tricolour go up in Rio', said Gopi, 'but yes, I missed listening to the national anthem being played at the Olympics. I am sure it will happen someday. That's what we athletes live for, and if Sindhu can do what she did in Basel and keep her focus, it will surely happen in Tokyo.'

At the Rio Olympics, Sindhu had a steeliness about her game; an unflappability that was unusual. She has always been pegged as a talented player, dangerous but brittle, and as likely to beat herself as to be beaten by an opponent. Where Saina Nehwal is a product of perspiration – a manufactured player, if you like – Sindhu was always a natural. But in the ruthless world of competitive professional sports, 'natural' alone doesn't cut it.

Sindhu had the tendency, sports psychologist Vaibhav Agashe said, 'to get negative, to overthink things.' She would become cautious when the heat was on and matches got close and would end up handing the initiative to her opponent, losing matches after being in the winning position. There was little evidence of this trait in Rio as she dispatched Wang Yihan, conqueror of Nehwal four years prior in London and a badminton superstar in her own right, in the quarter-final. She then outplayed Nozomi Okuhara, who was ranked higher than Sindhu at the time and had also won the All England Open, arguably badminton's most prestigious title.

Most of India came to a halt during her final with Marin. That Sindhu could cope with the pressure and weight of expectations perhaps had something to do with Gopichand confiscating her phone for the duration of her Olympic training. Her eventual loss had nothing to do with her old Achilles heel: mental frailty. She may need to improve her defence, as experts and coaches have observed, as well as her close-to-the-net game, but she seems to have acquired a winning mentality. This is perhaps the most important ingredient.

In Sao Paulo, on her way back to India, Gopichand finally let Sindhu have her phone back, and within seconds, she was on WhatsApp. Rewards had already been laid at her feet and a new-found celebrity status now awaited her – Gopichand would soon long for the days when a smartphone was her only distraction. #Sindhustan was the trending hashtag online. It was the delirium and hysteria of a country starved of Olympic medals and craving international respect on the sporting field that P.V. Sindhu had to deal with after Rio.

She will be twenty-five in Tokyo, at the prime of her career. And it may well be her moment that ends up transforming Indian sports forever. And then she can shout, standing alone in the middle of the seven courts in the Gopichand Academy in Hyderabad ... or even cry. Gopi too will be crying. In the satisfaction and celebration of a mission fulfilled. The journey started in Rio and picked up momentum in Basel – Tokyo is the home stretch.

Sindhu, by the look of her, is determined. Giving up on ice cream and biryani and even on her phone is acceptable to her. Losing out on gold is not. 'I really want to change the colour of my medal at the Olympics,' she said. 'Win an Olympic gold medal for India in 2020.'

Celebrity also awaited Dipa Karmakar, who has now documented it all in her autobiography, co-written by Digvijay Singh Deo and Vimal Mohan, two of India's best Olympic journalists of all time. Unlike Sindhu and Malik, Karmakar didn't win a medal. But the audacity of landing the Produnova – a vault that her mother rather cheekily said even Simone Biles, the American phenomenon, won't risk – stunned the country and established her stardom.

Karmakar is the second child and second daughter, much to the distress of some family elders, of Dulal, a weightlifting coach with the SAI, and Gauri. Her parents took her to a gymnastics coach when she was five and made the conscious decision to enrol her in a Bengali medium school because they believed there would be less academic pressure. They went in a direction opposite to the one most Indian parents might go in. Yet, Karmakar was studying and sitting for a political science exam right after her return from Rio. Her story is of the kind that happens, as they say, only in India. Karmakar first learned some of the skills that enabled her to perform a Produnova on the grandest stage of them all – a vault fashioned out of old scooter parts.

Even at a young age, her coach and parents knew she would win medals. At five, she would stay behind after her lessons and practise for up to three hours. At seven, she won her first gold on the balance beam. Part of her prize was a sports kit full of goodies that was too big for her. 'Dipa wouldn't let anyone else carry that bag', her mother remembers, 'she wouldn't ever part with anything she won as a prize. She was so proud.'

Soma Nandi, Karmakar's first coach, said, 'Dipa would never rest until she had got a move perfect. It was such a rare quality in a child that she stood out from the very beginning.' She took the Indian gymnastics scene by storm, winning medals – mostly gold – at every meet. She competed in the 2010 Commonwealth Games as a teen, finishing seventh and promising her father that she would bring home a medal the next time. Four years later at the games in Glasgow, she won a bronze in the vault. By then, she had been practising the Produnova for two years.

As with so much else in her still-young career, Karmakar learned to perform the Produnova despite the naysayers, despite conditions entirely unfavourable to practising such a risky vault. From the very beginning,

Karmakar's family says, she had her doubters. A coach and a doctor told them she would never be a competitive gymnast because she had flat feet. Foreign coaches doubted an Indian gymnast's ability to pull off a Produnova, and her coach, Vishweshwar Nandi (Soma's husband), said, 'they thought she would end up mangled.' And you can understand why. 'Tripura', Soma said, 'had no infrastructure to practise the Produnova, no foam pits. On mattresses and hard surfaces, the limbs are under tremendous pressure and can only take four or five landings; on a foam pit you can try fifty.'

Even three months before Rio (having qualified for the Olympics in March), it took the intervention of Sarbananda Sonowal, the chief minister of Assam, to ensure Karmakar had adequate facilities to practise. The result was six- to eight-hour practice sessions and 1,000 Produnovas in just ninety days. Having cut out all ice creams and sweets from her diet in the run-up to Rio, Karmakar, having become the first Indian to qualify for a gymnastics final, asked her coach if she could celebrate with a strawberry sundae. 'He looked at her', Soma laughed, 'and promised that if she could wait till after the final, he would lock her up in one of the ice cream fridges in their village.'[1]

More seriously, Soma points out that while Karmakar has 'inspired every young girl in Tripura, there are children whose families cannot feed them an egg or a glass of milk'. The success of Karmakar and the medal-winning exploits of Malik and Sindhu cannot mask the intrinsic problems India faces as an Olympic nation. But that's a larger thread running through this book. For now, let's take pleasure in these extraordinary female athletes and their respective moments in the sun, thousands of miles away from home in Brazil.

2

Gopichand's Revolution
Turning India into a Badminton Superpower

P.V. Sindhu had just won her quarter-final in Rio against the legendary Wang Yihan of China, and all of us, members of the Indian media contingent, were euphoric. One more win and Sindhu could finally end India's medal drought. Later that evening, Gopichand bumped into Boria by the gate of the Olympic Village. It was past 9 pm and the coach was alone, pacing around rather aimlessly. He hadn't expected a run-in and looked somewhat surprised. In all these years of knowing him, very rarely had he looked as anxious and frail. 'Let's talk after the match tomorrow,' he said. 'I am tired of Indians coming fourth. I really can't take another fourth place finish. If she wins tomorrow she is sure of a medal, and once that happens I will come with you to Christ the Redeemer and celebrate.' Gopi was in a flow. 'I have not properly smiled for months now. Lost eight to ten kilograms in the last few months for this one day. Time we win a medal,' He tailed off before walking back into the Village, leaving many unasked and unanswered questions in his trail.

We had been following Kidambi Srikanth, who was ranked number one in world badminton in 2018, and Sindhu closely in the months leading up to the 2016 Olympics and could immediately relate to what Gopi was saying. Between January and August 2016, his days would start at 4.30 am with Sindhu and continue till 11.30 am with Srikanth and the rest of his wards. Sindhu and Srikanth had their dedicated times with him, having qualified for the Olympics. Gopi had separately assigned each of them practice times for particular strokes. Srikanth, for example, worked for hours on the smash and more specifically on his jump to time the smash to perfection. Gopi also worked on his defensive technique to get him up to speed and now, many say Srikanth has one of the strongest defensive techniques in the game. 'The best thing about Gopi sir is he doesn't leave things to chance. "God doesn't play dice," he says, and all that he is keen on is practice. That's how you come close to perfection,' Srikanth said at one of our visits to Gopi's academy in Hyderabad's Gachibowli area.

While Srikanth lost a closely fought quarter-final against Chinese legend Lin Dan in Rio, Sindhu won a much-needed silver to partly fulfil Gopi's ambition. I say 'partly' because it is not about one gold or one silver for Gopi. It never was. It is about producing multiple champions and nurturing talent to make India a badminton superpower. 'The Chinese don't depend on any one particular player. That creates pressure. Once you have several players in the top ten, not only does practice improve because they keep playing against each other but you also have a far greater chance to win medals,' Gopi maintains.

So how does he produce a champion, we ask him. The question doesn't have a straightforward answer. It is not a mathematical formula, or else it would simply be replicated by every country that can afford it.

'What does a champion mean to you?' Gopi asked in return. And before we could respond, he started off again. 'A champion to me is a player who knows how to keep winning consistently. To know how to win is an art. Everyone at this level can play well. But not everyone knows how to win. At 17–17, all you need is to be a little more than a good player to close out the game. That's something I think I am good at – working with them backstage. That's what has helped me nurture these players. Once they learn the process, I will move on to working with younger men and women who need to be groomed going ahead.'

Typical Gopi: straightforward and simple. Decoding the process as if it isn't something really difficult.

True to his mission, Gopi is at his academy at 5 am every single day. After finishing his Pranayam between 4.30 and 5 am, it hardly takes him five minutes to reach the academy from his house, which is next door. Once there, it is one rigorous session after another with his famous wards between

5 and 11 am. Some evenings he is there between 5 and 8 pm too to finally end the day around 9 pm.

While Sindhu trains between 6 and 8 am, Saina Nehwal gets undivided attention between 9 and 11 am. After a thirty-minute break, Gopi is back with Sindhu for an hour before he breaks off for lunch. The few times he doesn't train with the players, he observes them from his little office on the first floor of the academy opposite the courts and makes notes to pass on to each of them after the session is over.

'The process is what is most important. All people see is what the players do in tournaments. Sindhu was hailed for playing a 100-minute match at the 2017 Glasgow World Championships. Saina is being hailed for having regained fitness, first evident at the 2018 Gold Coast games. Srikanth doesn't get tired after three long games. Prannoy can beat any top player on his day. Each of these things can happen because we have a robust process in place for each of them. They train close to five hours on most days, spread into two halves – morning and evening. They play long rallies, simulate match situations and work on perfecting particular strokes. That's why they aren't flustered in match situations anymore,' said Gopi and suggested that we visit the academy a few more times to understand the process he was talking about.

Guru Gopichand and His Gachibowli Formula for India's Badminton Champions

With the flight on time, it was just before 9 am that our car arrived at the Gachibowli crossing, just minutes from the facility. Situated among rocky outcrops and hillocks in Telangana's Ranga Reddy district, Gachibowli is a software hub located a fair distance away from Hyderabad's city centre. It is mostly populated by multinationals and tech companies and is full of lounge bars and international restaurants. It is also a sports hub that has hosted the BWF World Championships and the Military World Games.

Gopi, Sindhu and Srikanth have all moved to the area for easier access to one another and to avoid daily commutes through the heavy Hyderabad traffic, which would eat into their training schedules on most days. As our car reached the Gachibowli crossing, we saw the first signage to the left of the road: SAI Gopichand Academy. What it does not say is that it is also India's singular medal producing factory. Here, we are not using 'factory' in a pejorative sense. In this case, it refers to structure, discipline and clockwork precision – functions which are integral to a well-oiled corporate set-up.

However, all this is for later.

As our car took a U-turn to get onto the service road leading to Gopi's temple, we saw a few cars parked on both sides of the road. These cars can be seen as the first visual markers of the amazing success of Indian badminton over the last few years; recognition the country has accorded Gopi and his band of super achievers. For the record, the BMWs parked outside on most days belong to Gopi and Sindhu, presented to them after the 2016 Olympic Games, whereas the Audi belongs to Saina for having won an Olympic medal four years prior in 2012.

On entering the academy, the atmosphere felt somewhat aloof. There was a certain rugged feel about the place. A few posters on both sides of the stairs showcased achievement, but that's about all. Even the Yonex store selling clothing and gear at discounted rates was characterized by indifference. It was manned by one or two people who seemed completely disinterested in their jobs. As we went in further, there was an eerie silence which only added to the aura.

The ground floor has offices, storerooms and also a canteen, which serves food for all players training at the academy. All the badminton courts and changing rooms are on the first floor. Among the posters which take up wall space on the first floor is a sign that prohibits the use of media devices during practice unless prior permission is taken. A second sign disallows spikes on the courts.

The media sign is interesting because in the first four years after Gopi set up the Hyderabad academy, not a single sports journalist entered it. 'Yes, between 2004 and early 2008 the media wasn't interested. No one came and no one was really following what I was trying to do. Not that it mattered, because I could do my initial planning away from the glare of cameras, which is actually not such a bad thing,' said Gopi with a smile.

As we climbed up the stairs, we heard the first sounds of activity from the courts: the sounds of shuttles being tossed up by some of India's best and the heavy thuds coming from their lunges. The sight was unforgettable – playing in the four courts in front were P.V. Sindhu, Saina Nehwal, Kidambi Srikanth, H.S. Prannoy, Sai Praneeth, N. Sikki Reddy, Parupalli Kashyap, Satwiksairaj Rankireddy, Chirag Shetty, Sameer and Sourabh Verma. Five of these men are ranked in the top twenty of world badminton whereas two of the three women are in the top ten – these players have dominated the sport for a while now. One cannot see such a sight anywhere else in India. And in over two decades of sports coverage around the world, we don't remember seeing a similar sight anywhere else either.

'You are kind,' said Gopi. 'We are doing well, but to say this is something revolutionary is overdoing it. We need more wins to call it a revolution. We need doubles wins, more super series wins, Olympic medals, an All England title ...' As Gopi went on about his dreams, something suddenly started happening on the courts. Five players on each side suddenly just started smashing the shuttle at each other and having fun. What on earth was happening? 'Last fifteen minutes of practice. Two teams of five players each and they will play attacking shots on every point. It builds stamina and endurance,' Gopi explained.

Gopi is one of the most down-to-earth superstars you will ever come across; completely relaxed and almost saintly. It is as if he is always at ease with himself and with life. Superstardom has not affected him and it never will. He always answers questions with a smile. You tend to wonder if this man really is the strict disciplinarian his students like Sindhu make him out to be.

WHEN COACH GOPI TOOK AWAY SINDHU'S PHONE AND TAUGHT HER TO SCREAM

The answer to what makes Gopi such a life-changing coach is best given by Sindhu.

'I had just lost a hard-fought first-round match at the Australian Open against former world number one and London Olympics silver medallist Wang Yihan in December 2015. Yet, Gopi sir wasn't flustered. In fact, he said to me that all restrictions on food and late nights were removed temporarily. It was party time. Little did I realise that these were my last few days of enjoyment before going into hard Olympic labour. Soon after we returned to India, Gopi sir called me to his office in the academy and handed me a letter. It was a first in our fourteen-year-old association and the letter listed the 'dos and don'ts' for the next eight months. And among them was a clause stating that I would have to surrender my phone to him.'

No phone and no gastronomic indulgences. Sindhu was twenty years old then and Gopi was coming down hard on his talented young student.

Talent, he argued, needed to be honed to win an Olympic medal and he was determined to leave nothing to chance. 'I had the 2010 Asian Games in mind. While coming back from Guangzhou I had called Sindhu and Ramana (her father) and said I would see her at 4.30 am the next morning. And all she said was "yes". That's what made me feel I could push her more. Yes, I was a little worried about the phone because, among all my students, she was the fastest to respond to a WhatsApp message. She is clearly hooked on the gadget. But it was a distraction we could do without,' said Gopi, looking back at those eight months that eventually made P.V. Sindhu an Olympic champion and what she is today.

How did Sindhu take it? 'I did not think he meant it seriously,' she said. 'Definitely not about the phone. How could I not have a phone!! And yet, when he gave me the letter I instinctively said "yes". So when I looked over it again in the evening, there was nothing much I could do because I had already agreed to all his conditions,' laughed Sindhu.

A second example helps demonstrate the point even better.

'In our house, it is always Vishnu and Gayatri (his children) who decide on the food,' said Gopi. 'I have no say and I really don't mind. But this wasn't the case during the lead up to Rio. For those few months, it was about me and me only. I wanted food of my choice because I was afraid of falling sick and missing training. It would mean that Sindhu would miss training and such things weren't permissible.'

Sindhu helped close the discussion. 'I felt the worst when Gopi sir made me stand in the middle of the courts one day at the academy in Hyderabad and screamed at me. He was instructing me to shout. There was no one there and he had never done this before. He was angry and wanted me to be aggressive. I hated it. Hated him for what I was being told to do. And I started crying but wasn't able to shout.'

She did eventually shout though. This newly cultivated aggression has since gone on to redefine Sindhu the player.

Srikanth, who in late 2019 was on a comeback trail having lost form and confidence after reaching the top of the world rankings the previous year, literally idolises his coach. 'Gopi sir has said to me that the world number one position is kind of a box tick. At the end of your career when you look back at your highest ranking, to think it will be number one is a heady feeling. But what is more important is how many tournaments you win and how consistent you are. That's what sir teaches us.'

H.S. Prannoy, one of the most improved players in world badminton, attributes this success to his coach as well. 'Gopi sir made us believe it was possible. We would be content with losing if we played well. It did not hurt much. Now it does. Every match lost hurts more and that's what Gopi sir is all about. He hates to lose and expects the same from us,' said Prannoy.

Things have not been easy for Gopi either. As we pressed him to tell us more about the challenges of being a coach, he called for lunch to ensure the thread of our conversation was not broken. Excellent chicken curry, aloo-bhindi, roti, rice, curd and achar constitute lunch. This is what the players get and it is all made inside the academy. 'We have eighty men and women who now live in the academy. Almost all of them eat breakfast, lunch and dinner here itself. The food helps them a lot because it means staying off outside food and also spares them the time of having to think of what to eat,' said Gopi's mother, who heads the administrative wing in the academy.

Once lunch was over, Gopi opened up about what is turning out to be a rivalry like no other: London 2012 bronze medallist Saina Nehwal versus P.V. Sindhu. Saina leaving his academy in 2014 to train in Bengaluru created one of the toughest challenges he has ever faced. It happened after the 2014 World Championships in Denmark, where Sindhu won a bronze while Saina, who was a favourite, lost early.

This is how an insider (who requested anonymity) recounts the story: 'Gopi and Saina were both in Copenhagen in 2014 and things were perfectly fine. On the way back, Saina was on a morning flight while Gopi was leaving later that day. Before his departure, he was told that she would be leaving Hyderabad for the Prakash Padukone Academy in Bengaluru and had decided on training with Vimal Kumar. Gopi had not expected this and must have felt let down and hollow. In staying true to his nature, he did not try stopping her. Sindhu clearly was the beneficiary.'

When pushed to open up on this issue, all Gopi said was, 'Every athlete should do what they think is best for them. As a coach, my job is to train them and wish them well. Prepare them for the best. If Saina felt that's what was good for her at that point, it is totally fine by me.'

He was maintaining professionalism by giving the diplomatic answer, but seeing his expression, it was better to let this one go.

So what about Saina's return to the academy in 2017? On the comeback trail, the original poster girl of women's badminton in Indian eventually returned to the Gopi fold ... but wasn't it difficult for the coach? Did he think of it as vindication of what he had initially done for Saina? And, on another level, was it a challenge because Sindhu had moved too far ahead by then?

'Yes, it was a challenge,' he responded. 'But that's why we are here, isn't it? If an athlete reaches out for help, it is the duty of the coach to try and do the best he can. I will always do that.'

We explore the Sindhu–Saina–Gopi story at length in the next chapter, but it's a complicated dynamic. It wasn't easy for Gopi. It still isn't and never will be. When Boria visited the academy soon after Saina's return in September 2017, he saw Gopi in his eight-by-eight-foot room directly opposite the courts, closely monitoring her movements. 'She needs to get fitter. She isn't able to reach shuttles and we need to work on that,' he was mumbling to himself.

Two months later, on a return visit, one could visibly notice a difference in Saina. She was much fitter and nimbler. The training had worked and her Commonwealth Games gold medal in 2018 – when she beat Sindhu 21–18, 23–21 – is evidence that she still has a lot to offer Indian badminton.

In this classic rivalry between two ace shuttlers, there is only one winner. India.

Gopi maintains that he has no favourites. 'I did not even watch most of the Commonwealth Games final in 2018. Only watched the last few points and have to say Saina played smart' was what he said on a call just moments after the Saina–Sindhu contest had ended at Gold Coast. 'I need both of them to do well. They are playing superbly and have a lot to offer to the sport. The more the merrier,' he said. His customary chuckle was back.

'I want them to set a benchmark for world badminton,' he said. 'A rivalry is very good as long as it doesn't turn unhealthy. Yes, the two of them are competitive and that's how it should be. In the academy, there are five men who are in the top twenty and it has never been an issue to coach them together. I am confident I will be able to manage the Saina–Sindhu case.'

With tension simmering all one can do is wish Gopi luck.

As we were talking, an exhausted Srikanth walked into Gopi's room. The two of them speak Telugu, a language we don't understand. But it looked like Srikanth was asking Gopi to come out and watch him play the jump smash.

Srikanth briefly ranked number one in the world in April 2018 but hasn't been the same player since. Gopi, however, hasn't lost hope. 'He has the potential to be a Lin Dan or a Lee Chong Wei,' he said. 'All he needs now is to be a little more consistent. But he has the shots, the ability and the mental strength. He can smash the shuttle and also retrieve it from impossible situations. What he needs to learn is that when you have momentum, you have to capitalise and close out a match. If you allow opponents like Kento Momota back into the contest midway into the second game, he will run through you in the third. That's what has happened with Srikanth time and again in the last two years.'

We have been welcomed with the same warmth on each visit. 'Please feel free to sit and watch. Come and train also if you think you can,' said Gopi. The jibe was harmless and the smile that followed was proof of Gopi's sense of humour.

As he walked out with Boria during his last visit to the academy, Gopi said, 'There is a lot left to do. We still don't have an Olympic gold. Or an Asian Games gold. Yes, the process is in place and we have taken steps in the right direction, but there is so much more left to achieve.'

Kashyap, one of his first real star pupils and winner of the Commonwealth gold in Delhi 2010, puts the last statement into perspective. 'I may not be at the top of my game anymore, but that doesn't mean I can't ask Bhaiyya for help. At any point, if you think you need to improve on something, all you do is go to Bhaiyya and ask for help. We assume that he has the solutions to all our issues,' Kashyap summed it up quite beautifully.

As Gopi and Sindhu start to spar and we enjoy watching from Gopi's room, we wonder what will happen if India does win a gold at Tokyo 2020.

Frankly, nothing much will happen as far as this monk-like guru of Indian badminton is concerned. Given the kind of person he is, we can guarantee things won't change. Even the day after winning a gold medal, Gopi will still be at the academy at 5 am with a racket and shuttle in hand trying to think how to improve further. 'The next super series is a month away,' he will say, but then go on to add (as he has explained to us before), 'The goal is not medals, you know. Medals are just one aspect of the story. Sport helps us in a number of intangible ways. It helps us become better men and women and, most importantly, deal with crisis better. When you fail an exam, you don't come out of your homes and in extreme cases commit suicide. Sports give you multiple chances. Your loss is public so you can't really run away from it. All you do is get back up, seek family support and come back the next morning trying to rectify the mistake. And when you do so you become a winner. Everyone who plays sports is a winner. Not always do you have to win medals. If we all come to terms with this aspect of sports, we would make a better society.'

What he left unsaid was that he would also produce champions in this process.

But we do know why he never said that. It is because champions are never satisfied. And Guru Gopi, in every sense of the word, is one.

How Gopichand Became Guru Gopi

Gopichand won badminton's holy grail, the All England Open Championship in 2001, becoming only the second Indian to reach these rarefied heights since Prakash Padukone's win in 1980. He was twenty-nine years old when he won and at the pinnacle of his career when he decided to set up a coaching academy. What made him make the shift?

'I was injured at the start of 2004 and, as a result, feeling restless at home', Gopi said while recollecting how he came up with the idea, 'I decided to get into coaching to keep me going. The start was nothing fancy. I just went to Lal Bahadur Shastri Stadium and picked out a few kids between the ages of nine and sixteen and brought them to the Gachibowli Stadium and started working with them.'

While the process wasn't simple, that was how it all started for him as a coach. Sindhu, at nine, was the youngest and Kashyap, at sixteen, was the oldest among the students who moved with him to Gachibowli. The rest of the crop included Saina, Sai Praneeth, Prannoy, Sikki and Sumeeth Reddy, Gurusaidutt, Sameer Verma and a few others. It is amazing to see just how many of the children from his initial batch eventually made it to the highest level of the sport in the years to come.

There were eight proper courts in the Gachibowli stadium at the time. Gopi found that everything else – from the availability of shuttles to proper nutrition for the students – was lacking. 'It is up to you to look at the glass as half full or half empty. I could either crib that there was very little government support or tell myself that whatever I had was enough for a start and it was on me to get more by pushing hard and showing results. Wallowing in self-pity would hardly get me anywhere and that's something

I have always believed in,' said Gopi as he looked at the players training in front of him in what is now a first-rate facility equipped with all the modern amenities needed to produce champions.

Things look great today at the SAI Gopichand Academy in Hyderabad. Multiple sponsors support the facility, students queuing up to become the next Sindhu or Srikanth and parents jostling for space in the already-cramped training schedule. Just as you enter, there is a huge Industrial Development Bank of India (IDBI) Federal Life Insurance board announcing the 'Quest for Excellence' programme the company launched with Gopi immediately after Rio in an attempt to support the academy.

In speaking about it, Vignesh Shahane, managing director of IDBI Federal Life Insurance, had a rather interesting story to tell. 'Karthik Raman (chief marketing officer) and I had gone to meet Gopi a few weeks after Rio. First, it was a challenge to get an appointment because he had a huge number of social engagements going on. And on the day we went, he was at one of these programmes and we had to wait for a while. Gopi sent us a photograph on WhatsApp to show that he was indeed at the programme and wasn't fibbing! When we did finally meet him, he was cagey. Talks started and he seemed to think we had gone there to speak about Sindhu. When we mentioned to him that we wanted to support him and the academy because we understand the importance of a Gurukul, he was a tad surprised. The meeting was inconclusive because Gopi was yet to be convinced. It was only when Karthik went back to him accompanied by a friend who is close to Gopi that the ice broke and he agreed to join hands.'

To think that the academy is just a fifteen-year-old story is startling. Soon after Gopi brought the kids to Gachibowli, he received a grant for Rs 10 lakh per annum from the government's sports council to develop the academy and its facilities. The state government also provided him with land, not too far from the Indian School of Business, on lease to set up the new facility. While the money wasn't much, it made a difference in the early days and was used to appoint three coaches to help out in training and give the facility some structure. 'I appointed Tom John from the UK, Govardhan and Siyadath, who is still with me, having started here in 2004. He is now a pillar of the academy. Tom had a salary of 60,000 a month while Govardhan and Siyadath were paid 15,000 a month to start with,' Gopi remembered.

Gopi's personal life was in turmoil at the time and how he navigated his problems while simultaneously building an academy and a new coaching structure for Indian sports is an extraordinarily mind-boggling story of grit and determination. Gopi's children, Gayatri and Vishnu, were born in 2003 and 2004 respectively. It meant Laxmi, his wife, had to devote all her time to taking care of them. His mother had just been diagnosed with cancer and her treatment had started in Hyderabad. 'You can very well imagine what I was going through. It wasn't easy. I would come to the academy early and be there all day. I would eat there and even sleep there on occasions. I would go home around 9.30 pm completely exhausted and this routine continued for months,' he remembered.

'There have been days when he slept in the car because he was fatigued. We were all working for a purpose though we did not really know what lay ahead of us,' said Siyadath with a smile. Things turned problematic when Gopi was informed in 2006 that the sports council had decided on revoking the grant for Rs 10 lakh per annum. 'It was a big blow and I had to let Tom John go for I couldn't afford his services anymore. Govardhan too left us because he was being paid double the money to coach at the Lal Bahadur Shastri Stadium. It was a facility that was being run by a few former players who literally came and poached him from Gachibowli.'

We asked if he had anticipated foul play in the sports council's decision to call off the grant and he just smiled. 'It is left to your imagination. You have followed Indian sports long enough to know what was going on and to what level people can stoop,' he said. While Gopi wouldn't say it explicitly, there is no doubt that he had his detractors in Hyderabad who did not want the academy to succeed. He had also been appointed national coach in the interim in 2006, which hadn't gone down well with a few senior players.

'It was still manageable', he said, before adding, 'I had been able to get the academy up to speed and by 2007–8 we had our first physio and trainer appointed with support from Manisha Malhotra of the Mittal Champions Trust. Little did I know that it would all come to a standstill when I was about to formally inaugurate the facility.'

The story goes that Gopi had gone to invite then-Chief Minister of Andhra Pradesh Y.S. Rajasekhara Reddy to formally inaugurate the academy. He had his iPad with him and was keen on showing the CM and the state's sports minister snapshots of their progress from the last few years. That was when he was told that the government had decided to cancel his lease and reclaim its land.

Officials informed him that the inauguration couldn't happen. He was reminded that the work he had got done until then to build his academy was on government property, which he would have to give up. Gopi pleaded with them to see the photographs but was politely asked to leave, implying that the meeting was over. The very next evening, which happened to be a Friday, senior officers of the government turned up at the academy to lock it all up.

The day of the week they chose is interesting. A weekday would have meant that Gopi could approach the judiciary the next day, but Friday meant he wouldn't be able to do much over the weekend. With few options left, Gopi moved court the following Monday and managed to get a stay to stop the academy from being closed down.

The backstory is that a builder well connected to the men in power was keen to build serviced apartments on the site of the academy. It is alleged that this support from the high and mighty allowed him to make life miserable for Gopi. Trouble continued for the next year and a half and it was only because of intervention from the Governor of Andhra Pradesh that India's medal factory survived the tumult.

Though trouble was brewing at the official level, things were gradually taking shape as far as the facilities were concerned. Gopi had managed to make a deal with Yonex to send his wards to train in Indonesia and even managed to hire three physios and three trainers at the facility.

Saina's ground-breaking quarter-final performance at the Beijing Olympics in 2008 helped. With media attention and corporate funding starting to trickle in, things started to ease up for Gopi. When he had set up the academy in 2004, not many had taken him seriously. In his words, 'not one journalist had set foot in the academy between 2004 and 2008, and it was only after Saina's quarter-final appearance in Beijing that people started to take notice.' Then, he was alone. He no longer is.

Once Kashyap won the 2010 Commonwealth Games gold and Saina won her historic bronze medal at the 2012 London Olympics, things changed dramatically. Sindhu and the men – Srikanth, Prannoy, Sameer and Sai – have added multiple medals since, making it a medal-winning factory of sorts!

Now, Gopi has sports science specialists, physios and foreign coaches to lend him a helping hand and the results are palpable. There are 150 children training at the academy every day and most of them are residents who have made the academy their home. Every morning the academy opens its gates at 5 am and by 5.30 am all of India's top stars are in action, honing their skills for the next major tournament. More importantly, there is a support system that runs 24/7, 365 days of the year.

It is a centre of excellence that India can be proud of. For years, Gopi's mother headed the administration of the academy, adding to it a personal touch and making sure that things worked to perfection. Students of the academy have the option of food cooked in-house. Personally speaking (and taking the liberty of digressing), we have to say that the food in the academy canteen is extremely tasty and sumptuous. Students have the option of rice or roti and there are multiple vegetarian options to go with the dal and chicken, not to mention the delicious egg curry that Gopi often serves when we visit.

It is no accident that Sindhu, who is an exceptional athlete with exceptional genes, has taken full advantage of the academy to reach the pinnacle of her sport. That she is able to sustain her position at the top is also because of the backend support in Hyderabad. Injuries are properly dealt with, rehabilitation is organized, diets of the high-performance athletes are closely monitored and all requirements are looked into with urgency.

This is why the Gopichand Academy is a disruption. With proper funding and necessary infrastructure in place, it is now systematically producing champions. Under Gopi, it is no longer about one or two individuals aspiring to do well at the international level.

While there is now a system in place, not all boxes have been ticked yet. The big positive is that corporate India has woken up to the potential of sports and several companies have started to invest money in Olympic sports in the last few years. The negative, however, is that corporate support continues to be ad hoc. Soon after Sindhu won the World Championships in 2019, corporate coffers began opening up for her. In August 2019, for example, *Forbes* magazine ranked her as the thirteenth highest-paid female athlete, with her earnings totalling up to $5.5 million.

For almost a month after her World Championship win, Sindhu had to attend felicitations and events. In almost all of them, she was being handed checks of a few lakh rupees for having reached the pinnacle of her sport. While the money paid to her is much deserved, it is valid to ask whether or not she needs this money anymore or if this support is now being misplaced.

Sindhu has sixteen brand endorsements to her name alongside support from the TOPS from the government. She no longer needs this kind of ad hoc support. What will make a real difference to the sport is if this money is poured into grassroots-level coaching and supporting the up-and-coming players aspiring to be the next Sindhu. This isn't happening yet and it is up to the government and a few private initiatives to take care of the next-generation athlete.

Gopichand himself sounds a warning, pointing out that just a handful of courts in Hyderabad have produced 'two world number ones, one world champion, two Olympics medals, Asian Games and Commonwealth Games medallists, but I am not a school that churns out players each year.' He emphasises that 'we need to churn out more coaches, more Gopichands.'

This is why he said to *Times of India* in September 2019, 'what I have been able to produce is difficult to replicate' unless the wider system itself produces 'many more coaches with quality and gives them the power to execute.'

No one is more aware than Guru Gopichand about how much India needs more grassroots investments in sports.

3

Saina, Sindhu and Tokyo 2020

The Dark Backstage of Success

It was just two days after P.V. Sindhu had won the world title in Basel in August 2019, beating Nozomi Okuhara in straight games. She had played the perfect tournament and her fitness had come to the fore yet again in the semi-final and final. India, as usual, was in a tizzy and celebrating the new world champion. She was the first-ever to win a world crown in badminton for our country and the celebrations were every bit deserved. At the same time, there is a tendency to overdo things in India and we end up losing perspective at times. And that is what players and coaches need to be careful of for they know the importance of remaining grounded to prepare for the next major competition. There are demands from sponsors, requirements of the 24/7 media as well as official protocol. Some chief ministers insist that athletes come and meet them for the customary photo-op even if the latter have been travelling all night and barely had any sleep.

Some of these things are unavoidable. In a country where success in elite high-performance sports is a rarity, such things are inevitable. At the same time, success has its dark underbelly. Just imagine what it is like to be like a twenty-four-year-old girl with sixteen brand endorsements and millions in your bank account. Imagine brands queuing up at your doorstep every single time you win a major competition. Tuhin Mishra, head of Baseline and Sindhu's manager, has had an incredibly difficult time juggling demands from sponsors in the post-world cup days. Imagine getting mobbed everywhere you go, having to click a few thousand selfies every month to satisfy your fans. Imagine having to deal with interview requests every morning and being told you are the greatest sportsperson India has produced. How is one supposed to stay rooted under such circumstances? How can Sindhu's coach get her to refocus and plan for the next competition? After all, she is human and it is only natural for her to enjoy the fruits of her labour. But in doing so, where does she draw the line? Can her coach force her to do so? Can her parents push her to get back to training when the entire country wants a piece of her?

While we are using Sindhu as an example, the same concern applies equally to every top player training at the Gopichand Academy in Hyderabad. Several of them are stars and have a life beyond the academy. At the same time, they can't have a life of their own if they are to be world or Olympic champions.

Parupalli Kashyap, who started the badminton revolution in India by winning the 2010 Commonwealth Games gold, put it in perspective: 'As a coach, you will need complete control of your students. You need to know when they are sleeping, what they are eating, what they are doing to be able to plan their training. You need to know their full routine and you can't expect surprises from them every now and then. Students, on the other hand, also deserve a life of their own. They can't always remain cocooned within the confines of the academy and that's where the problems start. These misunderstandings are a part of international sports. And to be fair, no one is at fault. While the coach has to have complete control to deliver results, the athlete does need space to not feel cloistered all the time.'

Gopi agrees with Kashyap but also feels that these distractions can derail India's Olympic quest in the short term. Countries with a proper sports culture, by contrast, can shut out these distractions from time to time. 'While I am aware that each of them has achieved a lot and it is fair that they enjoy their share of life's luxuries, they also need to keep in mind that there is a bigger goal ahead of them. They aren't normal people. They are high-performance athletes and they are different. Cheat days can wait. Events can wait. Parental pressures can wait. The Olympics won't. As a coach, it is my job to tell them exactly this and, if need be, force their hand; they are all formative minds. Unfortunately, in India, there is no mechanism by which I can do so. Each of them listens to me because of the respect they have for me. But that's where it ends. As a national coach, I don't really have the authority to tell them what to do unlike countries like Japan where the system allows the coach to do so. It is an issue in India,' he said with a sense of resignation in his voice.

In September 2019, with the Tokyo Olympics just a few months away, Gopi's frustration was palpable. He knows India is on the cusp of a breakthrough at the Olympic level but also knows that the chance could slip away with some rather rudimentary mistakes being made during the home stretch. Each athlete needs to make sacrifices to scale the summit and unless that happens, potential alone will never translate into medals. 'The challenge for Tokyo is not about going there and performing. The challenge is to be the best prepared we can. With the sport having achieved a certain status in India and with money pouring in, this journey has only become tougher,' he said.

SAINA'S BREAKTHROUGH AND THE BREAK WITH GOPI: THE INSIDE STORY

Saina Nehwal won Indian badminton's first Olympic medal with her bronze at the London 2012 games, but it was at the Beijing Games of 2008 that we first witnessed Indian badminton's potential. Saina, a student of the Gopichand Academy in Hyderabad, made it to the Olympic quarter-final only to lose to Indonesia's Maria Kristin Yulianti in a match she should have won. Gopichand had started to deliver results and this potential had made everyone hopeful. The credibility of the Beijing breakthrough was further strengthened by a gold medal-winning effort from Kashyap at the 2010 Commonwealth Games in Delhi. Going into the 2014 Guangzhou Asian Games, hopes had soared for badminton.

Gopi was determined to keep the medals coming and, in trying to do so, was relentlessly pushing his wards. 'That's what resulted in a misunderstanding between Saina, Gopi sir and I during the Asian Games,' said Kashyap, who married Saina in December 2018. 'Saina and I were going out at the time. While we were both 100 per cent committed to badminton, we also had a life of our own. Gopi sir was upset, thinking we might end up neglecting the game. It wasn't the best thing to happen and our performances at the Asian Games suffered as a result.'

Gopi, who had helped Saina grow as an athlete and had great hopes from Kashyap, sees it slightly differently. 'I am no moral police to tell them what to do and what not to do. They are all adults and they have a life of their own. But as a coach, it is my job to make them realize their potential and that's what I was trying to do. It was a rather complicated situation and none of us benefitted from what happened,' said Gopi.

With things starting to get ugly and them not speaking to each other, it was left to Gopi to get Saina back on track. 'In 2011, I went up to Saina and told her that together we could win that elusive Olympic medal. We had every chance of making history as long as she allowed me to fashion her training for the next twelve months. I have to say I was doing it for myself as well. I wanted that Olympic medal as bad as she did and did not want to leave anything to chance,' said Gopi.

'Yes, I clearly remember Gopi sir speaking to Saina and the two of them getting back together. He promised her he would not leave Hyderabad even for a day if she would be there and I have to say, he kept his promise. It was as important for Saina as it was for each of us. Without Gopi sir, we felt lost. We would even cry. Don't forget we were all young and she was, in fact, a teenager. We needed Gopi sir's guiding hand. Without him, there would have been no London,' Kashyap reiterates.

In the months leading up to the London Olympics, Gopi had added high-intensity training to Saina's schedule and both she and Kashyap benefitted from the change. 'We had never trained like that before and, as a result, we were fitter and ready for fast-paced matches going into the Olympics. Had Saina not had a bout of viral fever just before the Games, she would have been even better prepared,' Kashyap remembers.

While Saina lost a tactical battle to China's Wang Yihan in the semi-final in London 2012, it was yet another lesson for Gopi and the Indian contingent. 'She failed to understand what Wang Yihan was doing. It was part of her strategy to deliberately make Saina wait before every serve, and when it was Saina's turn to serve, Wang would start moving around the court and take more time, much to Saina's displeasure. Saina should have done the same and not allowed Wang to get away with what she was doing. Instead, she tried to push the pace and each time she wasn't allowed to do so, she lost momentum,' Gopi lamented.

'I even remember Gopi sir yelling at Saina, telling her what Wang Yihan was doing. But the enormity of the occasion had consumed her and she was unable to stem the tide. In the evening she was hugely depressed and, I have to tell you, it was an ordeal to speak to her. Gopi sir was determined to show her the recording of the match to be able to tell her what went wrong because she was playing another Chinese player in Li Xuerei the next day. It was the bronze medal match and she couldn't afford to slip,' explained Kashyap.

'It was very hard. She was depressed and just not willing to listen to anything I had to say. Losing a semi-final is the hardest thing at the Olympics. All of a sudden, you risk losing out on a medal despite making the last four. That's what was weighing on her mind and it took a lot of effort to push her to agree to watch the match and understand what went wrong,' Gopi recollected.

Saina was lucky in winning the bronze the next day with an injured Li retiring hurt from the playoff. Years of endurance and labour had finally translated into an Olympic medal for her and Gopi. 'We were waiting for her at the practice courts behind the medal ceremony,' remembered Kashyap. 'She finally had the medal around her neck and I can't describe what it meant to each one of us. More importantly, the effort we had put in made a difference to our games and within months I was in the top ten and Saina in the top five of the world. Seeing us break into the top ten, the next crop of players had all started to believe it was possible. Srikanth, Sai, Guru, Prannoy and the next lot of players training at the academy all benefitted from her medal. It was our real breakthrough moment,' Kashyap argued.

While things should have taken an upward turn for Indian badminton after the London Olympics, Gopi's life was soon caught in a quagmire as he was trying to help Saina while also helping the lot of upcoming players who had all started to make giant strides in their games. Sindhu, who up until then was in Saina's shadow, was making big statements on the world stage and had started to beat higher-ranked opponents in the circuit. From one star student in Saina, Gopi now had his hands full with a group of players all capable of winning medals for India.

With no one to back him up, it was becoming increasingly difficult for him to take care of each of the players who craved and needed one-on-one attention and guidance.

It was Sindhu's bronze medal at the 2013 World Championships that made things more and more complicated for Gopi. By this time people around Saina had started to influence her, suggesting that Gopi wasn't giving her undivided attention anymore. She was often left to fend for herself. After losing the World Championships in 2013, she went on a downward spiral.

'Saina felt Gopi sir was hers and hers alone. It was a very different bond that the two of them had. For years Gopi had worked on her. All of a sudden Gopi had a lot of players to look after and Sindhu had started to show good results. Again, I don't blame either Saina or Gopi for the fallout. I had started to see things go wrong and did my best to control the negativity. But I was helpless,' said Kashyap.

'Each time Gopi tried to discipline Saina she would take it as an affront,' he added. 'She wasn't willing to buckle down and do things the way Gopi wanted her to. She wasn't in the best headspace and nor was Gopi. When we look back and take stock of the situation, things could have been better handled by both of them.'

Things came to a head at the World Championships of 2014 in Denmark. Yet again, Sindhu did brilliantly to win a bronze, her second successive World Championship medal, while Saina failed to rise up to her favourite tag, losing out early. She, as Kashyap says, was shattered.

Gopi had promised to speak to Saina at the end of the tournament and sort things out but the situation had spiralled out of control. She wasn't willing to wait anymore and had made up her mind on leaving the academy. Gopi, on the other hand, was very keen to have her stay but hadn't done enough to salvage the situation. With a lot of negativity around, Saina decided to leave Hyderabad and move to Bengaluru to the Prakash Padukone Academy and train with Vimal Kumar.

'It was as if something very dear was being taken away from me. Earlier, I had literally begged her not to go. But by then she had been influenced by others and had already made up her mind. While I did not want to hold her back and stall her progress, I knew this was something that wasn't beneficial for either of us. Yes, I indeed had other players to look after and Sindhu had made serious progress in the two years between 2012 and 2014. But I had never intended to neglect Saina. Maybe I wasn't able to convey this to her,' said Gopi.

'Maybe Viren or Vimal or Prakash sir could have spoken to her. I don't know why they did not. In fact, they encouraged her to leave Hyderabad. It is a mystery to me why Prakash sir has never said anything positive about me while I have always looked up to him as my role model,' he said with a sense of disappointment.

'What I felt distraught about was that she wasn't willing to wait for me for half a day more. I called her multiple times from Copenhagen to say we would talk the moment I reached Hyderabad. She was on an earlier flight back to India and I was to reach Hyderabad twelve to fourteen hours later. By then they had worked it all out. Her tickets had been sent to her and she was asked to leave Hyderabad immediately without waiting for me. It was one of the worst days of my life,' Gopi added.

'There was a lot of negativity around,' said Kashyap. 'At the academy, Saina felt that she wasn't getting Gopi's undivided attention. Her game was stagnating and she was in a very negative headspace. And when such things happen, people tend to influence you more easily. That's what happened with her. I wish I could stop what was going on but as I said it was in no one's control. Gopi had a job to do for India and he was doing it to the best of his abilities. Saina too had her career to look after and she decided that moving to Bengaluru was the best option for her at the time. You have to understand she was deeply hurt in doing what she did. She would break down every day for Gopi was the most important man in her life. But the feeling she got was that he wasn't concerned about her anymore and she couldn't deal with the pressure of what was happening,' Kashyap added.

While it was a feeling of betrayal that forced Saina to move to Bengaluru, for Gopi it was a case of losing everything he had worked on for over a decade. He had lost his favourite student. Sindhu, however, benefited from this as Gopi started to invest in her, though it was a challenge for him to take her to the very top of the sport.

Sindhu, in turn, grabbed the opportunity with both hands and started doing exactly what her coach wanted her to do. While Saina always had the potential, her departure from Hyderabad worked wonders for Sindhu in that it gave her more time with Gopi. The duo soon started preparing for the 2016 Rio Games with single-minded determination.

Saina too wasn't to be left behind. To her credit, she became the world's number one player within three months of moving to Bengaluru and seemed to have sorted out her game. But with time, her training in Bengaluru lost steam and she started getting injured frequently. While trying to focus on the Rio Olympics, she was overdoing things without knowing the repercussions of pushing her body too much. 'I was alarmed when I went to Bengaluru,' said Kashyap. 'I was injured and trying to make a comeback at the time. My Olympic dream was over and I felt it would be good if I was able to help Saina get into the best shape ahead of the Olympics. But what I saw was very disturbing. While she was playing brilliant badminton and keeping pace with me all through her training, she was doing so under extreme physical stress. It was only a matter of time before she broke down and things went out of her control. That she was able to go to Rio and win a match is a miracle.'

Saina had a hairline fracture in her ankle just weeks before Rio and was in serious physical discomfort going into the Olympics. Truthfully speaking, Vimal and her support group should not have sent her to Rio. But this was the Olympics and they were unable to make the right call at the right time. In Rio, she was in agony and went to the local doctor to get a steroid injection just a day before her first match. But by then, Kashyap says, the bone was in bad shape and nothing could numb the pain. It was a heartbreak of humongous proportions.

With Sindhu doing brilliantly to win the silver, Saina, the original superstar, seemed to have all but disappeared from people's radar back home.

'It was clearly the worst phase in her life. She had lost early in the Olympics and it had wasted months and years of hard work. Gopi sir wasn't with her anymore and she was soon to have surgery to get things back on track. She had no friends in Bengaluru and did not really know what to do,' said Kashyap.

'It was her grit that got her back to badminton. I have to say that if there is one player in the circuit who can win matches by her sheer grit, it has to be Saina. She has the mind of Roger Federer and Rafael Nadal combined and I am a huge fan of her mental toughness,' said Gopi. It was this grit that pushed Saina to undergo surgery and complete rehab as quickly as possible.

We ask Kashyap why she didn't go back to Gopi at that point. His answer offers us great insight into Saina's mind and helps us understand why she is who she is and why she still stands a great chance in Tokyo. 'My wife is a perfect Haryanvi Jatni, if you know what I mean. She is just too headstrong and proud. She desperately wanted to go back to Gopi sir and say sorry. She needed him badly but she was just too stubborn to admit it and open up to him. She wasn't willing to go back to a situation where she had nothing to show for herself. She had to complete her rehab, make a comeback and then go back to him having proven herself,' he said with a chuckle.

Thereafter he adds, 'Please don't write all of what I have said to you; I need to keep my marriage going!'

The mindset Kashyap spoke about explains why Saina rushed her rehab and made a premature return to the circuit. While she had started playing again, her pain failed to subside completely. She would inevitably carry niggles to every tournament she played in and it mustn't have been the best feeling to play with pain every single day of her life. Being in Bengaluru wasn't helping her and it was starting to get to her. 'To think she won a World Championship medal in this state is simply unbelievable,' said Kashyap.

'Her diet was all messed up at the time and she was pretty much having anything she wanted. She was overweight and her body wasn't ready to take the rigours of a three-set match. However, she could have still won the 2017 World Championships had she closed out the semi-final in two games against Okuhara. She almost did before Okuhara staged a remarkable comeback, and in the third game she stood no chance.' The frustration in Kashyap's voice was obvious.

And it was at the Glasgow World Championships in 2017 that Saina finally spoke to Gopi. A bronze medal after coming back from her injury meant she had something to show for her efforts. That's what prompted her to approach Gopi and ask him to take her back.

'Yes, it was difficult. By this time Sindhu had become who she is now, but Saina is someone I can never say no to. It was complicated. I have always believed these two players are the best Indian badminton has seen in decades, and as their coach, I have equal responsibility for both of them. Once she said to me she wanted to come back, I didn't have it in me to say no to her,' said Gopi.

So, did Sindhu have something to say something on the matter? Or did she take Saina's return in good spirit now that she had moved far ahead in the pecking order? Could the two poster girls of Indian badminton coexist in the same academy and could Gopi give them both his best without being accused of bias? Was it even conceivable that Saina and Sindhu would not have ego issues and that their parents, who make up the support team, wouldn't feel a tinge of apprehension?

Frankly, it was only a matter of time before problems emerged between the two players. Gopi, in trying to find a balance, was stuck in the middle, and yet again things turned complicated during the 2018 Gold Coast Commonwealth Games. While Gopi stayed neutral and chose not to watch the final between Saina and Sindhu, the latter's loss prompted a reaction the moment the two girls returned to Hyderabad.

Gopi had no choice but to train the two players in separate academies so that they weren't exposed to each other's training routines. With both continuing to do well in the circuit, there was little he could do but try to make the most of such a complicated situation.

'It is what it is because at the end of the day both of them respect me for what I am. And I know their strengths and weaknesses better than anyone ever can. I am convinced both Sindhu and Saina can win medals for India in Tokyo and that's what I am determined to work towards in the next few months,' said Gopi to us in mid-2019. Days after this conversation, Sindhu decided to move back and train in the SAI Gopichand Academy again – a very mature decision on her part with the Olympics on her radar.

The question we had for Gopi was: did he really believe in what he was saying? While Sindhu had become the toast of the nation in the aftermath of her gold-winning performance in Basel, Saina was continuing to struggle with one injury after another as of October 2019. Does she really have a chance in Tokyo? Or is Gopi giving it one last shot for old time's sake? Can Kashyap make a difference to his wife's Olympic ambitions and can India win a historic two medals in Tokyo?

Gopi, who has always been objective and rational, said something startling in answering us. 'If the Olympics were to be played a month from now, Saina stands a great chance to win a medal,' he told us in September 2019.

Gopi, it was clear to us, believed in what he was saying. For him, Tokyo is about winning two medals in women's singles. He has spent the last fifteen years of his life getting two women to become the best they can at the sport.

While one got India its first-ever Olympic medal in badminton, the other went a step further and changed the colour of the medal. If Saina is the first Indian to reach the world number one ranking, Sindhu is the first Indian to have won a world title, not to forget her five medals at the World Championships between 2013 and 2019. The two made the Commonwealth

Games final at Gold Coast in 2018 where, for the first time in the history of the Games, it was an Indian one-two in women's singles badminton.

While it might be farfetched to expect the same in Tokyo, it is safe to say that Gopi and the two star women will give it all they have to make history. Saina will play with all her grit and determination while Sindhu will use all her physicality to negotiate the slow courts in Tokyo. And Gopi, for one final tournament perhaps, will be sitting in the coaches' chair thinking this is his chance.

While he has already given the country two medals in the last two Olympics, winning two at the same Olympiad will surely make up for his disappointing loss at the 2000 Sydney Games.

It will not be simple. Olympic medals never come easy and no one knows this better than Gopi. Yet again, there might be complications and heartbreak. Yet again, he might have to deal with the egos of two super achievers, but as he keeps saying, 'We will have to deal with all of this for the country. India needs both Saina and Sindhu and both are capable of winning medals in Tokyo. Both deserve the best and I am committed to giving them both the best guidance I can.'

While we haven't seen the last of this saga, suffice to say that in trying to outdo each other, both Saina and Sindhu might just end up playing the best they ever have. Or so we hope.

4

Abhinav Bindra

'The Quest to Be Perfect on an Imperfect day'

Sixteen months before the 2016 Rio Olympics, Abhinav and Boria were together at an event in Nagpur. They were discussing how he had dealt with adversity in his decade-and-a-half-long career as an international sportsman. Just as the organizers were making the initial announcements requesting people to settle down, Boria noticed something very disturbing. Abhinav, who was sitting in the chair next to him, looked uncomfortable. All of a sudden, his hand was shaking involuntarily. It was clear that he was trying his best to hide it. Each time they made eye contact, Abhinav tried to avoid the probing gaze. It was shocking and surprising. Here was a shooter of the highest pedigree preparing himself for the Olympics, yet his hand was shaking and he had no control over it! It couldn't be real. But it was.

Abhinav Bindra, to our utter surprise, could not stop it for a good few minutes and had a look of resignation on his face. His secret had been revealed and we were privy to something not many had known in the realm of Indian sports. The onstage conversation went on as if everything was under control. Abhinav spoke about his training, his willingness to give it one more shot and finally what Rio 2016 meant to him. But we were interested in none of this. Our minds were fixated on what we had seen a few moments back and we were trying to understand what was going on. Was it just something that happened then or was it something Abhinav had been dealing with for a while? If it happened in competition, what would it mean for his shooting career and more importantly his dream to make it to Rio? If his hand was shaking the way it was in a precision sport, he could well decide to not compete and save himself the embarrassment.

The moment the show was over, Boria asked Abhinav if he would accompany him to his room. Abhinav immediately understood why but surprisingly agreed. The moment he entered the room and was left alone by the organizers, he revealed the shocking news: he was suffering from epilepsy and that was the reason he had wanted to leave the sport soon after the Commonwealth Games of 2014 in Glasgow.

While he has since written about his medical condition in his updated autobiography published in 2017, it was one of the biggest secrets of Indian sports at that time in 2015. And to hear him say it in the most matter-of-fact tone was even more disturbing. How could he mediate his condition and get ready for Rio? How could he prepare while dealing with epilepsy? The truth is he did and that's what makes him one of the greatest athletes ever in the history of Indian Olympic sports.

In his words, 'Rio 2016 will always be the Olympics I was best prepared for. I had done everything I could possibly have. I managed to control the medical condition, train for every eventuality that may have come my way and was confident nothing could surprise me at the Olympic stage. That's why I have no regrets for all you can do as an athlete is prepare and hope the results go your way. It did not in Rio, but so be it.'

Having followed his training closely, we agree with him wholeheartedly. He even carried a portable machine to Rio, which would allow him to train on an unstable surface just in case there was a balance issue at the range. He had faced a similar problem in Athens in 2004, something that may have cost him an Olympic medal despite being in really good form. With experience, he had learnt to deal with every probability for that's what he felt would give him the best shot at a second Olympic medal.

BEING ABHINAV BINDRA: LONDON AND THE RETURN OF HUNGER

We have both known Abhinav for a decade now. At least one of us can claim to be close friends with him since 2012. Till then, he was India's only individual gold-medal winner and our biggest star, but not someone we could claim to know closely. Until the London Olympics, we did not know enough about what happens backstage, which is extremely important in understanding an athlete. It all started when Abhinav failed to defend his gold and win back-to-back Olympic medals in London.

Gagan Narang, another exceptional shooter with enormous potential, won the bronze in the same event and opened India's medal count. Narang was the present in London whereas Abhinav was the fallen superhero. While all of us were seeking out Gagan for interviews, Boria remembers walking up to where Abhinav was opening his jacket and observing his every movement. Any public display of disappointment could lead to a story. How was he dealing with failure? That is what fans back home would want to know. Would he do something dramatic and quit the sport? But Abhinav, as we have learnt with time, is not about drama. He can be rather boring to the extent of being predictable.

All he did was pack up his equipment, smile and quit the range. 'I lost and that's fine. I wasn't good enough. Maybe I did not train hard enough' is all he said. That's where we sensed something. Was he trying to say he was a tad complacent coming into London or that he lacked motivation? That seemed unlikely for we were talking about the Olympics and Abhinav had just squandered an opportunity to win back-to-back Olympic medals for himself and India. Was there something he did not want to speak about?

When we met a month later, Abhinav had regained focus. He seemed to be at peace with himself and had started planning for the 2014 Commonwealth Games and the Incheon Asian Games that same year. Abhinav had not won a Commonwealth Games gold medal and it was something he wanted badly. The hunger that had driven him to push the limits in Beijing had disappeared in London, but it was back again and he was mentally ready for one more crack at sporting glory.

For the record, he did win the gold medal at the Commonwealth Games of 2014 in Glasgow and followed it up with a bronze medal at the Incheon Asian Games. Soon after the Asian Games, he tweeted saying he would henceforth shoot only as a hobby and that his days as a professional athlete were over.

When we quizzed him on what he meant by a hobby shooter, he said, 'My tweet is pretty clear. Let us not complicate it too much. My professional career from here on is over, which means training six hours a day, forty hours a week will no longer be there. I will not be doing it henceforth. I will train twice a week. I will compete at the national level and only if I am good enough will I participate in international competitions. I don't know if a hobby shooter can compete at the Olympics. Please don't take it that far. Please understand it bit by bit,' he said at the time.

In hindsight, it is clear why he said what he said at the time. He had been managing his medical condition for a while and was unsure if he could do so in the long term. At the same time, he did not want public sympathy by announcing he had epilepsy. 'I did not win a medal in Rio not because I had epilepsy but because I wasn't good enough on that day,' he maintains.

That is classic Abhinav – a proud athlete who will never hide behind an excuse. In the aftermath of the Incheon games, he was unsure if he could compete any further and still chose not to publicly talk about his medical condition. The part about shooting as a hobby was his way of buying himself time. And only when he was convinced about being able to manage the condition did he start competing in the Olympic quota events to give himself one more opportunity at Olympic glory.

It is necessary to state here that even if Abhinav had retired after Incheon, he would have still been remembered as one of the greatest athletes to have represented India. Whether or not Abhinav made it to Rio, he would still be remembered as the central architect of India's shooting revolution. The fact that nine of India's medals at the 2014 Asiad had come from shooting was largely a by-product of the 'Bindra moment', the gold that Abhinav won at the 2008 Beijing Games, not to forget Rajyavardhan Rathore's silver at the 2004 Athens Games.

In his autobiography, *A Shot at History* (with Rohit Brijnath), Abhinav has repeatedly emphasised the importance of timing – a state of full preparedness before the big moment arrives. Being the nation's first-ever individual Olympic gold medal winner will always make him special. But what makes the 'Bindra moment' pivotal for Indian sports and shooting is that it has encouraged thousands to take up the sport despite its lack of popular appeal and television coverage.

And with the many medals at the Asian Games, the fact that his gold unleashed a revolution in Indian shooting became far more significant than his triumph. Indian shooters winning on the world stage was no longer surprising. In fact, it is almost expected now.

His gold medal suddenly awakened the country to the idea that India can win at the Olympics as well. It helped satisfy a national yearning and, in the process, made a statement about the significance of sports in an era of escalating political turmoil. Olympic success, the victory demonstrated, held the promise of uniting Indians across the country. For the first time in

Indian Olympic history, the media appropriated this victory in a manner commonly associated with cricket.

With Bindra going on to add an Asian Games silver in 2010, a Commonwealth Games gold in 2014 and the two medals at Incheon to his repertoire, it was natural that his achievements, analysed for hours on television, made him India's most feted shooter ever. If the media frenzy that followed his bronze medal win was any indication, shooting, it could be said, had managed to capture the public imagination in the country.

What stands out in the Bindra story is that his legacy has never come easy to him. Not many know that Bindra shot a 4 in his first sighting shot before the final in Beijing. The second was an equally baffling 4.2. While we still can't pinpoint the exact reason, his first shot of 10.5 in the final against this backdrop helps demonstrate the enormity of the achievement.

Even in Incheon, when almost everyone had written him off before the last shot and thought he would end up fourth, he shot a top-class 10.5. And his Iranian opponent, then up by 0.7 ended up shooting a poor 9.6, giving Bindra the bronze medal.

Equally interesting is the reason why he lost in Athens after making the final for the bronze medal position. The floor below his position at the range 'was unsteady'. His coach later discovered it and reported it to the technical committee in attendance. 'They discovered the glue wasn't glued tight and a bubble had formed. It meant the tile had a slight bounce. Slight in shooting was fatal. Slight meant I was doomed ...' Abhinav has written in his autobiography.

Born in affluence and with an indoor shooting range in his backyard, he emerged as a shooting star only to taste initial defeat at the Sydney Olympics in 2000 and then again in Athens four years later. He could have given up, blamed the system and been content with his World Championship and Commonwealth Games medals. But he persevered. His is a story born out of the pain of loss and an iron will to succeed.

WHEN ABHINAV BINDRA PLASTERED HIS JAW TO SHOOT BETTER: LIFE LESSONS FROM THE MAN WHO IS ONE IN A BILLION

It had just been an hour since a fateful shot of 9 had shattered Abhinav's Olympic dream at the Rio Games. Close to four years of preparation had resulted in nothing. Ten hours each for 365 days across four long years, all for one shot which lasted a second. And one micron separated Abhinav from his second Olympic medal. If there was ever a heartbreak, this was it. If there was ever a sportsman who took it on the chin and moved on, it is him. 'What else can I do?' he said. 'I have done all that I could have. Trained, worked hard, battled pain, stayed away from home. I couldn't have done more and I am happy I made the final and the fourth position. It was close.'

We were curious to see if he was hiding his emotions. If there was something inside that we as journalists weren't able to capture. For one shot had relegated him to an also-ran position – made him a martyr. But no. Abhinav, the proud athlete that he is, did not want to give anything away. Just like the now-fabled last few shots that got him through the qualifiers, all he did was slightly shake his head. 'It is done. I now need to get this out of my system. Twenty-one years is a really long time, isn't it? Enough. Now I will go back and console my nephew who cried for one whole hour because his uncle lost. He is six and wants to be a shooter,' he said as he was packing up his equipment.

Was this his way to unwind and come to terms with the heartbreak? No. Was he jabbering? Not at all. He is Abhinav Bindra, India's only individual gold-medal winner and he had to be different. He was already trying to distance himself from the loss and move on. 'I will have my last meal in the Olympic Village. I won't come back here again. I've been here five times in the last sixteen years – Sydney, Athens, Beijing, London and Rio – and I think I have done my share. It's been a decent career.'

Let's go back to the last few shots for qualification in Rio. After three solid relays, Abhinav had suddenly started to falter. From fourth to fifth to twelfth, his Olympic dream was almost up in flames. His supporters had started to chew their nails. Shake. Stamp their feet. Pray. Imagine what he must've been going through. 'Yes, of course I was shaking. More than all of you. I am a human being after all. Why do you think I wasn't nervous? Of course, I was. I was feeling the pressure, the heat, the nervousness, and yet I couldn't move. I couldn't allow my body to move because I needed to shoot a good last relay to make the final. But that's what I had trained for. Worked on my body, my technique, my mind. And I tried to refocus because I knew these were the last ten shots of my shooting life. I had been there and done that for twenty-one long years and I wanted to do the last few shots well. That's all I was thinking about and it worked.'

It did indeed work. Three 10.8s in his last few shots and Abhinav made his third Olympic final. And while it did not end in glory, it did not end in disgrace either. Coming fourth means only three men in this entire world across two hundred plus nations were better than him. Six were better than him in Athens, by Beijing there were none and three in Rio. To be in the world's top eight across a period of twelve long years isn't bad, is it?

While he has now embarked on a new life, there is no doubt that it was a career unrivalled. He has had his lows as well as his highs. That's how it is. And the lows, as is always the case, are far more than the highs. Yet he did not give up. He would get up at 5 am every morning and reach his range by 8.30 am for electrical muscle stimulation (EMS) training and everything else that he possibly could do to get himself ready. To make the Olympic final and shoot to win India another medal. He was almost there. Almost.

The problem is that in sports, the 'almost there' is practically non-existent. It is a winner-takes-all situation, whether we like it or not. And no one knows this better than Abhinav. And that's why he is so matter-of-fact. So candid. So poised and composed. He was not in Olympic depression after Rio. Rather it was a liberation of sorts for him. It was all done. And he was relieved because he couldn't have done things any better. 'There is literally no fuel left in the tank. I have given it my all,' said Abhinav. He had indeed.

As he was walking back to the Village one last time in Rio, we kept asking him questions. Would he still watch the Olympics? Is there any particular event he would watch now that he had the time? Would he dabble in eating well once he was back in India after almost two months away from home? What is normal life for Abhinav Bindra? Has he led anything of the like in the last two decades?

We kept pressing him and Abhinav kept smiling. 'No, I won't watch the Olympics. Maybe an event here and there on television. But no, nothing in particular. Also, I am not a big foodie. Yes, I have missed home food and will eat at home but it is not something that attracts me a great deal. I don't really know what I will do in the morning after I wake up. I'll have to wait and see.'

As Abhinav was speaking, we kept thinking – how boring can one be? Is he not interested in the more mundane pleasures of life? But then the realization dawned on us one final time. No, he is not ordinary. An ordinary man does not win an Olympic gold medal. Does not make the final three times. Make it to the shoot-off and then remain composed after a heartbreak. He is a genius and Indian sports should celebrate him. Well done, Abhinav.

Looking back, he put it nicely: 'Twenty-two years of competition, 180 medals, five Olympics, three Olympic finals, one Olympic gold. All of it seems like a daze. Until it doesn't. I can now see all this much more clinically and dispassionately. I am no longer a stakeholder in my shooting career. I have exited my investment, as venture capitalists would say. That is my past. And I have a future to think about. But that makes retrospection all the more interesting for me. I was not a natural athlete. In fact, I was a reluctant sportsperson. When introduced to shooting, I felt it was for me. Something I could see myself doing, making a life of and a career from. For this chance, I navigated my way from dream to reality and built the personal skills that were necessary to win ... Athens 2004 was a wake-up call. In perhaps the most defining incident of my career, I came a disappointing seventh in the Olympic final after shooting what I thought was the perfect game. Only much later did I find out that the lane position I was allotted had a loose tile underfoot, which reverberated every time I shot. In a game of micrometres, it was amazing that I even hit the target! I went into depression (literally) after Athens. Months later, I had two obvious choices – one, quit the sport, or two, carry on and accept the incident as 'bad luck'. I chose a third option and it defined me. I chose the quest for adaptability – to try and be perfect on an imperfect day. I started training under deliberately imperfect conditions, even installing a loose tile in my home range and practising regularly while standing on it. I trained under low lights and bright lights, adjusted bulbs and added peculiar shadows, painted the walls the same colours as the relevant Olympic ranges. Extreme behaviour perhaps. But it worked for me and came to my rescue even in Rio when my carefully chosen sighter broke minutes before my event. I was able to remain composed and made it to fourth. Had I chosen option two after Athens, I would have probably accepted it as fate and given up!'

And when he speaks of extreme behaviour to try and make it to the top of the Olympic podium, it is important to understand what all he did. For that's the real backstage – the story that is not yet out there in the media for all to read and consume.

'To give you one example, I was made aware that in Germany people believed that the misalignment of the upper and lower sides of one's jaw can contribute to biomechanical errors and the misalignment of the body. So, I

visited a dentist who X-rayed my jaw and made a splint for me to wear while
sleeping and training. A sort of plastic denture. The result was incredible!
When I wore the splint, the range of motion in my neck improved by 1,520
degrees and this helped me perfect my alignment. I wouldn't have believed
this until I experienced it,' said Abhinav.

For Abhinav, 'high performance' was about being able to stay in the
moment and letting the body take over with no interference from the
mind. No new thoughts. No thoughts of unattended practices, inadequate
equipment, fear of failure or the outcomes of success.

He continued: 'Sight, Aim, Trigger. Sight, Aim, Trigger. All body. No
mind. No regrets. I would have loved to train in India and find all that I
was looking for, here. Unfortunately, given the nature of my quest, that was
not possible simply because the ingredients I was looking for were largely
missing. I couldn't make training in India my Plan A; it was always a Plan
B. At the same time, I could go abroad for a few weeks and access what I
needed elsewhere, but home was home and where I wanted to be based.
How do we make local training the Plan A for our athletes, as is the case for
a majority of athletes in the top five or six most successful Olympic nations?
To win a medal, you are competing with almost 200 countries. If we have
the aspiration, we need to be among the countries in the top one per cent in
any event. For that, things need to change.'

'So, what can we do to give more Indian athletes a Plan A that would
help them train locally?' he asks. 'It is easy to say money and funding
and quote the amounts spent by developed nations on "creating" medal-
winners. But that is a lazy answer because money, while essential to bring
about what is needed, is merely the enabler. The devil lies in the detail of
what you do with it. Athletes are human. Each is unique. Plan As will take
shape when options are created and made available to athletes who deserve
these options.'

To Abhinav, it came down to three things – culture, information and
infrastructure.

When we asked him to elaborate, this is what he said: 'By culture, I
mean as people, what do we aspire for? What messages do we give each
other? Do we believe and communicate that elite sporting achievement is
of societal value and act on these beliefs? Are coaches both inspiring and
wise enough to know when it is time to let go of an athlete? Are there
parents who don't throw the education card at every opportunity? The

way we live and the language we use creates cultures and environments. If we indeed expect excellence from our athletes, do we create for them the cultural milieu where that is the norm or at least a valid aspiration? Do we respect the idea that their careers and achievements might not be linear? Do we give them space to make mistakes, experiment and become the best versions of themselves? These ways of thinking and doing make a culture – the environment in which a successful athlete lives, trains and competes.

'By information, I mean having access to the best knowledge about technique, equipment, training and nutrition. These form the bedrock of a system that equalizes and levels the playing field before the innate talent and degree of preparedness can take over in contributing to results. If we are unable to be on the cutting edge of knowledge, we are asking our athletes to use their talent to equalize rather than exceed the competition. A serious commitment to enabling access to these is an absolute prerequisite.

'Finally, world-class infrastructure and equipment need to be more ubiquitously available if we are to encourage more youngsters to transition from recreational sports to elite sports. Increasing access not only involves creating infrastructure and purchasing equipment but also lowering the barriers of accessibility for our athletes. Making the best-of-class available locally reduces costs, increases the depth of the talent pool and competitiveness. All vital factors that play into sustained success on elite stages.

Ultimately – contrary to what some might believe – no self-respecting athlete wants everything on a platter.'

Abhinav was always ready to fight, to improve and to excel. Before signing off, he said, 'What we need to avoid is our athletes fighting the unnecessary battles of access, choice, knowledge and attitude. Of red tape. To me, those are the changes that will foster a high-performance culture in this country.'

Abhinav remains one in a billion. And will always remain so going forward.

5

Mother Mary
India's 'Ali' from Imphal

It was a month and a half before the 2012 London Olympics and Boria had a telephone interview set up with Mary Kom at 7 am. She was at home in Manipur on a break from her training in Balewadi. The interview had been organized by Viren Rasquinha, one of her closest friends and CEO of Olympic Gold Quest (OGQ), a foundation that has made a serious difference to Indian Olympic sports. We were keen to speak to Mary so we could document her journey. We did not know Mary well at the time and were concerned about whether or not she would want to open up on the first day itself. She isn't the best communicator and we needed her completely focused for the interview. At the same time, it wasn't fair to ask for more considering she was at such a crucial juncture in her preparation for the Olympics, which added to the anxiety before the call.

On picking up the phone in Imphal, Mary first said to call her back in an hour. She said she was busy with household chores and needed a little time to wrap it up. Our initial thought was that she was avoiding the interview. It often happens that athletes don't want to talk and, without being impolite, ask to be called back later. However, after sending a message to Viren it was soon clarified that this wasn't the case with Mary. It was enough to arouse our curiosity and when she got back on the phone in an hour, that was the first thing we asked her about. Was she avoiding a chat? 'I was making breakfast for Renca and Nainai (her children)', she said laughing, They wanted to eat paranthas for breakfast and when I am home I try and make them breakfast, lunch and dinner. I am a full-time wife and mother when I am home, you know.'

Mary takes pleasure in taking charge of the household. 'The maid hasn't come today and I will also be doing the dishes in a while. Onler (her husband) takes care of me all through the year when I am boxing. This is the only time I can take care of him.' A five-time world champion doing the dishes a month ahead of the Olympics – there could not have been a better start to the interview. This was one of the reasons why Mary, irrespective of what happened at the London Olympics or thereafter, was already a legend.

Mary, not many remember, had almost missed qualification for the London Olympics. She eventually made it as a lucky loser and had Nicola Adams, the eventual gold medallist, not beaten Russia's Elena Savelyeva in the semi-final of the World Championships in May 2012, Mary would have missed the cut, having lost to Adams in the quarter-final. However, the back story of this defeat is what is startling. For many years, Mary was the poster girl of Indian women's boxing and was regarded as the favourite to qualify by winning yet another medal at the World Championships.

The officials who accompanied the team to the qualifiers did little to make her journey smooth. On the day of her bout, which was scheduled for the evening, Kom was asked by the leaders of the Indian delegation to cheer for her teammates and was subsequently left to sit in the stands for close to six hours ahead of her bout. Not only was her food routine messed up but she was also exhausted going into her contest. These factors played a role in her defeat to Adams. While it is fair to say that Adams was a better and stronger boxer, it is also fair to say that Mary wasn't the best prepared for the quarter-final at the World Championships.

Things hadn't been easy for Mary going into the Olympics. Winner of five World Championship titles by then (six now) and awarded the Rajiv Gandhi Khel Ratna in July 2009, she returned from a two-year sabbatical to take a shot at the Olympics.

Women's boxing had made it to the 2012 Games and Mary desperately wanted the most coveted medal of all. During the interim, she had given birth to her twin sons Renca and Nainai. Since her comeback, she had done everything in her capacity to prepare the best she could. This included dealing with an emotional storm while preparing for the 2012 Asian Championship in Mongolia. Busy training in Patiala, Mary heard the devastating news that one of her sons, Nainai, had a heart problem and had been admitted to a hospital in Chandigarh. Emotionally drained but reluctant to miss practice, she used to visit Chandigarh every day after practice to spend time with her child. Onkholor Kom, her husband and biggest support system, was with her all the while and they stood together against an adversity they had little control over.

Her simplicity and humility were borne out yet again when we met her in Liverpool at the end of July where she was training for one final week before moving to the Olympic Village in London on 2 August to join the Indian contingent. Her first fight was on 5 August, which as it turned out was a day of special significance to her. Five years before, she had given birth to her twins on that very date. She hoped to not only make them but her entire country proud on their fifth birthday. It had all been very scientifically structured for her by Team Mary Kom. She trained in Balewadi in India till 25 July after which she travelled to Liverpool for a week of acclimatization.

She looked excited and upbeat after reaching England. '*Yeh* Emirates *wale bade acche hain. Inhone hume apna* rice cooker *lane diya* without charging for extra luggage,' Mary looked delighted. 'I am happy I can eat my sticky rice everyday. It makes a big difference in my training and preparation.'

Mary, it was clear, was still rooted in her upbringing in Imphal and the accolades she had won in her life had not changed her much. She still wanted her sticky rice, which she made herself in the rice cooker she carried from India, and that's what made her the happiest while training in Liverpool under the eyes of her coach Charles Atkinson.

In London, Mary Kom was already a legend. She was a rare international athlete who was sought out by the British media. People wanted to know how a mother of two could come out of a two-year sabbatical and mount a strong challenge for a medal at the Olympics. This curiosity over 'Magnificent Mary' had filtered down to the spectators who made their way to the ExCeL convention centre on 5 August 2012.

It was as if Mary was fighting a home bout. The noise inside the arena became deafening as the bout was about to start, creating quite the atmosphere as most cheered for Mary as she entered the ring. The entire Indian contingent was in the stands and as Mary punched her way past Poland's Karolina Michalczuk to a 19–14 win, we were in raptures. It was as if all of us were living the dream with her. While the first round was a close 3–3, the second went to Mary at 5–4. It was in the deciding round that Mary unleashed a flurry of punches and built up a sizeable lead. By the end of the bout, most of us knew who the winner was and it was only a formality for the referee to lift Mary's hand. But we have seen strange things happen in boxing and must say the countdown to the announcement of the result was a strain on our nerves.

This was because Mary was not simply a boxer trying to win a medal for India. She was a symbol of hope and empowerment with a never-say-die attitude that so defined contemporary India. For the longest time, we had heard that India was lagging in international sports from a lack of facilities and training opportunities. Here was someone who was born in Manipur with little or no facilities and had still made it to the top of her sport and remained there for over a decade. And here she was at the Olympics, fighting in a higher weight category than her own and still not overwhelmed by the enormity of the occasion.

Viren Rasquinha helped in putting Mary's challenge in context: 'Most people in India believed Mary was sure to win a medal in London because she had won five World Championship titles in the past. However, they did not take into account the fact that she won each of the titles in the 46 kg category. In London, she was fighting in the 51 kg category because there was no 46 or 48 kg category at the Olympics. It was a very steep jump for any boxer. As a result, we first got her to fight in the 48 kg category at the 2010 World Championships and finally pushed her to fight in the 51 kg category in 2011. Since Mary is blessed with talent, she adjusted to the new weight division really well.'

'Mary was never supposed to win an Olympic medal in 51 kg,' an *Indian Express* editorial later stated in admiration. It was an uphill task 'given the limitations of her diminutive frame and inability to pile on muscle weight. But Mary went on to do precisely that.'

Mary needed an Olympic medal to complete her story and the win against the Polish competitor was an important step in the journey. She followed up with yet another convincing win over Tunisia's Maroua Rahali and, much to everyone's relief and excitement, was assured of a medal. Though she lost in the semi-final to the formidable Adams, the Olympic medal was a fitting addition to an already glittering career. Mary wanted to become a boxer when she saw a Mohammad Ali fight on TV. Now, she had turned into India's Ali.

WHEN MARY KOM WANTED TO PUNCH A LONDON TAXI DRIVER

It turned out that Mary was only partially satisfied. We discovered this in an interview she gave to Boria the day after she won her Olympic medal. The interview itself unfolded under rather bizarre circumstances. The story started with a call from Viren Rasquinha to Boria around midday, asking if he was around the Westfield Mall in Starford. He was, for it was right next to the Olympic Village. Viren sounded relieved. 'Mary is lost. She had to go to some felicitation in the morning and the taxi driver dropped her off at a distance from the Olympic Village. She has made it to Westfield and is waiting there. Can you please go and find her and take her to the Village?' pleaded Viren.

Journalistic scoops are sometimes built on such coincidences. Finding Mary was delightful. It also gave Boria uninterrupted time with the newly crowned Olympic medallist as he walked her back to the Village.

The Mary in front of the Omega store in the middle of the mall was a very different Mary from the one we had met earlier in Liverpool. She was fuming and was red with anger. 'The taxi driver left me and disappeared,' she said. 'Had it been a little longer, I would have punched him.' We were glad she did not. An Olympic medallist being booked for assault would not have made a very nice headline. It was only after she calmed down that she started talking about her medal.

'I couldn't fulfil the promise I made to you and my country, so please forgive me' was her first comment when she finally settled down for a coffee. We were stunned by her modesty. Here was an Olympic champion asking for forgiveness when she had, in fact, won a rare medal for her country – the first by an Indian woman in boxing.

'You gave it your all to win an Olympic medal. You should be in seventh heaven,' Boria said, trying to cheer her up. But Mary would not have any of it. 'Actually, yes and no. I wanted to win gold for India. On every occasion that I have spoken to you in the last three months, I said that I wanted to beat Niccola on her home turf and make amends for the defeat in the World Championships. I trained hard, prepared really well for the bout but it wasn't my day. With that kind of crowd support in her favour, she always had the advantage. I couldn't make it to the final but at least I have won a medal for my country. Olympic medals do not come easy and I feel proud that I have won the only boxing medal in this Olympics,' she said with a sense of finality in her voice.

Boria tried to lighten the mood and shift the focus of the discussion. 'You have been away from family – your husband and children – and everyone else for a long time. What now? Back to being mother and wife?' Family is her soft spot and it did not take much to guess that she would be in a better headspace in speaking of Onler and the children. Her face immediately lit up with a smile as she mentioned her boys. 'I have been sent a long list by my children of gifts I need to buy for them,' she said. 'I have already bought skateboards, Liverpool football club jerseys and a host of other things. I have to take all of this back to make up for being away! The medal isn't of any consequence to them. They are too small to understand its significance. They are far more interested in the chocolates that mom will bring home. And yes, I am definitely looking forward to going back and seeing them again. My family has stood by me at all times and nothing would have been possible without them.' Mary was back to being mother and wife.

Finally in a better mood, she even asked Boria if he wanted to hold the Olympic medal and click a photograph (though it looked much better round her neck). In any case, a photograph with an Olympic champion was a better picture than simply holding up her medal in your hand.

Then came the final and most important question. Was she planning to retire? Mary seemed to be expecting the question. 'So, do you want me to retire?' she shot back with a smile. Before he could blurt a loud 'NO', she started speaking again: 'I am playing well and I want to continue for two–three more years and then see how things go. I am feeling good about my sport. I've trained as hard as I possibly could, looked after my diet, did all the technical things necessary to improve my game so there is no point in giving up just yet. I will surely continue for some time and try and win some more medals for India. But make no mistake, if the Olympics had a competition in my weight category, which is 48 kilograms, I would have surely won gold for India.'

'Fighting in the 51 kilogram category', she added while shaking her head, 'was really difficult.'

The gold medal dream hadn't quite left her. It was clear that it would take her time to accept that she had to stop one win away from the Olympic final. Maybe that's why her bigger takeaway was not the medal itself. 'I sincerely hope the medal encourages many more women in India to take up boxing,' she said. 'Even when I won five World Championships, there was no interest in the sport. But the Olympics are different. There is so much hype and interest in the Olympics. My Facebook account is overflowing because people recognize the significance of an Olympic medal. This medal belongs to all Indian women and it will only be of real value to me if it inspires the next generation of women to take up the sport.'

THE SPECIAL IRRATIONALITY OF MARY KOM

Mary couldn't make it to the Rio Olympics in 2016. Had it been anyone else in her place, he or she would have given up and chosen a life of comfort and luxury. She is now a well-known celebrity, a nominated Member of Parliament, an in-demand after-dinner speaker and much more. Most importantly, she is an Olympic medallist and also a six-time world champion. Mary is the face of multiple brands in India and is one of the best stories to have come out of Indian sports in the last half-century. She is also a part of multiple government committees and has most recently been voted the best Asian athlete of 2018–19. A mother of three adorable children, she had her last child in 2015.

There is very little that she has not achieved in her career of over a decade and a half. But these acknowledgements come from a rational mind. And Mary isn't always rational. To start boxing with boys at the tender age of seven while growing up in Imphal in a rather conservative milieu isn't rational. Changing her name to Mary to avoid her father finding out that she was competing in a boxing competition isn't a mark of rationality either. Finally, to keep training while one of her sons was in the hospital fighting for his life takes the kind of courage that we will never be able to fathom.

You tell her this and all she does is smile. We pressed her a little more on the subject and she gave us a rather philosophical answer: 'Boxing is the only thing I know how to do well. It has given me everything I have today. Why else would a woman from Manipur with little to no resources be respected all across India? And it is important that women feel empowered in doing what they want to do.'

It is this steel that explains how and why she was able to write the following letter to her sons in taking a stand for women's empowerment in India:

Dear Sons,

Let's talk about rape. Let's talk about sexual crimes against women.
Every single day, women are being stalked, molested and raped. You,
my boys, are only nine-years old – and the youngest only three – but
this is the age where we must sensitise ourselves to how we treat our
women.

Let me start by telling you that your mother was molested, first
in Manipur and then again while she was out with her girl friends in
Delhi and Haryana's Hissar [sic]. I know it is shocking to learn that
even a woman who has earned her spurs, boxing her way through
life, was made to feel violated. I was on my way to my training camp
at 8.30 in the morning in a cycle rickshaw when a stranger suddenly
lunged at me and stroked my breast. I was angry, very angry. I leapt
off the rickshaw and chased him, holding my slipper in my hand, but
he managed to escape. My regret is that I could not catch him or the
karate that I had already learnt by then, would have come in handy.

I was only 17-years-old then and am 33 now. I have brought great
fame to my country and have been celebrated as a medallist but what
I also want, is to be respected as a woman. We women have scaled
heights and stormed male bastions but for some men, we are still all
about our bodies. Remember, dear sons, like you, we too have two
eyes and a nose. Some parts of our bodies are different and that's the
only thing that sets us apart. We use our brains to think, like all men
do, and we feel with our hearts, like you do. We don't deserve our
breasts to be touched or our bums patted. That's what happened to
my friends and me in Delhi and Hissar [sic], while we were taking a
walk outside our training camps ...

–Mom

In 2018, Mary, at the age of thirty-six, defied norms and won gold at
the Gold Coast Commonwealth Games, at the Asian Games and also at the
World Championships in Delhi, increasing her World Championship gold
medal count to six.

Soon after the competition, we met Mary in Mumbai. She was there
as the face of the Tata Mumbai Marathon and looked more focused than
ever. Not only did she sing on stage and bring the audience to its feet, but
she was also in a perfect headspace to speak about her future. 'People have

started to expect the gold medal from me in Tokyo', she said before adding, 'What people don't realize is that I will yet again have to fight in the 51 kilogram category with boxers who are taller and stronger. But I am not saying this as an excuse. All I am trying to say is it will not be easy to make it to Tokyo and win a second Olympic medal.'

That's when Boria decided to interrupt and tell her that nothing has ever come easy to her. Born in a lower middle-class household, she had to walk miles to make it to school, which was a fair distance away from her native village. She was beaten up by her father for wanting to pursue boxing and was racially vilified ever since she came to Delhi.

She became used to hearing 'chinki' taunts before she went on to win multiple medals at world competitions and became 'Magnificent Mary'. She overcame the odds and beat Nikhat Zareen, fourteen years younger, at the Indian Open in May 2019 and won gold at a World Championship preparatory event two months later.

It is important to note that there was a well-publicized controversy involving Zareen when Mary was given direct entry into the World Championships in October 2019 without having to fight her again.

A similar issue arose between the two over representing India at the Tokyo Olympics. Zareen, known for having won a bronze medal at the 2019 Asian Championships, made an impassioned plea to the sports minister and the Boxing Federation of India for a trial bout. Abhinav Bindra sided with her, saying that as athletes you are always judged in the present and not by what you have accomplished before. Hence, it was a matter of time before a trial was organized. The federation, while initially reluctant, did eventually give in, saying that the same rules should apply to everyone. This controversy should never have been allowed to fester. Their selection trial was scheduled for December 2019, by which time this book would have already gone to press. Mary, who had publicly opposed the trial match, wasn't pleased with the outcome but was left with no option but to accept the ruling. Frankly, this is the best way forward.

In spite of all this, few will dispute that Mary is still the best boxer in her category in India. She proved this at the World Championships by becoming the first-ever boxer in history to win a record eight medals, surpassing Cuban legend Felix Savon.

This medal, to the ones who saw her fight, was not easily won. She had a tough draw and, despite the first-round bye, the route to the medal was tough. Facing the spunky Thai Jitpong in the second round, Mary had to bring all her experience to the fore against someone who was throwing wild punches, hoping some would connect. Mary sussed her beautifully in round one before going to attack in rounds two and three, eventually winning by a unanimous 5–0 verdict. It was the same story in the quarter-final against her Colombian opponent, who many thought was capable of causing an upset. But Mary was all over her in the second round and by the end of the bout, there was clearly one winner.

When the referee raised her hand saying the customary, 'And the winner in the red corner …', all she did was smile. There wasn't any over-the-top celebration. Mary knew that the World Championships were not her mission. Tokyo 2020 was.

6

India's Paralympians
Untold Tales of Deepa Malik and
Devendra Jhajharia

She was given seven days to walk. Literally, seven days. That is what the doctors said to Rio Paralympics silver medallist Deepa Malik when she visited the Indian Army's Research and Referral Hospital in Delhi on 25 May 1999. Twenty-one years old at the time and a mother of two young girls, she was informed that her spinal tumour was at breaking point and doctors were not confident enough of giving her more than seven days. Her soldier husband was serving in Kargil and her in-laws weren't keen on medical treatment. They preferred, in her words, *'Babaji's bootee* or *doodh-haldi'* (a baba's herbs or milk and turmeric) to combat the growing pain. Her father was in South Africa and Deepa had no option but to go to the hospital alone to get herself diagnosed. 'The pain was becoming unbearable and I was forced to go to the hospital. They said I could walk for the next seven days and that was all. I actually prepared myself for paralysis and never getting up and walking again' said Deepa.

She had two options left. The first was to give up on life and wallow in self-pity. Asking the 'why me?' question blaming fate wasn't going to help. The second option was to go home and use the remaining seven days to get her house ready to deal with what was coming. 'I got a customized bed made, had a ramp installed, bought a microwave so that my young daughters, nine and four, could heat their food and have it, bought

74

tupperware, which were all microwave-safe and got ready for a life on the wheelchair if I survived,' recollected Deepa. On the eve of the surgery, she was forced to inform her parents for she was told it could take her close to two months to get back home.

It is well known that Deepa was operated on for her spinal tumour and ended up having three back-to-back surgeries. She had 183 stitches and was in a coma for forty days before she opened her eyes and managed to get home. What most people don't know is that when she was being taken to the operation theatre, Deepa had two requests from her team of doctors.

First, she wanted to speak to her husband for what could potentially be the last time. Second, she wanted to walk to the operation theatre unassisted for that was the last time she would be doing so. Both her wishes were granted. Deepa remembers that Bikram Malik, her loving husband, tried to placate her by saying, 'Don't worry about walking. I will forever carry you in my arms when I am back from the war.'

From fighting against all odds to winning a silver medal at the Rio Paralympics in 2016 to winning the Rajiv Gandhi Khel Ratna award in 2019, Deepa Malik embodies what Indian paralympic sports are all about: the courage of conviction and a special kind of grit that is almost impossible to comprehend.

'The Extraordinarily Abled': India's Paralympic Breakthrough at Rio 2016

In nearly a century of competing at the Olympics, never before had two Indians draped in the tricolour celebrated winning medals together at an Olympic stadium in front of a near-packed crowd. It was to this rarity that the country woke up in September 2016 when Mariyappan Thangavelu and Varun Bhati won the gold and bronze in the high jump category at the Rio Paralympics.

However, compared to the national outpour of emotion in the aftermath of Sakshi Malik's bronze and P.V. Sindhu's silver medal wins just a month earlier in August, the reaction to wins at the Para Games was relatively muted.

How we treat our Paralympians like Mariyappan, Varun, Malik or Devendra Jhajaria (two Paralympics golds in 2004 and 2016 each) is a reflection of what we value as a society and who we are. Our attitude towards these exceptional athletes and their predecessors like Murlikant Petkar (gold-medal winner at 50 m freestyle swimming at the Heidelberg Paralympics in 1972) defines us as a 'people'.

In the West, para-athletes have for long been accorded the same respect as the able-bodied Olympians. Medal winners have been feted in the same manner and the Para games receive similar prominence in the media. In India, however, this has never been the case. We, as a society, have always looked down on our para-athletes, invested little in facilities that would encourage them to take up sports and done very little to decorate and turn them into national icons.

For the longest time, people have seen specially-abled athletes as langda, apahij or andha (handicapped, physically disabled or blind). They were either the subject of pity or scorn. The absence of respect has relegated para-athletes to the status of virtual outcasts. Such a mindset – appalling to say the least – betrays the very ideals of equality and civil liberty that our country stands for. This acute insensitivity is only now being rectified.

Para-athletes were not considered for the Khel Ratna, Indian sports' highest honour, until recently. Devendra Jhajharia broke through the glass ceiling when he was honoured with the award in 2017, followed by Deepa Malik in 2019. Murlikant Petkar was finally given his due with a Padma Sri only in 2018, forty-six years after his amazing feats in Heidelberg. These are important moves for creating a truly inclusive society.

The successes at the 2016 Rio Paralympics, in that sense, presented the opportunity to overcome the abominable ground realities that India's para-athletes face. It was an opening for redemption. With Indian athletes winning an unprecedented two gold medals, one silver (the first ever from a woman) and a bronze, the 2016 Paralympics went a long way in bringing Paralympic sports to the centrestage of national consciousness. The attention the medals engendered meant that the climate was finally ripe to start creating facilities for Paralympic sports in India and to sensitize our society to the treatment of para-athletes.

Despite there being a rich history, not much is known, for example, about India's first Paralympic gold-medal winner Muralikant Petkar. A war hero who had to give up on sports having suffered multiple bullet wounds in the 1965 war with Pakistan, his was a story of exemplary courage. Not only did he win a gold at swimming in 1972, but he also participated in several other events at those games. Yet, his story remains a lost historical relic. That he was not considered worthy of a national award like the Padma Sri until more than four decades after his achievement is a travesty given the iconic status accorded to personalities such as Abhinav Bindra or P.V. Sindhu.

Similarly, Thangavelu, who won India's first Paralympic gold in Rio in the high jump category, lost a leg at the age of five. He was playing outside his house when a state-owned transport bus hit him. Abandoned by his father before his teenage years, he was brought up by his mother who sold vegetables on a cycle in Tamil Nadu's Salem district and does so even to this day. He struggled to make ends meet but still managed to emerge a Paralympic champion. His is a story that can perhaps only happen in India.

Deepa Malik is yet another stand-out story. From getting operated on while her husband was serving the nation in the Kargil war and getting 183 stitches between her shoulder blades, she has been an inspiration for years. Having won sporting laurels on the international stage for close to a decade, the only accolade missing from her repertoire was a Paralympic medal. At the Rio Games, she fulfilled her dream.

Deepa has never been daunted by adversity. When she was told at the age of twenty-nine that she had to choose between paralysis and death, anyone else would have had a meltdown. Deepa, however, faced the challenge of life head-on. Seven broken vertebrae and frequent MRI scans in the absence of titanium plates could not stop her from throwing the shot put.

For the record, Mariyappan Thangavelu did not speak English. His coach Satyanarayana had to take on the role of his translator when foreign journalists wanted to report his story. However, language barriers did not stop him from seeing the *Rocky* movies and feel inspired. In his mind, if Rocky Balboa could do it, so could he. Sports, it is evident from this example, speak a universal language that cuts through class, geography and money.

Taking a cue from Mariyappan, Devendra and Deepa, Indian sports can take a giant leap in Tokyo 2020. It can help transform the way we look at sports and, more importantly, how we look at disability. As Sachin Tendulkar said at a function he helped organize in October 2016 to celebrate the Paralympic medallists, 'These athletes are not disabled. Rather, they are extraordinarily abled.'

A confession is in order here. While we are acutely aware that Paralympic athletes are an inspiration to millions of able-bodied men and women, it is also true that we aren't yet equipped to document every medal-winning story in detail. A lot more research still needs to be done on these athletes. Their stories merit a new book altogether, let alone a chapter. At the same time, we need to accord the Paralympics equal importance. It is something we deeply believe in.

The two stories we know well are of Deepa Malik and Devendra Jhajharia, the only two para-athletes to have won the Khel Ratna. We decided to document their stories in this book to set the ball rolling. It is a small start.

As our systems become more sensitive to para-athletes and the government and private foundations start investing in Paralympic sports to provide athletes with the facilities they so badly need, it is a matter of time before someone documents India's Paralympic story in totality. The next few pages should serve as the starting point for this endeavour.

The Lady Who Got Her Chair Welded: The Extraordinary Story of Deepa Malik

Soon after returning home from hospital in 1999, Deepa had to find a new purpose in life. An active kid who played every conceivable sport while growing up and was addicted to riding her bike, the reality of disability was a difficult one to adjust to. 'I had fallen in love with Bikram because he was a biker,' smiled Deepa. At the time, Bikram was a young major in the Army with a fondness for bikes. One day, Deepa walked up to him, asked for the keys to his bike and proceeded to roam the neighbourhood on it as if she was a pro. Bikram, intrigued and smitten, met Deepa's father, who was also in the Army, the very next day. He asked for her hand and told her father that he wanted to buy his would-be fiancé a bike!

For an active sportsperson, life on a wheelchair was extremely difficult to come to terms with. Problems mounted for Deepa when her elder daughter, Devika, suffered a head injury and was paralyzed for a while. She needed physiotherapy and constant care, which an ailing Deepa was unable to provide. While staying in Ahmednagar, where her husband was posted at the time, she was struggling to find a balance between her treatment and the responsibilities of a young mother. 'Sir, *mere* life *mein tabhi* sport *dobara waapas aaya*,' said Deepa. (that's when sport came back to my life.) 'It started rather strangely,' she added. 'One day a retired cook from the

Army came to visit us and said to me "Madam *aap toh itna* active *the. Mujhe aap koh aise dekh ke accha nahi lagta*".' (Madam, you were so active. I don't like seeing you like this.)

Deepa, not one to feel depressed, asked him if he knew of any restaurants or eateries nearby where she could take her daughters in the evening to add a bit of variety to their lives and cut the boredom. 'That's when it started. This man said to me that while there were no restaurants in that area of Ahmednagar, he was willing to start cooking for me if I was ready to fund him. Soon enough we started a home delivery service, which subsequently became a restaurant, and we called it 'Dee's Plate'. I was told that the Maharashtra government was giving loans for people with disability to do things on their own and it was with this loan that I started the food delivery service. To those who had said to me that my life was over and I couldn't feed my kids anymore, I was now ready to feed them and their children as well,' she said with pride. 'We soon started getting bulk orders and also did catering for school parties and birthdays.'

Army officers often frequented the restaurant for it was also a place to relax and Deepa, who loved biking, soon decided to write a piece on the officers' bikes for a magazine. Once it was published, the junior officers asked her how she knew so much about bikes. One of them asked why she didn't get a customized bike made for herself and apply for a license. 'A junior officer said to me one day that I should go to the Spinal Injury Centre in Vasant Kunj in Delhi and do some strength training, for then I could ride a bike better. That's where my world opened up. They allowed me to swim as part of my rehab and said it was the best way to build shoulder strength,' said Deepa.

Just as she was contemplating making swimming her sport, Deepa was told that she wouldn't be able to train in water during the winter. The doctors said that her condition increased the chances of a cardiac arrest in the cold. 'Given the absence of heated pools in India, swimming wasn't an option. I had made the World Championships in Berlin and had come tenth. But I was unwilling to walk away from swimming without leaving a mark. That's when I asked my coaches to think of what I could do to get recognized and one of my coaches who came from the Malhar community in Allahabad came up with the idea of swimming across the Yamuna,' she went on.

Rigorous training for four months got her ready for the challenge and she finally informed the officials of the Limca Book of Records to come and see her make history by crossing the Yamuna. 'They insisted I have a lifeboat tail me in case something went wrong. We had a doctor and a medical team in the boat. We got a lifeboat from the Army but the ripples caused by it meant I wasn't able to swim. What happened thereafter is not something you'd believe. Men from the Malhar community, most of them boatmen and known to my coach, stationed their boats every few metres so that they could come to my rescue in case of a medical emergency. The Army boat was following me at a distance and I managed to cross the Yamuna and conclude my swimming career with a flourish,' said a proud Deepa.

'By then, however, the sports bug had bitten me. Satyanarayana sir, who had seen me then, told me that I had long arms and I was tall so I should start doing throws if my medical team allowed me to. That's how javelin started.' It was around the same time that her restaurant closed down in Ahmednagar with neighbours complaining to the police, citing a possible security threat. 'The German Bakery blast had just happened and my neighbours, who weren't very pleased with the success of the restaurant, complained to the police, who asked me to shut it down. Bikram too had left the Army by then and I needed to do something to stay occupied.'

The 2010 Commonwealth Games in Delhi were around the corner and Deepa was excited by the opportunity because every participant in the Para-Commonwealth Games stood to get Rs 2 lakh from the government of India. She entered herself in the javelin throw competition. 'I can't deny that it was an attraction. I was nearing forty and I needed the money to support my daughters,' she said. 'It was at the Commonwealth Games Village in Delhi that I learnt how a javelin was thrown while sitting on a chair. I had no idea for we had never been told or taught how. My friend Pratik, who was accompanying me, had to get my chair welded overnight in Delhi and it was no surprise that I did not win a medal. However, it was a real eye-opener in the sense that I learnt all about the international Paralympic committee, the events it hosted and the process of qualification. I learnt that I had to be a registered Para-athlete for my scores to be counted and I also learnt about the way the quota process worked.'

She put her learnings to good use and in two months won a bronze medal at the 2010 Asian Para Games in Guangzhou. More importantly, the medal earned her a reasonable amount of money to support her family. It was motivation enough to continue with sports. Multiple records and medals at international competitions followed.

It was almost expected that Deepa Malik would be India's first woman Paralympian at the 2012 London Games. 'While I don't want to blame anyone, it was a disappointment that I wasn't able to go to London. My fate was such that I received my Arjuna Award from the President of India on the same day the London Olympics started. I did not know whether to feel happy or sad,' said Deepa. 'The naysayers said to me "Madam, *ab bahut ho gaya*. (this is enough.) You are lucky that you have received the Arjuna without going to the Olympics. You are forty-two now and should retire.'

Deepa, however, was far from done and was determined to make it to the Olympics in the next four years. In the interim, she managed to keep on winning medals in javelin-throwing events at the Asian and world levels.

Just when she seemed confident of making it to the Olympics, news broke that javelin had been replaced by shot put in her category at the Rio Games. It meant that three years of hard work wasn't going to get her to the Olympics and that she would have to learn a new sport from scratch to realize her dream. '*Main haar nahi maani. Mujhe* Olympics *jaana tha aur maine thaan liya ki* shot put *karna shuru karungi*.'(I did not accept defeat. I wanted to go to the Olympics and I decided that I would start learning shot put.)

'It is a very different sport,' said Deepa. 'When I started with shot put I couldn't control my bowel movements. I would pass urine or stool on each throw and would need to change my diaper. There were days when I had passed urine and couldn't change my diaper for hours because my daughter wasn't there to help me. In the absence of a nurse or a proper doctor, these things were deeply embarrassing. While I can change clothes on my own, I need a bed to do so. I can roll out of my clothes and get into a new set, but there was no bed available in the stadium for me.' In her words, 'it was a difficult time', and for a while, 'it seemed like the forces were conspiring against me.'

Things started to change for her with the initiation of the TOPS by the SAI in 2014. 'It meant that I could now hire my own trainer, nurse, physio and have a doctor with me all the time,' said Deepa. 'Money from the TOPS allowed me to customize my equipment and chair and that made a huge difference to my training. With the amount of training I had put in, I was very confident about clearing the Rio qualification mark of 3.67 metres and making it to the Olympics.'

At the trials, Deepa managed a throw of 4.48 metres, which at the time ranked her at the very top of her sport. While she was delighted and was looking forward to seeing her name in the media the next day for having breached the Olympic qualification mark, she woke up to a headline which read, 'Deepa Malik taken to court for tampering the trial results.' One of her competitors had lodged a formal complaint claiming that Deepa, using all her clout, had manipulated the process and had unfairly made the cut.

'Sir, *mera dimaag ghum chuka tha. Mujhe* hate mail *bheje ja rahe the,*' said Deepa. (My mind was going crazy. People were sending me hate mail.) 'Some of it said that there was no way one could better the distance in shot put, so how was it that I had managed to throw 4.48 metres? One of the trolls challenged me by saying, *"Dum hai toh* Rio *mein phek ke dikha."* (if you have the strength then throw like that in Rio.) When I should have been preparing for Rio, I was busy fighting a court case and trying to clear my name. Without much support it was a real ordeal, and just when I was starting to lose hope, the verdict was passed in my favour. In fact, it was just days before the final cutoff date for Rio that the high court ruled in my favour, allowing me to compete.' Tears flowed freely down her cheeks as she recounted the story.

'At forty-six, I was competing in the biggest sporting stage of all. *Main aur kya maang sakti thi*? (What else could I ask for?) To wear the national blazer and march at the opening ceremony was a dream come true,' Deepa said. Things were different in Rio. Everywhere the Indian contingent went they were met with warm cheers. For Deepa, it was an opportunity to answer all her critics who had doubted her for years. 'I had to throw the shot put to more than 4.49 metres,' she said. All of a sudden, we sensed a change in her voice. It was as if her steely resolve was back as she got ready to recount her moment of Paralympic glory.

'There are days when great things are destined to happen. 14 September 2016 was one such day. I had never thrown the shot put to 4.61 metres and to do so at the Olympics was a dream come true. There isn't a greater feeling than to see your flag go up for you at the world's greatest sporting stage and to know that you are the first-ever Indian woman to win a medal. It meant my journey had turned full circle,' recollected a proud Deepa.

So, did things change for her after Rio? Is she happy with the sensitization that we have seen in India in the last four years? Have things improved for para-athletes or do they still put up with the absence of basic facilities in training and sports science?

'As I mentioned earlier, with TOPS things are very different. I can now afford every modern facility and have my own coach and trainer and physio. Men and women with special abilities taking to sports will not have to struggle in the same manner that we did and that's what Rio has done,' Deepa said.

However, the struggle was not yet over in 2016. Even after Rio, there was a national debate as to whether or not para-athletes deserved the Khel Ratna. After much deliberation, Devendra Jhajharia, India's only double gold medallist at the Paralympics, was presented the honour in 2017. While able-bodied athletes were awarded the Khel Ratna in 2016, it can be asked why it was restricted to one para-athlete in 2017? Nevertheless, it was a good start.

Deepa, who was disappointed at having missed out, finally received the award in 2019. 'Sir, *maine kya nahi kiya? Logon se galiyan khayi, beijjati sahi, apman saha, paagalon jaise training kiya, har* international platform *mein maine* medal *jita. Iske baas bhi log kehetein hain main* Khel Ratna deserve *nahi karti hoon.*' (What did I not do? I was abused by people, bore insults, trained like a mad person, won medals at every international platform. Even then, people say I didn't deserve the Khel Ratna.)

The anger in her voice was palpable. There will always be detractors, we told her. That's how life is and all she needs to do is what she has done for a decade and a half. Defy every odd and keep proving people wrong.

It is not simply about Deepa Malik but the thousands of specially-abled women who aspire to be the next Deepa. She agreed and concluded the conversation by saying, 'I am very happy that I finally got the Khel Ratna. This whole journey has been more about changing the attitude of people towards disability and the hidden potential in people with disability. I think the award is going to be a huge inspiration to disabled women athletes. It took seventy years for independent India to win a medal by a woman athlete in Paralympics. The next medal shouldn't take more than four years.'

THE MAN WITH THE RS 300 JAVELIN: THE INSPIRING STORY
OF DEVENDRA JHAJHARIA

'When I went to the Athens Paralympics in 2004, all I had was a pair of spikes that cost me Rs 400 and a javelin priced at Rs 300,' said Devendra Jhajharia. 'That's all I had. I paid for the trip myself and was one of the twenty-five athletes who represented India in Greece.' We had asked him to recount the journey to his first Olympic gold medal and his response was heart-rending.

'Every other athlete participating in Athens would come to the stadium with his personal coach, trainer, physio and support team,' he said with a smile. 'They had better javelins, which were very similar to the ones we use now. But for me, it was never about facilities. It was never about the quality of my javelin or spikes or coaching. It was always about hard work and more hard work. Working the hardest was my weapon against adversity and I am glad it worked for me.'

Devendra Jhajharia lost an arm at the age of eight when he accidentally touched an electric cable while climbing a tree. 'The shock was more mental than anything else. When I came back home from the hospital I was depressed. For the first month, I refused to leave my house.'

It was a sense of inferiority and peer pressure that started to weigh on the mind of young Devendra. It was only when his mother motivated him to go out and play with the neighbourhood kids that he finally started stepping out to socialize. His mother was clear: Devendra was a victim of certain circumstances and was in no way inferior to anyone else. She inspired him to do everything that he did earlier. He remains indebted to her for the early confidence she was able to instil in a confused and scared eight-year-old child.

The turnaround for Devendra happened when he was in tenth grade in school. At the annual school athletic meet, Javelin was one of the events. A young Devendra, always keen to play sports, was eager to try his hand at the javelin throw. But he faced serious rejection at school. As he put it, 'Sabne hume manaa kar diya. Kehne lage main kya kar raha hoon wahan pe. Javelin mere se nahi hone waala hai aur mujhe ye sab nahi karna chahiye. Mera ek haanth nahi hain, maine aise kaise thaan liya ki main javelin phekunga. Bhagvaan ki daya se main padh raha tha, yahi bahut tha.' (Everyone dismissed me. They asked what I was doing there. They said I couldn't do javelin and that I should let it be. I didn't have one hand, so how could I think of throwing a javelin, they asked. By god's grace, I could still study and they felt that was enough.)

Even the teachers refused to come out in support of Devendra. In fact, they asked him to leave the field and cheer from the sidelines. They feared he might end up injuring himself and were unwilling to take the risk. *'Maine bhi thaan liya tha. Main javelin khelna chahta tha aur main khel ke hi rahunga,'* he said. (I was also determined that I would throw a javelin and that I would do it.)

He went home and the first thing he did was convert a piece of wood from a nearby tree into a makeshift javelin. That was his first real piece of equipment, which he used to practise for the next few weeks. Soon after school got over in the afternoon, Devendra would run back home to be in time for practice before it got dark. Little did he know that the five kilometres he was running each day was working perfectly as his endurance training. *'Mujhe yeh sab nahi pata tha. Main jaldi se ghar pahoounchna chahta tha kyonki ghar mein bag rakh ke main ground mein practise karne jaata tha. Agar main thoda tez bhaad saka toh main aur thodi der practise kar sakta tha,'* he remembered. (I didn't know all this. I wanted to reach home early so I could leave my bag there and go to the ground to practise. If I ran fast, I could practise more.)

When it was time for the inter-district championship, Devendra was ready to shock everyone with his skill in the javelin throw event. When he won a medal at the meet, things started to change at his school as well. *'Yeh competition, main aap se keh sakta hoon, mere liye Olympics ke samaan tha. Yeh mere atma-sammann ke liye mujhe jeetna tha. Main able-bodied athletes ke saath khel raha tha aur sabke saamne kar dikhane ka yeh mauka mujhe dobara nahi milta.'* (This competition, for me, was like the Olympics. I had to win this for my self-respect. I was competing with able-bodied athletes and would not get another such opportunity to showcase what I could do in front of everyone.)

Winning a medal at the inter-district championship transformed his athletics career forever. This competition had given him the necessary confidence to train harder. That's when he started to think of an athletic career and making a name by representing India. He was also included in his school team thereafter and accorded respect as an athlete. By the time he entered college, javelin had become his first love.

The next major athletic meet was in Jamshedpur and that's where the next chapter of his story was written. Devendra, who was being trained by R.D. Singh at the time, had gone to Jamshedpur as a promising athlete confident of winning a medal. Singh, who had seen him train and improve, mentioned him to one of the coaches present only to be ticked off for backing someone '*jiska ek haanth nahi hai .*' (who doesn't have one hand.)

In the words of Devendra, '*Main* Coach sir *ke saath khada tha jab unhone ek dusre* coach *se kaha ki ispe nazar rakhna, yeh bahut accha* athlete *ban sakta hai. Unhone mere taraf dekha aur haske mere* coach *se kaha ki* "Sir *aap bhi na. Yeh kaise khel sakta hai? Isse* government job *mil jaaye aur wahi badi baat hogi*".' (I was standing with Coach Sir when he told another coach to keep an eye on me, that I could become a great athlete. He looked at me, laughed and said to my coach, 'Come on, sir. How is he going to play? It'd be a big enough deal if he gets a government job.)

Little did the man realize that he had further tickled Devendra's ego. Once again, the javelin would do the talking. 'I told my coach I was used to such comments and that they did not bother me. By talking one gains nothing. Talk is cheap and real talk for me happened on the field.' True to his words, Devendra won another gold at the event and the coach who had ticked him off was forced to apologize and acknowledge his mistake. '*Yeh* competition *jeetne ke baad maine socha ki main* India *ke liye zaroor khel sakta hoon.*' (I thought I could play for India after winning this competition.)

At the turn of the millennium, facilities for para-athletics were virtually non-existent in India. People with disability were mostly subject to scorn and pity. To watch them play sports was virtually unheard of. It is no surprise that the government did little to facilitate their training and participation in international events and the best a para-athlete could aspire for was a clerical level government job. In the absence of proper facilities, it was left to the athletes to come up with novel methods of training and practice.

Why Devendra Jhajharia Got an Axe and Cut Wood For Months

Devendra didn't have the therabands (latex bands or tubes commonly used for physical therapy and light strength training exercises by athletes) that he had seen his foreign rivals using. So he found his own method of training – getting an axe and cutting wooden logs to build his shoulder strength.

'*Bahar ke* players *sab* theraband *se* practise *karte the*,' he said. (All foreign players practised with a theraband.) '*Voh bahut* important *hai* shoulder strength *badhane ke liye. Mere paas toh* theraband *thi nahi. Maine socha main kulhari se* theraband *ko* replace *kar dunga.*' (It is very important to build shoulder strength. I didn't have a theraband. So I decided to replace the theraband with an axe.)

In something that is clearly unheard of, Devendra would cut wooden logs with an axe every single day of the month and repeat the action close to 500 times a day. With each swing of the axe, he would expend considerable strength. By the time he was done with his training, he would be completely exhausted.

From 2002 to 2003, he stopped attending social engagements, watching films or attending family parties. For him, it was all about his training and mental focus. 'When I went to Athens, I was very well prepared,' he said. 'I had already broken the world record in 2003 and was confident I could do it yet again at the Paralympics.'

What made a difference for Devendra was him being asked to be the Indian flag bearer at the opening ceremony. '*Maine socha ki agar main* flag-bearer *hoon toh mujhe aur accha khelna chahiye.* Flag *toh mere haanth mein tha par mera rashtra gaan mujhe sunna tha aur yeh tabhi ho sakta tha jab main* gold medal *jitta. Bhagvaan ne meri maang puri kar di,*' he said with a sense of satisfaction. (I thought if I am the flag-bearer, I should play well. The flag was in my hand but I wanted to listen to my national anthem, which would only be possible if I won gold. God fulfilled my wish.)

What is shocking is that even after the Athens Games things hardly changed for para-athletes. A chance meeting with Prime Minister Manmohan Singh and then-Union Minister of Sports Sunil Dutt helped to a degree. Devendra was able to request them to grant recognition to the Paralympic Committee of India. He was promised money but it came much later. '*Mujhe Rs 30 lakh rupiya* promise *kiya gaya tha. Par yeh paisa mujhe mile* 2010 *mein. Mujhe yeh manna hai ki che saal baad yeh paisa milna koi kaam ka nahi tha.* (I was promised Rs 30 lakh. But I only got this money in 2010. Getting this money after six years was of no use.) This did not help me in any way and did nothing to contribute to my training.'

In these years, it was Devendra's commitment and passion that kept him going. With a life partner who is also a high-performance sportsperson, Devendra always had support at home to draw upon in times of need.

When his event was left out of the Beijing Games in 2008 and then again at the 2012 London Games, he thought of retiring and supporting his wife, who was a national-level kabaddi player. 'She said that I should wait another four years. We would get to know by 2014 if there would be javelin in Rio. In 2010, we had our daughter. My wife sacrificed her career and started bringing our daughter up. One of us had to leave our careers and she wanted me to keep playing,' he said with a tone of affection.

Things took a positive turn when javelin was included in the 2013 World Championships and then at the 2016 Rio Games. Once again, Devendra was the Indian flag bearer in Rio. This time round, he was leading a very talented contingent. 'Even before me, Meiyyapan had won gold in high jump. Our team was doing well. This gave us a sense of positivity and confidence,' he said as he recounted the three best throws of his life.

'My first throw wasn't the best. I had thrown 57 metres and was in third position. We are allowed six throws, as you know. It was very important I did well in the second and third throw. In fact, when I went to the top of the mark for my second throw, I was determined to do something big. For this to happen, everything has to be perfect. Your release, your follow-through, your arm action and the harmony between each of these steps has to be perfect for you to achieve the maximum distance.'

His second throw was 60.70 metres and catapulted him to first place. In getting him to the gold medal position, this throw had done two things for Devendra. First, it had put the pressure back on the Chinese athlete who was now in second position, who now had to throw his best to catch up. Second, it allowed Devendra to go for broke in his third throw and attempt something phenomenal. When we asked him to recount his third throw in as much detail as possible, there was a slight pause.

He gradually looked up and said, 'The way you mentioned it is giving me goosebumps. When I was walking up for my last throw there were a lot of things on my mind. I knew I was in the gold medal position and I was aware that I still had three more throws left. It was best to take a chance with the third throw. If you see the video you will see I was constantly talking to myself. And when I released the javelin, I knew it was the perfect throw. The javelin hit the ground swiftly and there was hardly any jerk. My instant reaction was to raise my hand because I knew the world record had been broken. All I needed was the official confirmation. When that came, I couldn't control my emotions. I was jumping and screaming like a kid for I had broken my own world record and had done so twelve years after winning gold in Athens.'

By now, his eyes had started to swell up with tears of joy. He concluded, 'This was a big achievement not only for me but also for my country and I was proud of it.'

What is important is that this time round things did change. Devendra was celebrated for months after Rio. It seemed like things had finally turned for Paralympic athletes and para-athletics in India. 'We now have every facility,' he said. He continues to train in the SAI centre in Gandhinagar, away from his young family, for one last mission.

'After coming back from Rio I told my mother that she was responsible for giving India two gold medals at the Paralympics. She said the gold medals did not matter to her. What mattered was that her son could grow up a normal human being. That is what it is all about – pursuing your dream and doing what you want to do. I know little other than playing sports and that's why I am here one final time, away from my wife and daughter, training for Tokyo. I speak to them every night at 9 pm and often feel a pang of guilt as to whether or not I am doing the right thing. My daughter is growing up and I have hardly seen her grow. But I can promise you that after Tokyo I will give her all the time in the world.' There was something in his voice in this last bit; as if he was trying to reassure himself more than anything.

Till then, however, it is all about India and the javelin. With proper training, coaching and his team in place (thanks to government support and support from the GoSports Foundation), Devendra has finally left behind the days when he had to use spikes worth Rs 400. But what he remembers the most is seeing the tricolour go up and hearing the national anthem being played. 'For an athlete, nothing can better that sensation', he said before going on to mention with a silent prayer, 'I want to see it one final time. I hope god will allow me to do so.'

7

Ad Hoc or Professional?

The Promise and the Problem with India's Sporting Systems

When sports minister Kiren Rijiju went to the National Institute of Sports in Patiala in 2018, he noticed that one row of athletes was being served a single piece of chicken each whereas another row was being served three pieces of chicken per person. When he asked officials why, he was told that the athletes being served only one piece of chicken were younger. Hence, the difference in quantity. As the *Times of India*'s guest sports editor for a day in October 2019, he told editors that this was 'not just unsporting and unscientific, but inhuman too. Logic suggests that a sixteen-year-old wrestler will eat more than a chess player. If he is a weightlifter, how does age matter? Only nutritionists should decide one's diet.'

Rijiju's comment is indicative of the vast distance our sporting systems still need to travel. A lot has improved, but the basic DNA of officialdom must also change.

When the great Usain Bolt was asked in Rio why Jamaica is an athletics powerhouse despite its size, his answer was simple: the island has a unique sporting culture. The key, said the greatest sprinter in history, was Jamaica's annual school sports competition, 'Champs', which makes kids the focus of public attention in a competitive setting early on, performing in front of packed stadiums and on TV. 'It is just that we have a good system,' said Bolt. 'Boys and girls, Champs keep producing more athletes. For years to come, we will have great athletes to win.' Bolt considers schooling to be so important that he once even attributed his dominance over fellow countryman Asafa Powell to the fact that the latter's school did not always qualify for Champs!

His analysis should put into perspective the national hand-wringing that accompanies the heroics of P.V. Sindhu or Sakshi Malik. Our four-yearly obsession over why a billion-plus India doesn't win medals is rooted in the fact that we don't have a decent sporting culture or a grassroots pipeline to attract young talent in Olympic sports.

Our six-medal haul at the 2012 Olympics lulled us into thinking we were racing towards sporting excellence, with official predictions of at least ten medals in Rio. India's medal tally regressed in Rio and it was a major setback. Yet, a deeper look showed that there was a silver lining despite the structural bottlenecks.

First, Indian sports significantly increased its width in Rio, with several Indian athletes appearing among the top ten or twenty for the first time in disciplines we have not had a presence in for decades. Dipa Karmakar's awe-inspiring Produnova and her coming fourth in the vault event are the gymnastic equivalent of the US beating India at Test cricket by an innings. Lalita Babar's creditable tenth place finish in the steeplechase can only be appreciated if we remember that no Indian woman has reached the finals of an Olympic athletics event since P.T. Usha in 1984 (on a field curtailed by the Soviet boycott). This happened despite no major improvement in sporting facilities. Karmakar's physiotherapist was not allowed to accompany her to Rio and was flown in only when she qualified for the final. Athlete Dutee Chand flew to Rio on an economy-class flight for thirty-six hours while sports officials flew business class. Rower Dattu Bhokanal from drought-hit Talegaon reached the quarter-final in sculls and said he'd 'never seen so much water' in his life till he joined the Army in 2012.

Second, as sportswriter Deepak Narayan has pointed out, in Beijing 2008, three Indian athletes reached the medal rounds and all three won medals. In London, eleven made it to the medal rounds and six won medals. In Rio, though only seven reached the medal rounds, three fell just short of bronze – Abhinav Bindra, Dipa Karmakar and the team of Sania Mirza and Rohan Bopanna. Among our three traditionally strong disciplines, the shooters were below par but boxing and wrestling suffered from atrocious politicking. Vikas Krishan, who lost in the quarters, was right in saying that Indian boxers have had very few chances to compete outside the country since 2012, when the world boxing body suspended the Indian federation for manipulating elections. This was one of the reasons why only three Indian boxers qualified for Rio as opposed to eight in London.

Third, Olympic medals are a consequence not of access to facilities, not population. On July 26, 2016, the then-sports minister Vijay Goel told the Rajya Sabha that his ministry had spent Rs 49.2 crore ($7.3 million at 2016 exchange rates) on India's Rio athletes (including Rs 25 crore under TOPS) apart from another 49.2 crore ($7.1 million) spent on sixty-seven sports federations since 2012. This was nothing compared to the £350 million spent on the 2016 Olympics by the UK (who stood second on the medals tally), $340 million by Australia or $139 million by Canada. Dipa Karmakar, for example, only received Rs 2 lakh under the TOPS compared to UK gymnastics, which alone received £14.6 million, built 1,300 gymnastic clubs for those under the ages of twelve and went on to win seven medals in Rio.

For a country with less individual medals in a century than Michael Phelps alone, having over 120 athletes qualify for Rio in so many new disciplines despite a moribund system was evidence that something new was happening in India.

Apart from the critique of inefficiency and politics at the top, the issue in Indian sports has always been that most of our population will remain outside the formal sporting net unless we have a wider network of organized sports at the school level. Since Rio, there has been a new beginning with the Khelo India initiative.

It was created in 2016, when the Modi government combined three existing schemes – the Rajiv Gandhi Khel Abhiyan, the Urban Sports Infrastructure Scheme and the National Sports Talent Search System – into the Khelo India scheme. Sports minister Rijiju said Khelo India is the 'biggest thing to happen to India in the last seventy-two years.' He told the *Times of India*, 'Every country has a structure in every discipline … Next year we will activate the School Games Federation and the Youth Games Federation. All under-seventeen players will go to the School Games Federation and those under twenty-one will go to the University Games Federation.'

Like Usain Bolt's example of Jamaica, a strong school-level structure is essential and any more organized sports in schools should always be welcomed. But what about our federations and other organized structures of Indian sport?

SHOOTING SYSTEMS: THE REVAMP AFTER RIO

Abhinav Bindra had just made the final of the 10-metre air rifle event at the Rio Olympics in 2016 and Raninder Singh, the president of the National Rifle Association of India (NRAI), was relieved. Till then his shooters had flattered to deceive. Abhinav was a ray of hope. In the one hour between the qualification stage and the final, Raninder looked excited and was confident of a medal. Shooting was India's premier Olympic sport in Beijing and London. Raninder couldn't afford to come back from Rio empty-handed when as many as twelve of his shooters had qualified for the Olympics. When Abhinav lost the shoot-off and missed out on the medal, Raninder was crestfallen. It was as if all hope had been lost and this sense of dejection was evident to all.

Indian shooting had taken a backward step in Rio and the NRAI couldn't let things drift any further. Soon after the contingent was back in India, Raninder put correctives in place. He appointed a four-member committee chaired by Abhinav Bindra himself to take stock of the Rio debacle and to chart out a road map for the next few years. Besides Abhinav, the committee included Manisha Malhotra, a former tennis player and sports management professional with in-depth knowledge of Indian Olympic sports, as well as Digvijay Singh Deo and Kamesh Srinivasan, two of India's best known Olympic journalists and men who know the grassroots better than most. Raninder was clearly serious – the committee wasn't designed to mask the poor performance in Rio and placate the masses. None of the committee members could be influenced and the reform process had commenced.

This committee, as expected from the likes of Bindra, went deep. Its final report was a critical eye-opener on the NRAI and the way it had operated in the last few years. The thirty-eight-page study summed up the shooting story in Rio unambiguously, stating, 'It can be said with no reservations that Indian shooting "over achieved" at the Rio Olympic Games. The formula for success was wrong and Indian shooting had ridden its luck over the last few years, no doubt helped by some extremely talented shooters. It is the sincere wish of this committee that the NRAI closely look at its processes and the free hand given to individuals to avoid another embarrassing no-show in four years time in Tokyo.'

The committee members spoke to every shooter present in Rio as well as coaches and support staff to understand what went wrong. The report, which is a fascinating read, made it clear that not only was there no systemic plan in place, but there were cases of financial mismanagement and lack of accountability and transparency.

For example, the committee's observations on Ayonika Paul, who had qualified for the 10-metre air rifle event, were scathing: 'The committee feels that Paul's approach to the Olympics shows the flip side of allowing athletes, especially young ones, the power to chalk their own course. They are clearly not equipped or mentally ready to shoulder the responsibility. The projection of Thomas Farnik as the coach and Suma Shirur only as the mentor (Paul had claimed that Farnik was her personal coach and Shirur was just the mentor during her preparations) was purely for financial gains. The records and documents presented to the committee proved that Suma was the full-time coach. There has to be absolute honesty of effort while preparing for the Olympics. The NRAI needs to address confusion over the presence of two coaches, one in person and another on paper.'

Having already highlighted issues of financial impropriety, the committee emphasized the critical need for a professional juniors programme. This was essential to take care of the shooters as they made the transition from the junior to the senior stage.

It also emphasized the need for proper coaching and noted that the absence of a good coach may have cost Jitu Rai, India's best medal prospect in Rio, his Olympic medal. 'The committee feels that the foreign coach Pavel Smirnov did not have the expertise in the precision events to help Jitu Rai win an Olympic medal. Rai's admission of his inability to find a working relationship with Smirnov further put the shooter in a precarious position of coming up with his own training plans. The lack of expertise for the best shooter in India despite no dearth of support from the Army and the government further highlights the lack of proper planning.'

Finally, it made note of how athletes competing at the Olympics need to be taken care of so that they approach their events in the best physical and mental state and are properly rested before doing so. Highlighting the case of Apurvi Chandela in Rio, the committee noted, 'The lack of experience and monitoring caused Apurvi to have an accidental injury during her cryotherapy session. It must be noted that all cutting-edge scientific training must be under the guidance of suitable experts, which was obviously lacking. The committee also feels that lack of sleep or disturbances on the eve of the competition should have been visualized and the athlete could have been protected or better prepared. (On the night before her competition, people were knocking on her door as a fresh batch of Indian athletes had arrived in the Olympic Village. As a result, she was unable to sleep and was exhausted going into the event in the morning).'

The members rounded off the report, concluding unanimously that 'Indian shooting needs to change; change its attitude, its policies and practices ... At present the system is ad hoc. There is no systemic framework in place.'

To recommend is one thing, but to implement is a fundamentally different task altogether.

To its credit, the NRAI, under President Raninder Singh, was open to the criticism, took the recommendations in its stride and set in motion a slew of changes advocated in the report.

A look at the Indian contingent for Tokyo draws attention to the impact of the reforms put in place. With Jaspal Rana and Suma Shirur, both of whom made the transition from the junior coaching structure to a senior role, taking care of the shooters, Indian shooting is no longer ad hoc. While much can still be done, it is now a structured system with its heart in the right place.

It allows for a healthy mix of experience and youth. Hence, youngsters like Manu Bhaker and Saurabh Chaudhary are accompanied by seniors like Apurvi Chandela and Sanjeev Rajput. While the system isn't perfect yet, it is good enough to empower the shooters to try and be 'perfect on an imperfect day' as Abhinav Bindra always aspired to be.

When we went back to the committee members to check if they were satisfied with the reforms put in place, this is what they said: 'The committee's recommendations after the debacle at the Rio Olympics provided the blueprint for the NRAI to introspect and implement course-correction for the future. It was not our intention to pin the blame on a particular individual but to adopt a holistic approach to ensure that Indian shooting cut the flab and became a professional organization with respect to delivering medals at the top level. There have been a few systematic changes with the NRAI drafting in senior shooters such as Mansher Singh and Suma Shirur to replace redundant coaches who were largely seen as political appointees. The appointment of Ronak Pandit as high-performance manager and NRAI observer is also a welcome one.

'The biggest takeaway, though, remains the success of the junior programme. The committee had recommended that the junior programme be allowed to develop at its own pace and today it is that very programme set up by Jaspal Rana and Dipali Deshpande that is delivering results at the international level. Not only have promising teenagers started winning junior competitions, but the likes of Manu Bhaker, Saurabh Chaudhary, Anish Bhanwala, Elavenil Valarivan and others are delivering results consistently in the senior competitions as well. The record haul at the 2019 World Championships is a testament to the success of the junior programme.'

Jaspal Rana reinforces this assessment: 'The junior programme is really robust. Close to sixty per cent of the funds are spent on this programme and there are multiple coaches, physios and trainers in the camps. Earlier I had to look after all the shooters myself. It was impossible to give personalized attention to fifty or sixty shooters. Now we have about four or five coaches, physios and trainers to give me a hand. We are now able to give the athletes international exposure as and when required. Things have undergone a sea change in the last few years.'

Joydeep Karmakar, who trains Mehuli Ghosh, alluded to this change and said, 'Participation has increased twenty times in the past few years. We have thousands wanting to compete in the national competitions and it is only natural that with proper coaching and sports science India will start doing well at the international level.'

The work, however, isn't done just yet. With fifteen quotas for Tokyo 2020, hopes have soared yet again. Indian shooters were number one in the medals tally in all four world cups in 2019. That's what makes the months leading up to Tokyo so important for the shooters and the NRAI. As much as the shooters need to compete and train, they also require adequate downtime to be in the best shape for the Olympics.

We often obsess about training and hard work and tend to forget the importance of letting bodies recover and refocus. Diet, mental hygiene and training regimes need to be monitored for each of the men and women who now have the opportunity to make India proud at the world's biggest sporting event.

The best part is it that we are no longer focused on one individual. It is not about a Bindra or a Narang. In each of the events that India will participate in at the Tokyo Olympics, we stand a good chance if we have a good day. To have the best day we need to be the best prepared. That's what training is all about.

The NRAI, with the help of the government, the SAI and private players like the GoSports Foundation, Gagan Narang Sports Foundation, JSW, OGQ and others, have done the hard work. We finally have a professional system in place. We have talented men and women who aren't satisfied with just a medal. They want the best and are focused on getting there. All they need now is the final honing to make them battle-ready.

The Bindra committee concluded with a few words of caution for the federation: 'The NRAI now faces its biggest challenge as it will not just have to monitor the preparations of the shooters for the Tokyo Games but also find a way of integrating the senior and junior programmes. The transition of a shooter from junior to senior was earlier a big problem with many promising shooters getting lost as they made the step up. Today there is a lot of overlap with many of the junior shooters making the senior team and there has to be some element of flexibility and continuity to ensure that they do not find themselves in an alien environment when picked for a senior tournament.'

They are right. With cricketing legends like Sachin Tendulkar also tweeting about the achievements of the shooters, the media interest in these men and women, some of whom are still teenagers, can be relentless and daunting. The 24/7 media is always in search of a story and each of these achievers make for one.

While Elavenil Valarivan had to shoot without proper equipment for a while and is grateful to Gagan Narang for helping her out, Saurabh Chaudhary fought against all odds, coming from a lower middle-class household in Meerut, to emerge as a shooter of repute. Mehuli Ghosh, also a teenager, had to undergo counselling to overcome the trauma of inadvertently hitting a person at the age of fourteen when she was just about to start her dream of becoming a shooter.

'These things can be daunting. You have to protect them. See how young they are. Manu is eighteen. Saurabh is even younger. Fame and media interest can be really scary at times. It is a heady feeling to be talked about and mentioned in the mainstream media. From nowhere you are suddenly a star. People want to click pictures with you, speak to you, know your story. While it is all very good, this isn't the right time for any of it,' said a cautious Bindra.

From here on, the role of coaches is of paramount importance. While most coaches at the turn of the century were playing the role of a manager, what makes the NRAI's programme tick is the involvement of coaches who have all achieved significant international success in their careers. Be it Jaspal Rana or Dipali Deshpande or Suma Shirur – each of them currently employed by the NRAI as coaches and mentors – they know what it is to be a shooter of repute and what it takes to win medals on the big stage. With them in charge, Manu, Saurabh, Anjum, Apurvi and the rest are in good hands. 'This is one of the most important factors,' said Bindra. 'To have shooters of pedigree groom the next generation is one of the best things the NRAI has done.'

How many medals can India win in Tokyo? While we debate this, it has to be said that as of late 2019, things seem good. At the same time, the signs tell us to be cautious – to nurture these men and women with care and not waste another opportunity.

WRESTLING ON THE MAT

One of India's favourite sports, wrestling, made national news in 2008 when Sushil Kumar won a bronze medal in Beijing in the 66 kilogram category. Sushil, who had lost his opening bout, came back through the repechage route and eventually clinched India's third medal of the games, the first two going to Abhinav Bindra and Vijender Singh. Sushil followed up this performance by going on to better the colour of his medal in London, making it India's best Olympics ever.

Having covered each of his bouts in London, we can confirm that Sushil was the Indian media's favourite Olympic story in London besides Mary Kom. Soft-spoken and humble, Sushil is all about simplicity and hard work. 'I will now go back to India and have my mother's aloo parantha' was his reaction when asked how he was planning to celebrate his silver medal.

India's most decorated individual Olympian, Sushil was a national icon in the aftermath of the London Games. Several people in Chattarsal stadium, where he trains, worshipped him as their idol. With time, Sushil became a system unto himself. A superstar athlete with performances to back up his reputation, it was hard for the federation to look past Sushil. He inspired a generation of wrestlers and the sport was considered to have a bright future in India after the 2012 Olympics, with the government and the SAI investing in it.

Things turned complicated for Sushil and the federation when Narsingh Yadav, a talented wrestler from Mumbai, won a quota for the 2016 Olympics by virtue of his bronze win at the Las Vegas World Championships in 2015. While the federation named him as India's official entry to Rio, Narsingh's road to the Olympics was fraught with obstacles because he had been chosen to represent India before Sushil Kumar.

Sushil dragged Narsingh to the Delhi High Court and a bitter courtroom battle followed. The judgement went in favour of Narsingh, clearing the deck for him to participate in his very first Olympics. There was, however, more drama in store for Narsingh after his results returned positive for a banned substance following a test by the National Anti-Doping Agency (NADA) in June. Narsingh's roommate at the SAI centre in Sonipat also tested positive for the same substance, but the Wrestling Federation of India (WFI), led by Brijbhushan Saran, backed Narsingh's claims of sabotage and foul play.

By then the WFI was firmly aligned against Sushil for having taken the matter to court. For them, this was more an ego issue than anything else. Failing to see the writing on the wall, they sided with Narsingh and challenged the NADA finding while refusing to field either Sushil or anyone else at Rio.

Days before the Olympics, Narsingh was cleared of doping charges by the NADA, who accepted that the wrestler was indeed a victim of 'sabotage' and deserved the benefit of doubt.

However, Narsingh's hopes of participating in Rio were dealt a massive blow when the World Anti-Doping Agency (WADA) challenged the NADA's decision and moved the Court for Arbitration for Sport (CAS), demanding a ban of four years for Narsingh. It was a day before his event that the CAS panel ruled against Narsingh Yadav, banning him for four years and ending his hope of competing in the Olympics.

'The CAS panel did not accept the argument of the athlete that he was the victim of sabotage and noted that there was no evidence that he bore no fault, nor that the anti-doping rule violation was not intentional. Therefore the standard four-year period of ineligibility was imposed by the panel,' declared CAS in its verdict.

'Narsingh Yadav was sanctioned with a four-year ineligibility period starting today and any period of provisional suspension or ineligibility effectively served by the athlete before the entry into force of this award shall be credited against the total period of ineligibility to be served,' it added. 'Furthermore, all competitive results obtained by Narsingh Yadav from and including 25 June 2016 shall be disqualified, with all resulting consequences (including forfeiture of medals, points and prizes).'

Soon after the announcement, we met Brijbhushan Saran in Rio to discuss the repercussions of the ruling. Saran maintained that Narsingh was the victim of a conspiracy. 'This is an unfortunate decision. We didn't have time to get our lawyers here and that worked against us. Narsingh will have to leave the athletes Village tomorrow,' he said. When asked about Narsingh, we were told that he was not in a state to speak. 'This is a conspiracy against him. There is a nexus in India which has to be stopped. We will have to return to India and explore legal options. We demand a Central Bureau of Investigation (CBI) inquiry into the case so that no athlete has to go through this in the future,' Brijbhushan Singh ranted.

We eventually located Narsingh the next day in an apartment on the outskirts of Rio. He was waiting to fly back to India the next day. He seemed shocked and devastated. It seemed like he had lost weight overnight. He said, 'To say I am devastated by the decision of CAS would be putting it mildly. I have gone through so much over the last two months off the mat, but the thought of fighting for the glory of the nation kept me going.' As we tried to console him, he broke down saying he had lost everything. Once he gathered himself, he said in a tone of resignation, 'My dream of competing and winning the country a medal at the Rio Games was cruelly snatched away from me twelve hours before my first fight, but I will do everything it takes to prove my innocence. It is all I have left to fight for.'

This whole episode was a story of mismanagement. At no point should the WFI have challenged the NADA verdict and supported Narsingh's bid for participation in Rio. And even though Narsingh had got clearance from the NADA, the claim that he never intentionally took the banned substance during his stay at the SAI centre in Sonepat was always going to be challenged in front of a higher authority.

The WFI made it a fight for prestige against Sushil, who, on his part, shouldn't have taken the matter to the high court in the first place. No athlete should put himself above the system and Sushil, who is a legend in Indian sports, should never have done so.

Once the decision was challenged by the WADA in CAS, Narsingh and the WFI stood no chance. In the hearing, the WADA argued that Narsingh should have been banned right after failing the dope test. They also rejected the theory that his food was spiked at the SAI centre. The WADA said it was impossible to spike a player's food due to CCTV and high security at the SAI centre in Sonepat. With Narsingh and the WFI failing to counter these arguments, the four-year ban was the most logical outcome.

In hindsight, it is disappointing to note that just a few days before the Rio Olympics, all talk in India revolved around dope, sabotage, cheating, intrigue and personal interest. Egos had taken precedence over everything else and the only loser in this entire sordid saga was Indian sports.

Despite the drama surrounding Narsingh and Sushil, India deserved better. The remaining 121 athletes deserved better. They needed to be in a zone days before they faced the glare of the world's cameras for the greatest show on earth. But all they read and saw days before their departure was their fellow athletes fighting and spewing venom at each other.

Take the case of Yogeshwar Dutt. He was India's best bet in wrestling at the 2016 Olympics, having already won a medal in London. Ranked at number twelve in his category by United World Wrestling, Yogeshwar feared no one except the Italian top seed. He had trained exceedingly well and had tried to take his physical fitness to a different level altogether. But when he boarded the flight to Rio, everyone around him was fixated on Narsingh and Sushil Kumar – men he knew well and couldn't distance himself from.

The air was thick with intrigue and questions about whether or not Sushil and his camp had spiked Narsingh's food were doing the rounds. Some even suggested that a police case be filed on the matter to figure out what really happened.

This was not what Yogeshwar or any of the other wrestlers needed before boarding the flight to the Olympics. Each of them had worked for years and had given up on every form of recreation. It should've been the greatest journeys of their lives but all they got in return from the federation and the country was bad blood and internal bickering.

The questions that we need to ask as we approach the Tokyo Olympics is where is Narsingh Yadav today and what happened to him in the past few years? Who is responsible for prematurely ending a promising athletic career? Is it fair to argue that without the federation's support he wouldn't have challenged the NADA ban? Could he have returned to wrestling after a much smaller suspension period that way? Can the federation explain what they gained out of this whole controversy when egos took centrestage at the expense of Indian sports? Finally, what are the lessons we have learnt from this and can Indian wrestling regain its lost glory in Tokyo?

What we see before us today is a great improvement. India has a group of supremely talented athletes in Bajrang Punia, Deepak Punia, Ravi Dahiya and Vinesh Phogat. Both Sushil and the WFI have made amends in the greater interest of Indian wrestling. If Punia or any of the other wrestlers win a medal in Tokyo, wrestling will have been redeemed of all the ignominy heaped on it during and after Rio 2016.

SARKARI SYSTEMS AND THE PRIVATE SECTOR: A MUCH-NEEDED SYNERGY

For the longest time, Indian sports suffered due to the absence of structured support from the government. Initiatives put in place in the last few years have ensured that funding will be much less of a concern for India's high-performance athletes. The TOPS, administered by the SAI and funded by the sports ministry, has made a fundamental difference to Indian sports since it was started in 2014.

While it needs fine-tuning in that the disbursal of money can be more efficiently monitored and better orchestrated, the fact that it has facilitated high-quality training and coaching is undeniable. In 2018, Rs 100 crores was earmarked for TOPS athletes training for Tokyo, a sizeable sum by every yardstick. Neelam Kapur, former director general of the SAI, made this announcement on 30 December 2018. 'We have kept a ballpark approximate figure of Rs 100 crores for the 2020 Olympics. The sports minister has instructed that there shouldn't be any shortage of funds for the athletes in TOPS. With the TOPS, we have tried to take a holistic approach. We are consulting the national federations, national observers, taking their feedback and after going through all the data the final selection is made by the Mission Olympics Cell,' she said.

She went on to say that a TOPS secretariat has also been set up in Delhi to closely monitor India's preparations for the 2020 Olympics and build a sustainable sports ecosystem in the country. Active since September 2018, the secretariat consists of seasoned sports professionals with management and sporting expertise. They now oversee the functioning of the TOPS.

Of course, a great deal can be improved, including changing old attitudes, but on balance, it is fair to say that the sports ministry is relatively more active than it was a decade ago. With Rajyavardhan Rathore, an Olympic medallist himself, leading the ministry for five years, perceptions started changing. Kiren Rijiju, who was appointed as sports minister during the Modi government's second term, has carried forward the process by bringing in a system of efficient talent scouting and accountability. What has also helped is the willingness of the government and the SAI to collaborate with private entities to create a synergy in taking sports forward.

Deepthi Bopaiah, former banker and current CEO of GoSports Foundation, considers this the big plus in the last few years. 'The government and SAI are now open to listening to us and working in tandem. While there is little doubt they have a lot more facilities than we can ever have, it is a major positive that now there is dialogue. We can complement each other and help our athletes.'

Federations too have started to become relatively more professional and are better managed than they were a few years ago. While it started with hockey under the current Indian Olympic Association (IOA) President Narendra Batra, things also changed for the better in shooting between 2014 and 2019. This also applies to wrestling, badminton and track and field to a certain extent. Boxing too is in better shape than what it was a few years earlier. The fact that the IOA now puts up most memos and announcements on its website in an attempt to be transparent is a good sign.

Gone are the days when the Indian contingent for the Olympics or the Asian Games would include a slew of officials and babus with little or nothing to offer the athletes. Earlier, a mega event was only a junket for officials. It was a paid holiday at the government's expense and Indian sports benefitted nothing. Whereas some of this still happens, such cases have reduced with more vigilance and a better-administered IOA.

While we give credit where it is due, multiple caveats are also in order. Things can certainly get better and more professional. The NADA was pulled up by the WADA in August 2019 for mismanagement and inefficiency and there was a ban on the NADA testing athletes' samples in its laboratories in India. With cricket now under the NADA, it faced a whole host of questions.

What was startling was the following announcement from the NADA on 9 November 2019 posted on its Facebook page: 'The #BCCI had some reservations earlier regarding the quality of the NADA's anti doping programme. Over the last one year, NADA has taken a number of steps to allay their concerns. A system of Lead Dope Control Officers (LDCO), who are medical graduates, was approved in the last meeting of the NADA's governing body, after which many such #LDCOs have been empanelled by the NADA. Another scheme of LDCOs on retainership has also been recently introduced. Only #WADA approved dope testing kits are being used by the NADA. It has been decided to also make available premium services wherever required.'

Some key questions must be asked: Why did NADA have to wait for the BCCI to raise concerns to adopt these measures and not do so on their own? Why is it that things have improved only in the last year or so? Does it mean India did not have a robust anti-doping programme during the 2016 Olympics or Gold Coast 2018? Is it fair to suggest that the NADA needed a push from the BCCI to get its house in order? Aren't India's Olympic athletes a good enough reason to have the best facilities in place? How can the ministry stay silent on the matter? Finally, why was the IOA or the sports ministry silent if things weren't up to the mark and what will the ministry do now with the WADA ticking the NADA off for mismanagement and inefficiency?

The IOA too can improve its dealings with individual federations, which in turn will impact the overall health of Indian sports. Archery, for example, was a sport where India regularly won medals at international competitions. Today, the sport is in disarray. The national federation is poorly run and has lost recognition and credibility. Talented athletes like Deepika Kumari, Atanu Das and the entire team missed out from making it to the Archery World Cup final in Moscow on 6 and 7 September in 2019. Like in every other sport, an archer can make it to the prestigious events if he or she picks up enough points over the year and wins major competitions. While the Indian archers were inconsistent, the inefficiency of the federation did not help either.

The following example will highlight this point. Ahead of the Archery World Cup in Medellin in March 2019, a fourteen-member Indian team was picked but was unable to travel. The team, which was selected at the very last minute by the national federation, went to the airport in Delhi only to be told by the KLM authorities that their flight was delayed and that there was no certainty they would be able to board the connecting flight to Medellin which was scheduled to depart an hour and a half after the KLM flight was to land in Amsterdam. As a result, the entire batch of archers had to cancel their trip and miss the competition.

Things only turned worse thereafter as highlighted in the following report published in *The Bridge*: 'The controversy escalated further when the Archery Association of India (AAI) decided to send a B team to the world cup leg II event in Shanghai. There has been no national coach for years, so the AAI used to send coaches of selected archers with the squad all this while. But this time, the AAI picked wrong coaches to accompany the team. Ved Kumar and Kailash, who were active archers and who competed at the National Open selection trials for the world championship and the world cup in Rohtak, failed to find a berth in the squad and entered the team as coaches with no coaching experience.'

ROLE OF PRIVATE FOUNDATIONS

When looking at the role played by private foundations like OGQ, GoSports Foundation, Gagan Narang Sports Foundation, JSW Sports Foundation, Anglian Medal Hunt or the now-defunct Mittal Champions Trust, it is essential to understand what came before and what Indian athletes lacked earlier while competing at the Olympic Games.

The classic example will always remain that of Limba Ram in 1992. Ram, one of India's most talented archers, was considered among India's potential medal winners in the 70-metre archery competition in Barcelona. Having never participated at an Olympics before, Limba Ram was overwhelmed by the occasion. The story goes – and here we can't vouch for its authenticity – that Ram, after losing to his opponent fairly early in the competition, went up to an Indian official and requested him to organize a rematch. He had no idea that he was out of the Olympics and that his medal hopes had been dashed!

From someone who had never been exposed to the glamour of the Olympics and had come up the ranks from a very modest background, such a statement wasn't entirely unnatural. For the world, it was an act of naiveté. For Ram, it was what he was used to. No one had explained to him what the Olympics were and how there is no second chance on the world's biggest stage.

At the core of this story are three fundamental truths. Firstly, talent without proper grooming and nurturing will never lead to an Olympic medal. Second, an athlete's mental preparedness and confidence are as essential as anything else and it can only be strengthened through international exposure. Lastly, it is of paramount importance that athletes are prepared for the biggest stage of their lives. Every kind of preparation – nutrition, diet, mental equilibrium, physical stamina and form – needs to be at its best during Olympic competition. This is where the private foundations have made a difference and made changes to fundamentally transform India's Olympic performance.

If we read the mission statements of each of the foundations mentioned above, the synergies are striking. Each of them is committed to giving athletes the best coaching they can get, sending them to international competitions and giving them the necessary exposure. They are determined to provide them with the benefits of modern sports science and coaching and subsequently groom them for the biggest stage of their lives – the Olympics. While some like OGQ have the gold medal as their ultimate ambition, others like GoSports have laid more emphasis on the process and are focused on an athlete's all-round development, starting out very young.

JSW Sport, in a rare departure, has now set up India's best high-performance training centre for elite athletes in Bellary, which is equipped with modern training facilities and scientific coaching. They have also decided to set up the India House in Tokyo, a first for our country, where athletes and the media can come and relax whenever they find the time or feel the need. Athletes can now train in this institute and they no longer need to travel offshore for such facilities. Finally, the Gagan Narang Sports Foundation, set up by Narang himself in 2011, has groomed upcoming stars like Elavenil Valarivan, providing them with the best equipment and facilities at a formative stage in their lives. The work done by each of these foundations together with the set-up of modern infrastructure like the EKA Arena in Ahmedabad by Udit Sheth or the multiple high-performance centres set up by Abhinav Bindra across the country now mean that Indian athletes have every modern facility readily available to them as they embark on their quest for an Olympic medal.

While one might point to the large stadiums and other sports-related infrastructure facing the problems of underutilization, the fact remains that sportspersons till recently had to look beyond Indian shores to access proper training facilities and scientific coaching. This change is expected to make the difference between stepping on the winners' podium and returning home empty-handed.

What is also interesting is that two of the country's foremost athletes, Abhinav Bindra and Gagan Narang, decided to not just talk about moving in the right direction regarding infrastructure but actually acted on it. True to his promise after Rio, Abhinav Bindra initially launched a high-performance centre in Chandigarh, which has now spread its branches to Delhi, Bengaluru and Bhubaneswar. At these centres, athletes have facilities that are on par with any centre in the world. Narang too, in an attempt to give back to the sport, took time off while still an active athlete to focus on his foundation and the 'Gun for Glory' project aimed to train champions of the future.

Providing equipment that Bindra himself used for training while preparing for Rio, the centre has opened its doors to any athlete who wants to compete with the best. More importantly, the Chandigarh facility is free for any elite Indian athlete. 'For the longest time, we've lamented about the lack of facilities in our country. This is an attempt to redress the problem and this will not only get us on par with the West but will actually get us ahead of the curve. For twenty-two years of my life, I've been searching for something like this. Had I found it earlier I'd have won another Olympic medal,' said Bindra with a laugh.

From Ahmedabad comes another interesting development called The Arena from TransStadia. It served as the venue for the 2016 Kabaddi World Cup, which India had won. A spanking new sports infrastructure project, this multipurpose venue can house fourteen sporting disciplines, making it India's first and largest integrated convertible multi-sports facility. 'China has 1,000 of these high-performance centres. The US too has them in abundance. It's only fair our athletes have access to the best facilities to be able to compete with the best,' argued Bindra.

With the private foundations growing in strength and stature and the high-performance training centres increasing in number, Indian athletes now have access to high-quality sports science and rehabilitation along with other sporting facilities under one roof.

It is important to state here that none of these foundations have had it easy. We have seen Viren Rasquinha, the CEO of OGQ, put in days and months trying to convince corporates of the need for an organization like OGQ. Deepthi Bopaiah of GoSports speaks eloquently of the auction of sports memorabilia in Bengaluru that they had to resort to in getting the foundation going in 2010. 'We now have the funds to keep supporting 125 athletes for the next two years. But the aim is to ensure we have a five-year reserve so that we don't have to go back to donors year after year,' said Deepthi. 'Corporate social responsibility (CSR) monies have helped. With two per cent funds earmarked for CSR, corporates now see sports as a viable investment option,' said Viren. Narang, who invested his savings in getting the foundation going, agreed: 'The journey is certainly not over yet. Things have certainly changed for the better but there is a lot more that we can do as a country,' he said. 'With sports, you can make a statement to the world and that's what we need to make people see and realize.'

Tokyo can be a real game changer for these foundations. If India wins eight to ten medals and quadruples its Rio tally, the positivity created is sure to rub off on corporate India and benefit Indian Olympic sports in the long run. It is now upon the private foundations working with the government, the IOA and the SAI to make sure that each of our athletes and para-athletes are in the best shape going into Tokyo.

THE ORIGINS

8

Games of Self-Respect

The Nationalist Roots of Indian Sports Before Independence

There are so many communities, so many different religions, so many languages and dialects, so many different customs and ideals, that it is almost impossible to select a national team.

— Sir Dorabji Tata, President, IOA, 1929[1]

India was the first colonized Asian nation to take part in the Olympics. Its embrace of the Olympic movement, while still being a British colony, was no mere coincidence. Cricket, so central to Indian culture today, never gave our nation any significant international triumph until well after independence. It was in Indian hockey and the Olympics that colonial India found its earliest expression of nationalist aspirations on the sporting field. At a time when India was fighting for its independence from the British, the Olympics emerged as an international platform where Indian-ness could be projected on the sporting field.

Indians went to participate in the Olympics on equal terms with the British at a time when the colony was not even invited to the first British Empire Games in 1930 (later the Commonwealth Games) in Canada.

111

'100 YARDS ROUND A BEND TO ANTWERP': PEASANTS ON THE ATHLETICS TRACK

Sir Dorabji Tata deserves the credit for starting systematic Olympic activity on Indian soil in 1920. Son of the pioneering nationalist steel baron Jamsetji Tata, Dorabji was intimately involved in fulfilling his father's dream of creating an indigenous and modern steel industry in India. He is widely credited with the establishment of the Tata Steel Company in Jamsetpur (now Jamshedpur) that became India's largest private enterprise at the time. Simultaneously, in keeping with the great tradition of Parsi philanthropy in colonial India, some of his most valuable contributions came as benefactors for sports, culture and education.

Before taking an interest in Olympism, Sir Dorabji had already played a key role in the establishment of school and college cricket in Mumbai in the 1880s. He initiated the longest-running inter-school cricket tournament in India, the Harris Shield, in 1896. It served as a nursery for many Indian cricketers, most prominently Sachin Tendulkar. It was in a Harris Shield game that Tendulkar first made the headlines when he shared a world record partnership of 664 runs with Vinod Kambli.

Sir Dorabji was educated in England for the most part and his interest in sports was a product of his Western upbringing. The British saw sports as a form of becoming modern – a powerful but largely informal social institution that could create shared beliefs and attitudes between the rulers and the ruled. Playing a game also meant adopting the entire paraphernalia of modernity that went with it. It didn't just mean playing a foreign game, it also meant adopting European clothes, European rules and European notions of order and 'fair play'. Such was the power of sports as a cultural edifice that in 1902 Cecil Headlam could write of cricket:

> First the hunter, the missionary, and the merchant, next the soldier and the politician, and then the cricketer – that is the history of British colonisation ... The hunter may exterminate deserving species, the missionary may cause quarrels, the soldier may hector, the politician blunder – but cricket unites, as in India, the rulers and the ruled. It also provides a moral training, an education in pluck, and nerve,

and self restraint, far more valuable to the character of the ordinary native than the mere learning by heart of Shakespeare or an essay of Macaulay which is reckoned education in India.[2]

Sports became the playing field where tradition and modernity met, clashed and fused. And Indians saw in sports a way of taking on the colonizer on their own turf. In Sir Dorabji's words:

Having been educated in my youth in England I had shared in nearly every kind of English Athletics and acquired a great love for them. On my return to India I conceived the idea of introducing a love for such things there. I helped set up with the support of English friends, as General Secretary, a High School Athletic Association amongst numerous schools of Bombay, in the first place for cricket, and then for Athletic Sports Meetings which embraced nearly all the events which form part of the Inter-University contests every year in London.[3]

A good example here is that of the Deccan Gymkhana. After the successful start of the Harris Shield, the idea was modified in Poona (now Pune) with the creation of the Gymkhana. The committee that ran the Gymkhana was not conversant with the details of managing such athletic meets on European lines and wanted to develop their sports programme more in line with established Indian traditions.

Sir Dorabji, who was nominated the president of the Gymkhana, played a central role in the fusion of foreign and indigenous cultures that ensued. At the first athletic meet the Gymkhana organized, Dorabji found that the competitors were 'all boys of the peasant class working in the fields and living off poor fare ...'[4]

Naturally, they weren't familiar with European rules or modern training of any kind. On attending a meeting of the Gymkhana, Sir Dorabji found that they were proposing to run their 100-yard heats round a bend without strings. This was because their sports ground was very small and the track was part of a rough unrolled grass field. To the peasants, running was running, but now it had to be undertaken under standardized and controlled conditions. In Sir Dorabji's letters on the subject, preserved at the International Olympic Museum, the one thing that strikes the reader most is his sense of wonder at this clash of peasant and Western culture in the races at the Deccan Gymkhana.[5]

Other popular events included the long-distance race of about twenty-five miles, aptly named 'the Marathon'. The peasants who participated were used to running barefoot on hard macadamized or dirt roads. Despite their lack of training and primitive conditions, the first three or four men ran the distance in fair time. As Sir Dorabji observed, their timings 'would compare well with the times done in Europe or elsewhere'. In 1919, some of their times were close to those clocked in the Olympics.

Impressed by this, the Tata scion decided to send three of the runners to the Antwerp Games of 1920 at his own expense. This was the birth of India's Olympic encounter and nationalist sentiment was at its core. Dorabji Tata described his motives in a personal letter to the IOC president, Count Baillet-Latour, in 1929 as follows:

I therefore offered to arrange for the sending of three of the best runners to Antwerp to run the Olympic Marathon at the next meeting, when I hoped that with proper training and food under English trainers and coaches they might do credit to India. This proposal fired the ambition of the nationalist element in that city to try and send a complete Olympic team.[6]

But the peasant athletes barely had any idea of what was required to participate in the Olympics or the standard of performance essential to qualify for any of the events. For instance, a key member of the Gymkhana, when asked what time he thought was standard for a 100-yard race, replied that it could be anything 'from half a minute to a minute'. He was 'astounded' when informed that it was not a matter of minutes but rather tenths of seconds.

Despite their naivety on the rules of modern sports, Deccan Gymkhana members were all fueled by a strong nationalist imagination to send a team to the Olympics and started raising subscriptions to finance a team for Antwerp and set up an Indian Olympic association. Despite the enthusiasm of the organizers, public money at this early stage was not too forthcoming.

This meant that India's first tryst with international sports came to be financed largely by financial contributions from Tata, sundry princes, public collections (these increased substantially in later years) and interestingly, the government of India.

Apart from Tata's correspondence, a report published in the *Statesman* substantiates this point. The secretary of the Bombay branch of the proposed IOA sent the editor a letter appealing for support. The letter mentioned that a batch of six amateur athletes had been selected by a committee presided over by H.G. Weber and were soon to set sail for Antwerp on the steamer *Mantua* under the supervision of Dr A.H. Fyzee, India's national tennis champion. The cost of the adventure was estimated at Rs 35,000, of which only Rs 18,000 had been collected. The government of India subsequently contributed Rs 6,000 and also helped to secure a passage for the touring party.

Ranji, the great cricketer and Jam Saheb of Nawanagar, was expected to represent the country at the Olympic Council in Belgium and he too had assured the team all possible assistance. The *Statesman* report ended with an appeal to the public to contribute to India's Olympic cause. Contributions were to be sent to the secretary of the IOA located in Prag Mahal, Bombay.[7]

The public response, however, was lukewarm. In the end, Sir Dorabji bore a great deal of the expenditure and took a keen personal interest in selecting the participants. In return for his munificence, he was asked to become the president of the proposed Indian Olympic Association and head the Indian cause at the meeting of the International Olympic Committee (IOC) in Europe.

India's Olympic contingent was hurriedly put together and barely created an impression at Antwerp and, by extension, in India. India's first Olympic Games barely merited a mention in Indian newspapers. If it did, it was only as one-line news briefs. The following one-line update was probably inserted by a sub-editor at *Amrita Bazar Patrika*, published from Calcutta (now Kolkata): 'In catch-as-catch-can wrestling (featherweight) at the Olympic Games, Bernard (Britain) beat Shimpe (British India) in 19 seconds.'

Little else is known about the men who represented India in Antwerp, but one thing is certain – the Indian athletes did not do well and failed to catch the nationalist imagination their backers had hoped for. India's first appearance at the Olympics in Antwerp ended in sporting failure but the very fact that the athletes made it there was an achievement in itself. The journey had begun.

INDIA GOES TO PARIS

Not overly concerned with the failure at Antwerp, India once again entered a team at the Paris Games of 1924. This time, the nine-man contingent was better organized. The contingent for the Antwerp Games was more the result of a locally driven initiative, spearheaded by Tata and his experiences at the Deccan Gymkhana, but this time, a truly national effort had developed.

The team for Antwerp was selected largely by Tata after he saw some local runners in Poona. The Indian team for Paris was selected after rigorous screening at what was called the 'Olympic Games' in Delhi. These were the first national congregation of Indian athletes in any organized form. In the words of A.G. Noehren, leader of the Madras (now Chennai) Young Men's Christian Association (YMCA) and secretary of the newly established IOA, the Delhi 'Olympic Games' were a 'unique contribution made to the country... and it is fair to state that these have been far more successful, have created a wider interest throughout the country and have produced more permanent results than any of us dared to hope for.'[8]

In 1920, the money had largely come from Tata, the princes and the government. Back then it was an initiative largely driven from Poona and Bombay. But by 1924, the funding poured in from diverse regions across the country. The subscription drive undertaken to finance selected members for the Paris Games was a success. A detailed breakdown of public funding shows the marked progress of the Olympic idea in the public mind by 1924.

The Punjab Olympic Committee took the lead, contributing Rs 1,114, 'which represented contributions made by Punjab school boys through forty-seven schools'. Punjab, in total, contributed Rs 2,500. Uttar Pradesh, Bihar, Orissa and Madras contributed Rs 2,000 each while Central Provinces contributed Rs 1,500. Calcutta too contributed Rs 4,000 towards the fund. Across the nation, the Olympic ideal seemed to be catching the public imagination.

As before, the princes were also approached and the Maharaja of Patiala, the nation's leading sports patron, contributed enough to fund the participation of the Patiala long jumper, Dalip Singh. The Army too was sounded out to contribute to the passage of its representative and the government was called upon to put in a sum of Rs 5,000.

That Olympic sports were gaining currency in India is evident from the increase in press coverage between 1920 and 1924. Newspapers across the country carried news of multiple regional 'Olympic trials' and the 'Olympic Games' in Delhi were reported thus:

The All India Olympic meeting to be held at the Roshanara Club, Delhi on February 8–9 promises to be a unique event in the history of sports in India. Reservations have already been booked for the Indian team, which will proceed to France on the steamer 'Lancashire' ex-Colombo on 29 May. The team will be accompanied by a professional coach who will continue to train the players on [the] steamer deck and in France for a month before the Olympic begins.[9]

The detailed programme of the meet and the timings of all the events featured prominently in the dailies and provincial successes at the meet were greeted with considerable cheer in their respective regions. For instance, the fact that Bengali athletes made the finals in nine events was reported at length in the province and much was made of the fact that Bengal had beaten Madras (with six final qualifications) and Punjab (with five finals appearances). The two stars from Bengal, T.J. Pitt and J.S. Hall, were both eventually selected to travel to Paris.

The overwhelming popularity of this meet and the regional pride it evoked is evident in the following report in Calcutta's *Amrita Bazar Patrika* on February 1924:

The weather condition was excellent and spectators numbered several thousands. Viceroy and Lady Reading were present. In four events – hurdles, one mile, long jump and three miles, provincial and Indian records were beaten, although the world records have not been touched. Bengal was first in the composition of India's Olympic team having won three places ... At a meeting of the All India Olympic Committee held after the meet it was decided to send these men to Paris as the money is available –

Dalip Singh of Patiala for Long Jump
Lakshmanan of Madras (Hurdles)
M.R. Hinge of Bombay (Marathon)

T.K. Pitt of Bengal (100 and 440 Yards)

J. S. Hall of Bengal (220 Yards)

Sepoy Pala Singh of UP (Three Miles)

J. C Heathcote (Madras), High Jump

M.V. Venkatramaswamy (Madras), One Mile.

Patiala, Madras, Bombay and Bengal – the regional composition of the Paris team was already beginning to represent the disparate regions of India. H.C. Buck of the YMCA College of Physical Education in Madras, an American who had pioneered athletics coaching in India, escorted the athletes. Though the Indians did not win medals, they acquitted themselves better than at Antwerp, with two of them – T.K Pitt in the 400 metres and Dalip Singh in the broad jump – performing well.[10]

The organized planning for the Indian participation at the Paris Games was driven by the formation of a permanent All India Olympic Association. Sir Dorabji Tata was invited to assume the presidency of the new body but it did not survive for more than three years. In 1927, another body, the IOA, was formed and it continues to administer Indian sports to this day. Once again, Dorabji Tata was the president and A.G. Noehren the secretary.

It was the new IOA, with help from the YMCA, that led India's preparations for the 1928 Olympiad in Amsterdam where India had her first taste of Olympic success.

'IMPOSSIBLE TO SELECT A NATIONAL REPRESENTATIVE': THE NATION IN THE GAMES

Central to the challenge was the problem of creating a national consciousness in a land divided on issues regarding religion, caste and language. In 1929, a year after India had won its first hockey gold in Amsterdam, Tata wrote:

> ... India is not yet ripe for the International Olympic Games. The love of such things is not ingrained here. There are so many communities, so many religions, so many languages and dialects, so many different customs and ideals, that it is almost impossible to select a national representative that would meet all requirements.[11]

There were two other major problems: the lack of stadiums and the relatively small size of the leisured class that could patronize sports as an audience. As Tata noted at the end of his tenure as the head of the Indian Olympic movement, the foremost necessity was to have permanent stadiums, which would allow the organization for the Olympics in at least two of the provinces.

He had already approached the provincial municipalities and the government for funds to implement his projects of stadium building but nothing came out of his overtures. Local stadiums were an urgent necessity because it would be impossible for the poor to travel long distances.

The leisured class in India was much smaller than in Europe and the majority of Indians did not have the time to devote to sports, making the progress of Olympic sports increasingly difficult. Finally, each province had its indigenous pastime and people did not take much interest in other events.[12]

The Raja of Santosh in Bengal, Sir Manmatha Nath Roy Chowdhury, emphasized the following in the 1920s:

> Speaking for Bengal, I may say, without any fear of contradiction, that a sports stadium in Calcutta is the need of the moment. Sport in Bengal will receive a serious check if we fail to provide at the psychological moment a central home for sports. Besides, in a city like Calcutta where the huge sporting crowds always cause anxiety to the police and people alike, the problem of providing accommodation for spectators can no longer be ignored ... We must have a sports stadium, which could accommodate in its auditorium no less than 60,000 people.[13]

THE PRINCES AND THE POLITICS OF COLONIAL SPORTS

It wasn't long before the princes entered Indian sports. They already had a great deal of influence in cricket because sports were a form of cultural capital. Ranji serves as the best example of how important sports were for some princes. It is now well documented that Ranji, a disinherited prince, won back his crown of Nawanagar largely because of the social capital he had gained as a cricketing icon in England.

When Tata resigned from the presidency of the IOA in 1927, the position became a prize catch for several princes to fight over. With the princely influence over cricket and football already well demarcated and with Olympic sports gaining relevance, it wasn't surprising that the succession dispute became a battle royale between several Indian princes with an interest in sports.

Among the requirements necessary to become the successor was having the personal means and influence to visit Europe frequently. This was considered crucial to keep a tab on international developments, liaise with the IOC, learn of its plans and programmes and having imbibed new ideas, implement them back home. Sir Dorabji Tata repeatedly emphasized in all his correspondence with the IOC that a regular presence in Europe was a necessary prerequisite.[14]

This shows us two things. First, the global Olympic movement at this stage was still one of a league of gentlemanly elites from various countries. Second, though the movement rode on nationalist emotions within India, it was still mostly driven and controlled by moneyed and political elites. The democratization of the movement was years away and many would argue that this is a process that, at least in India, is still far from completion.

The IOC eventually suggested that the Maharaja of Kapurthala, a frequent visitor to Europe, be nominated the successor. Tata admitted in a handwritten letter (from Geneva on 16 June 1927) to the president that his presidency thus far had created a lot of discord in India from a rival section, which wanted Ranji, the great princely icon of Indian sports, to lead the Olympic movement. That crisis had only been averted because Tata, himself good friends with Ranji, heartily acquiesced with the idea of anointing Ranji only to be told by the Jam Sahib himself that he did not want anything to do with the IOA at that stage.[15]

Tata personally was in favour of the Maharaja of Kapurthala, who, he thought, was better qualified to represent India at the IOC. 'Kapurthala is every year in Europe and unlike me or Burdwan can be present at all European functions.' Because he travelled to India every winter after his European vacation was over, he was also in a position to closely monitor the day-to-day activities of the Indian Association.[16]

As the names of the Maharaja of Kapurthala, the Jam Sabhib of Nawanagar and the Maharaja of Burdwan were doing the rounds, the powerful Maharaja of Patiala, already a key figure in Indian cricket, threw his hat in the ring.

It can be surmised that Patiala's entry into the fray was the principal reason behind Ranji's backing off. This was because Patiala had been Ranji's strongest source of financial support in times of crisis. The connection between Ranji and Patiala was very well known in Indian sporting circles. Ranji had played for Patiala's team in 1898–99 and had been his aide-de-camp in the years before he won the crown of Nawanagar. While touring Bengal in 1899, Ranji and Patiala had been accorded a royal reception, with the Calcutta Town Hall spending the huge sum of Rs 3,000 on the occasion.[17]

Patiala's interest in Olympic affairs fundamentally transformed equations in India. By September 1927, Tata was informing his friend Count Baillet-Latour that the Maharaja of Kapurthala had already declined the presidency of the IOA and Burdwan too had decided to withdraw his candidature, clearing the turf for Patiala.[18]

The dispute lingered, and by early 1928, Tata had developed serious doubts about the suitability of princes, who themselves were not sportsmen, heading sporting organizations. In a letter to the count, he stated that though the maharajas were keen on shooting, hunting, polo and other sporting activities, they had little knowledge on track and field events and not all of them were frequent visitors to Europe. He emphasized that the only reason he had backed Kapurthala so far was because he visited Europe regularly. However, he had since realized that the maharaja had little knowledge of Olympic sports and would hardly be of any practical assistance to the IOC's cause. In Tata's words:

> The same applies to the Maharaja of Burdwan who has declined the Presidentship … It is going to be very difficult to find a prominent man in India who takes interest in running, jumping and this type of sport who can spare the time to come to Europe every year…I think that if the Maharaja Jam Saheb of Nawanagar could be persuaded to accept the appointment he would be the most suitable man as he is a good general all round sportsman.[19]

Worried about the leadership vacuum, in October 1927, the IOA once again requested Tata to reconsider his resignation. His refusal to do so meant that by the end of 1927, Patiala was the lone candidate left in the race for the presidency. As he had so often done in cricket with his affluence, he successfully out-manoeuvred the others and posited himself as the saviour of the Olympic cause in India. Soon after assuming charge, he took the perfect diplomatic step in appointing Dorabji Tata as the honorary life president of the IOA in recognition of his efforts to promote Olympism in India.

Aside from Ranji, if there was one Indian prince who was genuinely interested in sports for its own sake, it was Maharaja Bhupinder Singh of Patiala. He first became interested in Olympic matters in 1923 when a Patiala athlete, Dalip Singh, failed to make it to the Indian Olympic team for Paris. As Anthony de Mello writes:

> His failure was, apparently, because he had been unavoidably prevented from attending the trials, which had recently been held at Lahore. Dalip Singh appealed for help to the Ruler of Patiala, who not only helped the young man to get his rightful place in the team, but also ordered the formation of the Patiala State Olympic Association.

It was this incident that aroused Bhupinder Singh's interest in Olympic matters and 'already he was rehearsing for the role he was soon to play'.

Soon after taking charge as president of the IOA, Bhupinder faced the difficult task of sending a team to the Amsterdam Games in 1928. With virtually no official funds available for the purpose, the task was an onerous one. It was as a result of his labours that India managed to send seven athletes and fifteen hockey players to Amsterdam. As de Mello asserted, 'Without the efforts of Bhupinder Singh it is more than likely that our hockey wizards would not then, nor for many years to come, have had the opportunity so completely to baffle the game's experts from the rest of the world'.[20]

But Patiala's rise as the pre-eminent patron of Indian Olympism created serious resentment, not only among the other princes but also among the power players in the Indian Olympic structure. Efforts to discredit him and prevent him from appointing Punjab's G.D. Sondhi as India's delegate in the IOC continued. With the influence of Tata and the YMCA gradually decreasing, Sondhi, educationist and secretary of the Punjab Olympic Association, emerged as Patiala's chosen man at this early stage of India's Olympic encounter.

As early as 30 March 1931, Patiala urged the IOC president to allow Sondhi to stand in for Sir Dorabji at the IOC session in Los Angeles in case he was unable to attend. He argued that Indian representation in the IOC session was crucial because 'India is becoming more and more conscious of the importance of its position in international sport and we wish for as full a representation as possible on the international sports bodies'. India's success in hockey had strengthened the case for greater representation in the highest decision-making body of the Olympics and Patiala pushed further, demanding a permanent place for Sondhi at the international Olympic table:

> By winning an international event like hockey in the first year of its entrance into international competition, India has a good claim to have two members in charge of her affairs at the IOC ...[21]

The IOC's subsequent acceptance of Sondhi as the official Indian representative gave the formal seal to Patiala's dominance in India's Olympic affairs.

There were those who were not happy with this. Henry Gray, national director of the YMCA for India, Burma and Ceylon, sent the IOC a scathing critique of India's Olympic affairs on 28 December 1928. He lamented that the Olympic organization was sagging nationwide and ascribed the loss of steam directly to Patiala's ascent. Gray argued that the new leadership was not 'representative' and that control had passed to a very small group, chiefly three men in north India representing Punjab and the Army. He minced no words: 'This leadership does not have the confidence of the entire country, is not familiar with conditions nor acquainted with the leaders in the other parts of the empire'. He felt that this was because most local provincial committees had lost their voting rights after failing to pay their dues to the national body. Gray specifically criticized the management of the team sent to Amsterdam, where Patiala had played a central role. He argued that the 'masses continued to remain uninvolved in Olympic activity across the country' and went on to suggest that unless immediately checked, the 'top control of the movement will be secured by a semi-interested small group of people who do not represent the country as a whole'.[22]

Nothing resulted from any of these complaints because of the affluence and influence of the house of Patiala and the paucity of funds from other sources to promote Olympic sports in the country as a whole.

Patiala, as he had done in cricket, used his trusted weapon of patronage to gain control of Olympic matters in India. He had not only funded Indian teams for various international meets but had also built a grand stadium in Amritsar to promote track and field competitions.

Patronage worked well because the IOA was in a sorry financial state when he assumed the presidency. Most provinces were in arrears for their contributions; some of them for over two years. Rs 10,000 was all that was available to the IOA for sending the team to Amsterdam.

We can't understand how India went for the Olympics unless we understand who paid for it. As Noehren wrote before resigning from the IOA, 'It must be obvious that the whole success of India's participation rests on a financial basis and that the IOA will be powerless to send even a small team abroad, unless all Provinces pay up their outstanding obligations and that this revenue be further supplemented by private donations.'

In his much-acclaimed biography of the Olympic movement's founder Pierre De Coubertin, John J. MacAloon writes that he:

> ... failed to see that the games had become not something different from, but something much more than, what he had intended. From a small public novelty of the belle époque, an athletic competition wrapped in a prepotent historical conceit and adorned with verdant social claims, the games had been transformed in four decades (by the 1920s) into a crucible of symbolic force into which the world poured its energies and a stage upon which, every four years, it played out its hopes and its terrors.[23]

India had entered the Olympic family by the late 1920s, so a small part of this transformation was also enacted in the nation. Here, as in other parts of the world, control of Olympic matters resulted in fascinating battles of intrigue and power play that defined and transformed established contours of the domestic political landscape. Indian sports were global in the early twentieth century, long before the term 'globalization' became fashionable. Colonial India benefitted significantly from this.

Following Dorabji Tata, the Olympic torch was passed into the hands of the Maharaja of Patiala and his trusted lieutenant G.D. Sondhi. Having already fashioned a stranglehold over cricket by the late 1920s, control over the nation's expanding Olympic horizon allowed Patiala to establish himself as the patriarch of India's sporting world.

His monopoly was challenged on occasions, but such confrontations, more often than not, proved feeble and eventually fizzled out. Yet, such attempts continued through the 1930s and 1940s and are as much a part of India's Olympic encounter as the eight gold medals India won at hockey between 1928 and 1956.

GODS OF HOCKEY

9

The Golden Years

How Colonial India Became a Hockey Superpower

India claims to be the foremost in many things in the world. The world admits that she is foremost in hockey.

—A. M. Hayman, President, Indian Hockey Federation, 1932[1]

WHEN DHYAN CHAND FIRST BECAME A HERO IN NEW ZEALAND

India was once a hockey superpower. Between 1928 and 1956, India's hockey teams won six straight Olympic gold medals and twenty-four consecutive matches, a record likely to stand for the foreseeable future. In fact, it was at India's insistence that hockey was reinstated as an Olympics game at the Amsterdam Games of 1928 after being dropped four years prior. Amsterdam gave India its first Olympic gold, starting a golden run that lasted three decades. Indian hockey teams have won two more gold medals since – 1964 and 1980.

Now, as Indian hockey is once again resurrecting itself, it is more important than ever to understand how and why the early Indian hockey teams, representing a country that was still a British colony, ended up dominating the world.

Organized hockey in India started in Calcutta in 1885 when the first
hockey clubs were formed. Within a decade the great tournaments that
were to become the breeding grounds of the national team had been
established. The Beighton Cup in Calcutta and the Aga Khan Tournament
in Bombay were both set up in 1895. Having established itself in the
eastern and western regions, hockey moved north to Punjab, first to the
Army cantonments after which it made its way into the Punjab University
Sports Tournament in 1903. That same year, Lahore started its famous Hot
Weather Tournament.[2]

These tournaments were to be the lifeline of Indian hockey all through
its golden age. In 1952, the great Dhyan Chand, who had cut his hockey
teeth first in the Army and then with the Jhansi Heroes before going on to
wow the world with his hockey wizardry, explained why the Beighton Cup
was held in such high regard:

> In 1933, the Jhansi Heroes decided to participate in the Beighton
> Cup hockey tournament. My life's ambition was to win the Beighton
> Cup, as I had always regarded this competition as the blue riband of
> Indian hockey. In my opinion it is perhaps the best organized hockey
> event in the country. Calcutta is indeed lucky that it has at least three
> or four first class hockey grounds on the maidan, and this is a great
> advantage to run a tournament on schedule. Instituted in 1895, this
> tournament has had a non-stop run. World Wars I and II did not affect
> the tournament. Threats of Japanese bombs and actual bombings in
> Calcutta while the hockey season was on also did not prevent the
> tournament from being held. That being said, it is sad to think that
> the tournament had to yield to the communal frenzy, which gripped
> the nation in 1946–47.[3]

Like the Bombay Pentangular in cricket, these tournaments helped in
popularizing the game beyond Army cantonments.

The first attempts at forming a national association took place in
Calcutta in 1907–08. The political chaos that engulfed Bengal after
its partition in 1905, however, put paid to these efforts. The move was
revived in the 1920s when C.E. Newham, president of the Punjab Hockey
Federation, started a campaign to create a central organization to govern
Indian hockey. This second attempt at establishing a nodal organization

also ended in failure and it was not until November 1925 that a governing body for hockey was established.

The princely state of Gwalior was the new centre. In 1959, Anthony de Mello recounted the formation of the Indian Hockey Federation (IHF):

> In 1924, at the request of the now defunct Western India Hockey Association, Lieutenant Colonel Luard, who was then President of the Gwalior Sports Association, addressed all hockey associations, clubs and individuals interested in the game and invited them to a meeting in Gwalior. This meeting, which took place on November 7th, 1925, resulted in the official formation of the Indian Hockey Federation.

At the inaugural meeting of the federation, Gwalior, Bengal, Punjab, Sind, Rajputana, Western India, Punjab University and the Army Sports Control Board were represented. For the first two years, Gwalior was treated as the headquarters, after which it moved to Delhi in 1927.[4]

The formation of the IHF was a landmark event because it gave Indian players international exposure for the first time. Soon after its formation, the IHF organized India's first international tour – the trip to New Zealand in 1926. The Indian team immediately made its mark and their wizardry proved to be a commercial success as well. The New Zealand Hockey Federation made a profit of GBP 300 after paying the Indians a healthy sum of GBP 500. The Indians ended the tour with eighteen victories in twenty-one matches, with just one defeat. They scored a total of 192 goals, conceding twenty-four and averaging 9.31 goals per match. Astonishingly, the Indians registered a double-digit score in as many as nine games.[5]

It was on this tour that Dhyan Chand established himself as the premier star of Indian hockey. For him, an enlisted sepoy in the Army and a man not born into privilege like some of his counterparts, the opportunity to represent India was a windfall. The New Zealand tour turned Dhyan Chand into an Indian hero. His delight is beautifully portrayed in his autobiography:

> It was a great day for me when my Commanding Officer called me and said: 'Boy, you are to go to New Zealand.' I was dumbfounded, and did not know what to reply. All I did was click my heels snappily, give as smart a salute as I possibly could, and beat a hasty retreat.

Once out of sight of the officer, I ran like a hare to reach my barracks and communicated the good news to my fellow soldiers. And what a reception they gave me! I lost no time in getting prepared for the trip. I was not a rich man, my earnings as a *sepoy* being only a few rupees a month. My parents were not rich either. All thoughts of outfitting and equipping myself in the proper manner for an overseas tour of this nature had to be given up for want of sufficient resources. I clothed myself as inexpensively as possible, and my main personal outfit was my military kit…As soldiers, particularly those belonging to the Other Ranks (read lower ranks), it was a great experience for us. Prior to this tour we could never conceive of being feted and entertained at private houses and public functions in such a glorious and enjoyable manner. We were made heroes, and on my part, if I may put it quite modestly, I proved myself a great success and left behind a great impression.

Riding on this success and encouraged by the colonial British government's support, the IHF applied for and subsequently obtained global affiliation in 1927. This was crucial to India's participation at the Amsterdam Games. It was in Amsterdam that India started its uninterrupted reign over the world of hockey for the next three decades.

DHYAN CHAND AND HIS TROUSERS 'IN THE SUN': THE BEGINNING

Anthony de Mello writes that before leaving for Amsterdam, India's hockey players were 'confident that they would not disgrace themselves'.[6] At the same time, they did not approach the Games with any fantastic hopes. Jaipal Singh, who had a first-class degree from his native Ranchi and was then a student at Balliol College, Oxford, was appointed captain of the team.

A Munda tribal from Chhotanagpur, the forested plateau of undivided Bihar, Jaipal is a fascinating character in Indian history whose influence in later years extended far beyond the hockey field. As the historian Ramachandra Guha writes, he later became the marang gomke (great leader) of the tribals of Chhotanagpur and in the constituent assembly 'he came to represent tribals not just of his native plateau, but all of India'. It was his interventions in the constituent assembly that ultimately led to the reservation of seats for tribals in government jobs and legislative bodies after independence.[7]

Sent to Oxford by missionaries, Jaipal successfully led a team comprising of Indians studying at British universities for matches played in Belgium and Spain and earned a reputation as a great hockey player in the UK, as is evident from the numerous profiles published in *World Hockey* magazine. When the team for the Amsterdam Games was announced, it included Jaipal, S. M. Yusef and the Nawab of Pataudi Senior, all of whom were already in Britain. Thirteen players were set to sail from Bombay – nine of them Anglo-Indians – to rise to India's challenge at the 1928 Olympics.[8] However, before sailing for London, it was revealed at the last minute that because of insufficient funds, only eleven of the thirteen selected players could go on the tour. The shortfall, contemporary reports revealed, was Rs 15,000. The hockey federation even announced that in case sufficient funds weren't garnered, Shaukat Ali of Bengal and R.A. Norris of the Central Provinces would not accompany the team.

In the end, it was largely owing to the munificence of the sports-loving public of Bengal, who crowd-sourced public collections to make up the shortfall, that the two players were able to make the trip.

While he later became known as a prominent parliamentarian and adivasi leader, Jaipal described his hockey career in the UK fondly in his memoir:

> The effect of the tours of Indian students I conducted every year with the help of Aga Khan, 'Kanji' Baroda, Patiala, Bhopal and other Indian royalty was the formation of the Indian Hockey Federation ... India decided to send a team to the Amsterdam Olympiad in 1928. I was still at Oxford a probationer for the Indian Civil Service ... As after 1926 I could not play for the University team, I played for the Wimbledon Hockey Club ... As at Oxford I continued to receive publicity in the London press.[9]

In a clear reflection of how haphazardly that first Olympic team was put together, he goes on to narrate the strange manner in which he was appointed captain of the Indian team:

One early evening two Britishers, Colonel Bruce Turnbull and Major Ricketts, both of the Indian army, called at the Church Imperial Club. Turnbull was Secretary of the Army Sports Board in India and Ricketts was his lieutenant. I stood them drinks. They told me the Indian hockey team was coming the following week on its way to Amsterdam. 'We want you to captain the team.' I agreed but told them I would have to get leave from the India Office for absence during term time. I did not get leave! I decided to defy the ruling and face the consequences.[10]

Jaipal met his team when their boat docked in Tilbury on 30 March 1928. Having lived in England for a few years by now, he was unimpressed by what he saw as the players' rustic 'untidy dress and crude demeanor'. The team was put up in a pension in South Kensington and Jaipal invited them a couple of times to the well-known Veeraswamy's restaurant on Regent Street: 'It was expensive to feed them. The Indian dishes were Hyderabadi but not cheap.' Soon after their arrival, the players started addressing Jaipal as 'skipper' though he was yet to formally accept the offer.

In the first few practice sessions, Shaukat Ali and Dhyan Chand caught Jaipal's attention. Shaukat represented Calcutta Customs and could play in any position. Dhyan Chand, a lance naik in the Indian Army, had made his name in New Zealand, scoring the bulk of the goals for the Indian Army team in 1926. Jaipal states that Dhyan Chand:

...was humble. He had only one pair of trousers. I took him to Austin Reed on Regent Street. We went downstairs. Trousers galore were shown. 'Can I take them upstairs and see them in the sun?' That finished me. I told Shaukat the story. 'What else do you expect of a Lance Naik?' he laughed.[11]

The Indians played a series of matches in London against leading clubs and haphazardly put together national teams like the Anglo Irish. Dhyan Chand scored in almost every game. India's last engagement in England was at the Folkstone Easter Festival where they beat the English national team 4–0 and a team called the Rossalians 18–0. Following these victories, the British and French press both suggested that the Indians were favourites for hockey gold in Amsterdam. And they weren't wrong.

'THE WORLD'S GREATEST CENTRE FORWARD': AMSTERDAM 1928
AND THE MAKING OF THE LEGEND OF INDIAN HOCKEY

In Amsterdam, the onus was on the hockey team to lead the Indian challenge. The athletes – Chawan in the 10,000 metres, Hamid in the 400-metre hurdles and Murphy in the 800 metres – had failed to qualify for the second round. In hockey, India played its first match against Austria winning 6–0, an encounter reported in detail at home. Already, Dhyan Chand was being described as the 'world's greatest centre forward'. As the *Statesman* put it:

> The Indian Hockey team has successfully surmounted the first obstacle towards the prize for which they journeyed to Europe. India defeated Austria 6–0 with the world's greatest center forward Dhyan Chand giving another masterly exhibition. He scored all 3 goals in the first half. After the interval Dhyan Chand scored the fourth goal. The fifth was obtained by Shaukat Ali while Gately secured the last goal …

Dhyan Chand eventually scored fourteen of India's twenty-nine goals in Amsterdam. The very next day, the *Statesman* published another detailed report on India's 9–0 win over Belgium. The space allotted to the report was nearly double compared to the first, an indication of the growing popularity of the team back home:

> All India followed up their brilliant victory over Austria by defeating Belgium 9–0. The point about today's victory was it proved India can pile up goals even if Dhyan Chand does not think it necessary to improve his goal average. In his skilful manner he worked out scoring possibilities yet tapped the ball either to Feroze Khan or Marthins. Seaman, whose clever stick work on left wing has been the feature of the tour, bewildered Belgium's goalkeeper twice. Allen in India's goal did not have much to do. Jaipal Singh was brilliant and Penniger did all that was required of him with polish …

Subsequently, the Indians beat Denmark and Switzerland to set up a title clash with hosts Holland on 26 May 1928.

When the Indians trounced Holland 3–0 in the final, the press back home went wild. The *Statesman* had an entire report titled 'How India Won Honors' and went on to suggest that 40,000 people went into raptures over the brilliant exhibition of hockey displayed by the Indians in the final. It reported that despite having to reconstruct their side in the absence of Feroze Khan, who had broken his collarbone in the clash against Denmark, and Shaukat Ali, who was down with the flu, India won comprehensively.

Interestingly, the newspaper report did not mention the absence of captain Jaipal Singh. He had, for personal reasons, walked out of the team before the semi-final. This is one of the most enduring mysteries of the tour and perhaps the earliest political controversy within the national hockey team. Jaipal too was silent about this discord in his memoirs, one that raised doubts as to who actually captained the final victory – Jaipal or Penniger. Jaipal left the Olympic team on the eve of the semi-final and did not take part in the final either. He refused to discuss the issue ever again in public. Until new evidence emerges, the mystery of why he walked away from that first Indian Olympic team will remain unsolved.[12]

Another intriguing aspect of those years of Indian dominance at the Olympics was the conspicuous absence of previous champions, England. The colony had won in Europe but the colonizer was absent. Some questioned whether India would still have won if England had not chosen to sit out of Olympic hockey. Contemporary observers like the *Statesman* correspondent covering the games didn't think this would have mattered much. India's is 'no empty title,' the newspaper argued, 'for the critics are of the opinion that even if England had been competing in the Games, honors would have gone to India, though possibly not with the record of not conceding a goal remaining intact'.

Yet, despite having a strong hockey team, why did England not compete at the Amsterdam Olympics against India? England's hockey teams had won gold medals in 1908 and 1920 but stayed out of the Olympics thereafter till 1948. There was a rumour in Olympic circles that England had initially entered a hockey team for the Olympics in Amsterdam. According to this rumour, after the 4–0 drubbing they received at the Folkestone Festival at the hands of the Indians, the English were scared of losing on an international stage to their colony and withdrew from the event. This belief was known well enough for Dhyan Chand to refer to it in his recollections:

I reiterate that this is mere hearsay (that England dropped out of the Amsterdam Games fearing the Indians), although we fondly hoped that at least in future Olympics we would have the honor of meeting Great Britain and showing them how good or bad we were. It is my regret that this hope was never realized so long as I participated in Olympic events.[13]

The English team did not participate in Olympic hockey until the 1948 Games in London, by which time India was an independent nation. When India beat England 4–0, it unleashed great celebrations in the newly independent nation and the win contributed to national self-confidence and self-belief.

It was in Amsterdam that the legend of Indian hockey was created. Even the Dutch papers praised the team with generosity: 'So agile are the Indians that they could run the full length of the hockey field, juggling a wooden ball on the flat end of the hockey stick'.

England may not have participated but soon after the win, the viceroy, Lord Irwin, sent the following telegram to the team manager A.B. Rosser: 'Please convey to Jaipal Singh and all members of his team my heartiest congratulations on their magnificent victory. All India has followed the triumphal progress throughout the tour and rejoice in the crowning achievement'.[14] This telegram, which mentions Jaipal as captain, laid the captaincy debate to rest.

India scored twenty-nine goals in Amsterdam without conceding even one and averaged more than five goals per match. It is important to note that the Olympic hockey competition was played in May, while the actual Olympiad, including the opening ceremony and other events, took place two months later in July. As a result, the victorious Indian team did not have the good fortune of enjoying the Olympic atmosphere, the rituals of the opening ceremony and the ambience of the Olympic Village.

In London, the victory became the cause of great nationalist celebration for the Indian community. Indian women organized a tea party in the team's honour and presented them with turbans. Interestingly, as Jaipal pointed out, 'The Anglo Indians never wore them!'[15] They were also invited to lunch at Veeraswamy's by Dr Paranjpe, a member of the Indian Council. And when the team reached Bombay, a huge throng of adoring fans welcomed them. Mole Station overflowed with a wildly cheering crowd trying to get a glimpse of the new heroes. In the audience was Dr G.V. Deshmukh, the mayor of Maharashtra, who was there to accord the team a civic reception, and a representative of the governor of Mumbai who sent a congratulatory message.

Jaipal, who had broken his term at Oxford without leave to play in the Games, paid a personal price for the victory. He returned to Oxford after the festivities were over only to be confronted by angry dons. As he put it:

> I was told that as I had broken term I would have to stay for one more year. Captaining India to world championship was no prize for the British. I resigned from the ICS and refused to pay back 350 pounds. I was not put in gaol.[16]

Jaipal's resignation from the ICS after that first hockey win led him away from sports to a different arena – he gradually moved into politics and became the leader of the Adibasi Mahasabha in 1938.

The man who had looked at Dhyan Chand in derision for his rustic manners became the champion of India's tribals. He believed that the tribals were 'the original inhabitants' of the subcontinent, hence the term 'adibasi' or 'adivasi'. As Ramachandra Guha has pointed out, Jaipal went on to become the greatest defender of tribal rights in the constitutional assembly. His interventions were erudite as well as spirited, like when he opposed the prohibition of alcohol, which had been brought about as a directive principle. Alcohol, he said, was part of the daily and ritual life of the tribals of India and he denounced its prohibition citing it as interference:

> ...with the religious rights of the most ancient people in the country... it would be impossible for paddy to be transplanted if the Santhal does not get rice beer. These ill clad men...have to work knee-deep in water throughout the day, drenching rain and in mud. What is it in the rice beer that keeps them alive? I wish the medical authorities in this country would carry out research in their laboratories to find out what it is that the rice beer contains, of which the Adibasis need so much and which keeps them [protected] against all manner of diseases.[17]

Jaipal's hockey adventure led to his premature departure from the ICS, but their loss was independent India's gain. It was Jaipal who initiated the demand for the separate tribal state of Jharkhand, which was ultimately carved out of Bihar in 2001.

LOANS OF GLORY: EN ROUTE TO LOS ANGELES, 1932

The global economic depression, starting from the Wall Street crash in 1928, meant that India, Japan and the US were the only entrants competing for hockey honours at the Los Angeles Olympiad in 1932. However, that does not take away from the fact that the Indians were far superior to any of their contemporaries. Determined to defend the title won in Amsterdam, the IHF tried to pick the best team possible for the 1932 Games and organized an inter-provincial trial in Calcutta during March 1932.

Only Dhyan Chand was an immediate choice. Based on performance at the trials, the appointed representatives of the provinces affiliated with the federation picked the rest of the national team led by Lal Shah Bokhari. G.D. Sondhi was appointed as manager and Pankaj Gupta the non-playing captain and assistant manager of the touring side.

The effects of the depression were also felt in India and the IHF found it exceedingly difficult to raise funds for the tour. In the end, money came from a diverse range of sources: Viceroy Lord Willingdon, governors of the provinces, a few of the princely families, public collections by the nation's sporting public and proceeds from exhibition football and hockey matches played in Calcutta, Bhopal, Bombay, Madras, Bangalore, Singapore and Colombo. This was still not enough to cover all the expenses but at least the team was able to leave Indian shores.[18]

Picking the team was the easy part but sending it overseas was a huge financial challenge. To cope with the financial shortfall, the federation took a loan of Rs 7,500. It organized exhibition matches for the national team at Colombo, Madras, Bombay, Delhi and Lahore on the team's homeward journey and hoped that proceeds from these matches would wipe out the debt entirely. A sporting goods dealer from Sialkot, Uberoi chipped in by supplying the players with hockey sticks and balls. The sticks, it is evident from players' memoirs, were the very best by global standards.

Despite the challenges, the IHF was reluctant to forgo the opportunity of international glory. A measure of the obstacles faced in sending the team is reminisced by Pankaj Gupta:

Before the Los Angeles Games, I, in my capacity as Hony Secretary of the Indian Hockey Federation, and Mr. A.M. Hayman, the President, had more than our share of headaches. First there was the question of finance and secondly it was debatable whether it was worthwhile sending a team to play against such weak opposition as that provided by the USA and Japan. Several meetings were held and the IHF took a bold decision, prompted by the fact that if India did not take part the event might be deleted from the Games and possibly not revived ... I am glad that we, in the larger interest of international glory, decided to send our team.[19]

In the same article, he emphasized Bengal's contribution in promoting hockey in India and declared, 'it might be news to many that most of the money at the earlier stages of India's participation in Olympic hockey came from Bengal. I must not be misunderstood when I refer to Bengal, which I have not done from any parochial angle but public memory is always short and history and tradition should not be forgotten.' He went on to state that in his opinion the best Indian team ever produced was the 1932 Olympic team, which played on consecutive days despite having to undertake overland third-class travel on the continent to meet expenses.

India's newly picked team played its first pre-Olympic tour match at Bhopal on 15 May against a team from Aligarh University. The national team won easily, scoring five goals in each half. On 16 May they played the Bhopal team, beating them 8–2. While at Bhopal, the team was accorded royal treatment as guests of the Nawab. Prince Rahid-uz-Zafar Khan, who made a contribution of Rs 1,000 towards the tour fund, organized a reception in their honour. At the time of the visit, the Nawab of Bhopal was away on official work and sent the team the following message:

I extend a most hearty welcome to the members of the Olympic Hockey Team on their visit to Bhopal and my keenest regret is my absence from my state on this occasion. But my inability to show you and your team hospitality in person will not diminish the cordiality, which my state will offer you on my behalf, or the sincerity of my good wishes for the success of your mission. Our Indian team represents the true spirit of sportsmanship in India and carries with it the good wishes of all people. We are confident that all of you will ... keep the flag flying in all the countries you include in your tour. Your sporting achievements will ... add further glory to the fair name of India and enhance its reputation among the nations of the West ...

This message is indicative enough of the respect accorded to the players by the Nawab. For players like Dhyan Chand and Roop Singh, men from underprivileged and humble backgrounds, the game was a means to social respectability. Like in football and cricket, princely patronage played a crucial role.

The communal riots in Bombay, though, cast a deep shadow on the team when it moved there for three matches between 19 and 21 May. Attendance at these games was affected by the riots, after which the players moved on to Bangalore, Madras and Colombo. Travelling around the country and raising money for their Olympic journey, the guiding principle for these players was the idea of 'national self-respect'. Skipper Lal Shah Bokhari said in a message issued in Madras: 'I can assure my countrymen that we will bring respect to India and we will maintain our tradition as World's Champion Hockey playing nation'.

The money-raising drive did not end in India. En route to Los Angeles, the team played exhibition games at every port at which they docked. The aim was to raise enough money to wipe out the loans. The exhilarating stick work left dazzled onlookers in their wake everywhere they went. Watching them play in Ceylon, for instance, the governor declared in awe, 'Is it really over? I feel I have been watching your team play for only five minutes'. From Colombo, the team set sail for Singapore onboard the steamship *Haruna Maru*. The final destination of the pre-Olympics tour was Japan, where the Indians beat an unofficial Japanese team by eleven goals on 20 June. Having won hearts in Tokyo, the Indians proceeded to defend their crown in Los Angeles.

Their arrival in America was greeted with much fanfare, with Indians settled in California coming out in large numbers to fete the team. The citizens' forum of San Francisco organized a civic reception in honour of the Japanese, Philippine and Indian Olympic athletes when the boat carrying the Indian team stopped in San Francisco for two days on 6 July 1932. At the reception, the mayor presented each delegation with a key to the city. Finally, after a forty-two-day voyage, the Indians arrived in Los Angeles. Once settled, they were all praise for the Olympic Village and the training facilities at the University of California. What especially impressed the Indians was the wholesome food offered at the Olympic Village.[20] Local newspaper reports in the US mentioned that while the Indians indulged in light exercise, the US and Japanese teams practised all day long to improve their skills.[21]

INDIANS IN AMERICA: THE REAL ACTION

The first Indians in action at the Los Angeles games were the sprinters M. Sutton and R. Vernieux. Both athletes performed well and were successful in making it to the British Empire team picked to face the Americans after the Olympics. This was the first time Indian athletes made it to the Empire team. While the Indians acquitted themselves well in athletics, N.C. Mallick lost out in the 400 metres freestyle competition in swimming, coming fourth in his heat. However, his timing was considerably better than what he had clocked at home; a remarkable achievement in a short period of time.

In hockey, India's preparations did not go to plan with Hammond and Jaffar down due to muscle strain and Lal Shah, the captain, badly hurt following an injury during practice. Penniger joined the injured list on 2 August when he suffered a hit on his eyebrow, which required stitches. Finally, a day before the first encounter against Japan, India's goalkeeper R.J. Allen, who had distinguished himself at Amsterdam by not conceding a single goal, suffered a strained muscle that forced him out of the contest as well. Hind, the reserve goalkeeper, replaced him.[22]

11–1

In the opening match of the hockey competition in Los Angeles, the Indians overwhelmed the Japanese with a score of eleven goals to one. If contemporary reports are anything to go by, India's clinical display mesmerized the Japanese, who had no answer to the deft stick work and ball control exhibited by the Indians. Dhyan Chand scored four goals while Roop Singh and Gurmit Singh scored three goals each. Carr scored the final goal for India after a brilliant solo run. Match reports mentioned that the Indians would have fared better had it not been for the soft turf to which they were still not accustomed.

Having beaten the Japanese by a convincing margin, it seemed inevitable that the Indians would retain the gold they had won at Amsterdam. Their confidence was evident when they decided to make a series of changes to the team in the match against the US to ensure that all fifteen players in the squad played a hand in the victory. Olympic rules necessitated that a player had to play a part in the competition to be entitled to a medal.[23]

24–1

The match against the US, which saw the Indians make a mockery of the Americans by beating them 24–1, was reported back home as follows:

India has retained the world hockey championship. Today, before a crowd that sat amazed at the skill of the Indians, the US suffered a defeat by 24 goals to 1. It was greatly expected that India would win easily but not even her most optimistic admirers thought goals would come at the rate of one in every two minutes. The Americans worked hard but the game was a revelation to them. Amazingly clever stick work of the Indians, the perfect understanding between forwards, the manner in which half backs came up to support and strengthen each attack, the flick passes of both forwards and halves—all these were new to the Americans who often were so spell bound by these tactics that they could only stand and gape at their nimble opponents. Roop Singh scored 12 goals and Dhyan Chand 7, Gurmit Singh scored 3 and Jaffer [sic] and Penniger 1 each.[24]

In the immediate aftermath of the victory, there were spectacular scenes of jubilation when India's flag fluttered at the summit of the stadium and the band played the national anthem of British India. Newspapers across the world paid tribute to the incalculable superiority of the Indians and notably did not express astonishment at the magnitude of the score, which was an international record. Rather, newspapers in the US expressed satisfaction that the US was able to score a lone goal against the mighty Indians.

The US captain commented that for most of the game 'they were chasing shadows' and this aptly summed up the nature of the encounter. Finally, a special broadcast was arranged to comment on India's incomparable prowess in hockey and pay tribute to the Indian team's exceptional conduct and widespread popularity.

The Viceroy, who helped in raising funds for the team, sent a congratulatory message as well: 'I am delighted and proud to learn of the splendid victory of our hockey team. Please give all members of the side my warm congratulations upon retaining World's Championship'. The director of the Olympic Village wrote the following message to Pankaj Gupta: 'The Indian team being in the village longer than any of the others became part of the family. On behalf of all my associates and myself here I want to thank you, and through you the entire Indian delegation, for the splendid cooperation you gave us in the operation of the village.'

Not surprisingly, the Indian community in Los Angeles went berserk after the final. Many contributed generously to raise a pool of $400 needed for the Indians to travel around the country exhibiting their skill. The post-Olympic tour lasted for almost a month.[24]

WHEN DHYAN CHAND WAS AN 'ANGEL'

India started her post-Olympic tour in Philadelphia with a rematch against the US on 20 August. This time around the final score was a little more respectable for the opponents, with the Indians winning 20–1. This was followed by a return visit to California before the Indians embarked on a tour of Europe. Financial considerations were once again paramount here. When in Los Angeles, the advantages of returning via Europe were considered by the Indian delegation. Pankaj Gupta was determined to make this happen and did a great deal in obtaining quotations for rail and steamer fares. When the German Hockey Association came to know about the Indian team's intention to travel through Europe, they invited them to play some games on the continent. The Indians accepted the offer as it did not involve a substantially higher expenditure than if they returned via Japan.

The Indian Olympic team played nine matches in Europe on their way back and won each one of them despite Europe being a logistical nightmare, as reported by the president of the IHF:

> Every member of our party enjoyed the tour immensely, notwithstanding the strenuous travel we had to undertake. To play the match at Budapest on 15 September, we had to travel by bus from Vienna to that city and back, a distance of 500 kilometers. We left

Vienna at 10.30 am, arrived at Budapest at 5 pm., played at once, and returned to Vienna at 2 am the following morning.

The Indians received their warmest reception in Amsterdam. People at the Dutch capital were jubilant to have the team back in the city. Old acquaintances like Leming, attaché to the Indian team four years earlier, organized a civic reception for the Indians in which the players were presented with the local mascot – a monkey.

Contemporary reports make it clear that Dhyan Chand was an idol in European hockey circles. Germany held him dear, calling their best hockey player 'the German Dhyan Chand'. In Prague, a young lady insisted on kissing India's hockey wizard after the match, a demand that made him extremely uncomfortable. 'He is an angel,' she declared before kissing him.

In Germany, the Indians met the German national team in Munich and beat them 6–0. After the match, the Indian contingent presented a stick signed by the entire squad to their hosts at the German Hockey Federation.

In all, the Indian team played twenty-eight matches on tour and scored a total of 263 goals.

The Problem of the Rupee

Neither the Olympic title nor the spectacular display put up on numerous occasions across the world was enough to solve the financial crisis that plagued Indian hockey. At the start of the tour, the team was short of approximately Rs 8,000–10,000. The contributions received from matches played at various venues on the way to Los Angeles had made up a large part of this deficit. However, expenses in America were excessive compared to the estimate and transport charges for excess baggage throughout the tour weighed heavily on the touring party. Added to this was the extra expenditure incurred to play a series of exhibition matches in several European countries. In the words of the IHF president: 'We all took too much luggage with us. This involved us in avoidable expenditure in transport charges. This is a matter that should receive careful attention in subsequent tours.'

Tour expenses were paid for from the special fund and by drawing upon the few thousands from the main account of the federation. The final debt stood at a substantial Rs 12,000. The team was forced to issue a plea to sports fans and sporting clubs back home to come forward and make donations to the tour fund.

Interestingly, the managers of the team were determined to get the accounts of the tour fund audited immediately and were also keen to publish a summary of the receipts and expenditures incurred to ensure transparency.[25] Whether this was eventually done is not known.

THE NATIONAL GAME: WHAT WAS SPECIAL ABOUT INDIA HOCKEY?

Why was India so good at hockey in those early years? Commenting on the Indian success in Amsterdam, A.B. Rosser, the manager, declared in his report: 'The success of the Indian team was due to positional play, combination of forwards with halves, likewise of halves with backs, the tackle back, quick movement and first time passes, deft stick work both in attack and defence, frequent use of hand to stop the ball and the feint to baffle the defence.'[26] From this description, it is evident that the Indians were sound in the basics and adept at tactics and strategy.

The managers of the 1932 Indian touring team further elaborated on Rosser's comment. They argued that because the grounds in India were hard, it allowed players to develop a fast game. Also, they were supple of the wrist, making possible the dribble. They played in light footwear, which enabled quickness of movement.

Swami Jagannath, a player, organizer and future professional hockey umpire, offered a similar explanation. 'The chief factors which contribute to the success of the Indians in the field of hockey are the extensive plots of land available as playing fields, heavy rainfall over only a short period of the year giving generally dry and hard grounds, the light physique of the people and the supple movements of their bodies.'[27] The comparatively low cost of practice was another reason behind India's supremacy in world hockey.

In the 1960s, C.D. Parthasarathy wrote that it was only when a series of rule changes were introduced and a series of amendments passed that India's superiority was challenged. For example, the introduction of free hit for 'bully' made skill secondary. Also, the new penalty corner rule introduced in the 1950s made goal scoring easier, rendering ineffective the natural Indian flair with the ball.

Gradually, crisp, sharp, short passes and the dribble, a feature of India's play, gave way to long and powerful hits and first-time passes. Soon, power counted more than precision and the Indians lost out, unable to counter the innovative techniques of the Europeans.[28]

However, none of these explanations convincingly clarify the reasons for India's early superiority or subsequent decline in Indian hockey. For even after the rule changes were introduced, the Indians won silver in Rome in 1960 and gold in Tokyo in 1964.

It can be argued that apart from talent, the most striking feature of the successful Indian tours of 1928 and 1932 was the absence of divisions among players or officials on lines of class, caste or economic privilege.

In 1932, the entire touring party, with the exception of G.D. Sondhi, stayed together at the Olympic Village. This also included the president of the IHF, A.M. Hayman. In his review of the tour, Hayman singled out this sense of camaraderie among the players and officials as the central factor that contributed to India's continuing dominance in world hockey. He ended his report with the following words:

> I have been with the Olympic team throughout the tour. I lived with the players at the Olympic village at Los Angeles. I entered into all their frolic and fun. I have never lived with better companions. At all times and in all places everyone of them behaved as a true sportsman and gentleman.

It was this feeling of camaraderie among players that held the Indian team together during their amazing run of six consecutive Olympic gold medals between 1928 and 1956, and it partly explains why India could do it in hockey but was unable to scale similar heights in cricket or football in the 1930s–40s.

The camaraderie was perhaps a product of the players' backgrounds and professions. Unlike cricket, where the princes always had the upper hand because the players were dependent on them for patronage, the hockey players were mostly professionals in other fields, with an innate sense of discipline governing their lives. Hockey players who weren't part of the Army were professionals employed by institutions like the railways and on most occasions had graduate degrees.

A study of the class composition and professions of the players of the 1932 Indian Olympic team helps substantiate this point. While the captain Lal Shah Bokhari was a member of the Punjab Provincial Service, goalkeeper Richard Allen James worked for the Port Commissioners in Calcutta. Eric Penniger, who captained the team in the absence of Jaipal Singh in Amsterdam, worked for the North Western Railway, as did his second-in-command Arthur Charles Hind. Others employed by the railways included Carlyle Tapsell (Bengal Nagpur Railway), William Sullivan (Central India Railway) and Richard John Carr (East India Railway). Dhyan Chand, as mentioned earlier, was a lance naik in the Army while Roop Singh, Mohammad Jaffar, Aslam Bagga, Masud Minhas and Gurmit Singh were either in college or had just finished their bachelor's degrees from well-known institutions like Chief's College or Islamia College in Lahore.[29] In hockey, there was no one like Lala Amarnath or Mushtaq Ali, who could rise to prominence because the Maharaja of Patiala and the Nawab of Bhopal accorded them patronage.

In sharp contrast to the rosy picture painted by the hockey team, the Indian cricket team which toured England in 1932 was a divided house. The sharply divided nature of the team is portrayed in *Twenty-Two Yards to Freedom: A Social History of Indian Cricket*.

The team that was initially united under Patiala's leadership was deeply divided by the end. Soon after the tour was over, Vizzy donated a pavilion to the newly built Ferozeshah Kotla Stadium in Delhi, naming it after Lord Willingdon. These efforts to curry favour with the Viceroy were successful, and though Patiala was elected chancellor of the Chamber of Princes in 1933, his influence over Indian cricket was on the wane.[30]

Mihir Bose also draws attention to this deep-seated internal discord in his seminal work on the history of Indian cricket.

Willingdon's hostility to Patiala had coincided with the waning of the latter's cricket power. He had been the kingmaker of the 1932 tour, but in the winter of 1933–34 he was pushed to the sidelines. The emergency Board of Control meeting in Delhi on 1 May 1933 showed that the associations, which had once survived because of his generosity were now turning against him.'[31]

That the scenario had not improved is evident in a letter written by Mushtaq Ali when on tour in England in 1946 to his mentor C.K. Nayudu.

Written on 1 August 1946 from the Carlton Hotel in Taunton, the letter revealed the divisions within Team India:

> ...Now Sir I must tell you something from this end, how Indian cricket is and how we are doing in this country. In my humble opinion this tour is worse than 1936, the same old trouble: no team work at all. Every member of the team is for himself. No one cares for the country at all. Amarnath is the cause of all these things. Pataudi is a changed man ... and is very much against the Indian players. C.S. Nayudu plays in the team not as a bowler but as a fielder only ... Whenever a county player is set for a big score you will find the Indian captain back in the pavilion. As a captain he is worse than a school boy ... I am very much fed up with him as are the other members of the team. Believe me Sir, the second Test match was ours after such a nice start. We collapsed because he sent in Abdul Hafeez at No 3 instead of going in himself ... I think Merchant is a much better captain than this fellow.

The picture was similar in football as well, evident from the tremendous infighting between provincial football organizations in the run-up to the formation of the All India Football Federation (AIFF) in 1937. It started when the Indian Football Association (IFA) based in Calcutta, unhappy with its role as a regional institution, aimed to govern the development of football in the whole country and posed as the governing body for soccer in India. It was as a mark of protest against these intentions of the IFA that other state associations for soccer formed the All India Football Association (AIFA) in September 1935.

Indian football soon became engulfed in a battle for supremacy between Bengal on the one hand and the western and northern states on the other. Unfortunately for Indian football, players too were drawn into this conflict and were forced to take sides. When the Chinese Olympic team visited the country for a series of charity games before the Berlin Olympiad of 1936, there was a huge dispute over the venues and also over the players picked to represent India against the Chinese team. The fact that there was an overwhelming majority of Bengali players in the team did not go down well with soccer players from northern and western India.

It was only when the representative of the Army Sports Control Board, a key player in the whole controversy, decided to bring about a compromise between the provinces by taking the initiative to form All India Football Federation that the conflict came to an end. Eventually, the Army was forced to issue a circular to all the soccer associations of the country declaring that a conference would be held at Simla (now Shimla) in May 1937 where AIFF would finally come into existence. While this solution was not something Bengal desired, it was the best move under the circumstances. Bengal was in no position to alienate the Army Sports Control Board, whose support was key to the survival of the IFA. Bengal tried its best to postpone the formation of AIFF to September but the Army Sports Board didn't budge. In a personal letter sent to the Maharaja of Santosh, the president of the IFA, the representative of the Army Sports Control Board, declared his intention to go ahead with the formation of AIFF in Simla in May 1937, solving the crisis that had plagued the fortunes of football in India for almost a decade.[32]

In hockey, there were no early administrative and political divides like in the other two games. The players, unsullied by administrative wrangles, played as one unit. The hockey team rose to national prominence for its performances on the international stage as a national team. It was this nationalist link that bound it in the early years.

While the politics of nationalism operated in both cricket and soccer,[33] neither of these two games produced triumphs for the national team. The great 1911 victory of the Calcutta-based Mohun Bagan Club over the British East York Regiment is seen by a number of historians as not just a sporting but also a nationalist milestone that spurred on the Swadeshi movement.[34] By the 1930s, the noted literary figure Sajani Kanta Das had noted that three things personified Bengali colonial identity: Mohun Bagan, Subhash Chandra Bose and New Theatres.[35] Yet, soccer's triumphs were not the triumphs of a national team in the way that hockey's were and soccer remained enmeshed in regional rivalries between Bengal and other provinces until much later.

In sharp contrast, the astonishing success rate of Indian hockey in the late colonial and early post-colonial period turned the game into a symbol of nationalist sentiment as a whole. So much so that when the IOC toyed with the idea of dropping hockey as an event in the 1952 Helsinki Olympics, India offered to host the event separately in New Delhi. The success of the

Indian hockey in beating Western teams demonstrated that Indians could compete on equal terms with the West. After independence, the ministry of sports, not surprisingly, chose hockey as the official 'national game' of India.

ONWARDS TO BERLIN

India had established itself as the world's foremost hockey-playing nation by 1932. At the same time, there's little doubt that the absence of leading European and Australasian nations in Los Angeles had diluted the impact of the Indian triumph. Their absence transformed India's title defence at the 1936 Berlin Olympics into something far more significant than a quest for another Olympic gold.

That the Indian team wasn't yet ready to relinquish its hold on the world title was evident when on its second tour to New Zealand in 1935, the team stunned the world by winning all the forty-eight games played. The Indians scored a record 584 goals and conceded just forty. It was indication enough that India was ready to take on Europe at the Berlin Games. What made the Indian dream run at the Nazi Olympiad especially momentous was that for the first time in history the legendary Dhyan Chand was named captain, an appointment that hinted at the decisive collapse of what remained of the privilege barrier in hockey.

10

Hitler's Games

Captain Dhyan Chand and Indian Nationalism in the Third Reich

Nowadays I hear of the princely comforts provided for national teams travelling overseas and the fuss players raise if they happen to miss even a cup of tea! When we used to travel, the name of our country and the game were the only two things that mattered.

—Dhyan Chand on India's title defence at the 1936 Berlin Olympic Games[1]

'WILL INDIA LOSE UNDER MY CHARGE?': DHYAN CHAND'S DELHI DILEMMA

Despite having comprehensively beaten the world in 1928 and 1932, India's supremacy in field hockey was still in doubt on the eve of the Berlin Games in 1936. This was because all of Europe had stayed away from the 1932 hockey competition in Los Angeles on account of the Great Depression. European hockey had also improved quite a bit in the interim. This is why trying to defend the title in Berlin was the biggest challenge Indian hockey had ever faced thus far. That India was ready for it was evident when the Indian team won all forty-eight matches on its tour of New Zealand in 1935.[2]

152

But even the greatest of champions can have an off-day. There was a big flutter when the Indian Olympic team, picked after the inter-province trials in Calcutta between January and February of 1936, lost 1–4 to a Delhi Hockey XI on 16 June at the Mori Gate ground. This was unprecedented and the shocking defeat started dark murmurs.

Dhyan Chand, the newly appointed captain of the national team, described the after-effect of this brutal wake-up call in his autobiography, published sixteen years later:

> My experiences thus far had been to win matches and not lose them. I remember that in 1932, after our return from the Olympic tour, we beat Delhi by 12 goals to nil. I never recognized Delhi as a big hockey playing center, but on this day they were right on top of us and completely outplayed us. The news of this defeat created adverse opinions about us, and while we were touring other centers before we finally sailed from Mumbai, this particular defeat kept worrying me. For the first time I was captaining the Olympic team; will India lose the title under my charge?

Later generations would justifiably remember Dhyan Chand as a wizard who could do no wrong. But his musings after the Delhi defeat revealed the eternal truth of all sports: even the greatest of legends are only human. By now Dhyan Chand was worried about his legacy and suffered from moments of self-doubt.

In the run-up to the Berlin Games, Dhyan Chand's anxiety had reached great heights, for his appointment as captain was mired in controversy. A lowly soldier in the Army, Dhyan Chand had been passed up as captain in 1932 on account of what was seen as his inferior social status even though he was the best player on the team and its talisman. By 1936 the sheer weight of his exploits and his towering presence on the field prompted reconsideration. But he was too conscious of the new responsibility and the tremendous burden on him at a time when social divides still largely governed public life. One small slip and the knives would be out for him. As he noted, 'I was bypassed in 1932 possibly because of my academic handicaps and so-called social position in life. I was still an ordinary soldier, holding a minor rank.'

Palwankar Baloo, the great Dalit cricketer at the turn of the twentieth century, whose social origins initially denied him entry into the Hindu Gymkhana in Bombay, would have sympathized. Baloo overcame high-caste derision to become one of the Hindu Gymkhana's greatest stars in the Bombay Pentangular but was never made captain. It wasn't until 1923 that his brother Palwankar Vithal broke the captaincy barrier in cricket. In Dhyan Chand's case, class barriers too had been a major obstacle and the fact that he was finally given the captaincy placed him under enormous pressure in Berlin.

TO THE FÜHRER: AN INDIAN IN BERLIN

Of all the Olympics before the world wars, none is better documented on film than the Berlin Games. This can partly be attributed to advances in film technology, but one can't overlook the propaganda value of the Games for Adolf Hitler, who had ridden on the Weimar Republic's post-Versailles treaty discontent and humiliation to achieve power through the Berlin putsch of 1933. Berlin had won the bid for the 1936 Games long before Hitler and the Nazis came to power, but for a leader who had just openly repudiated the Treaty of Versailles, the Olympics became an occasion to promote Nazi ideology. Joseph Goebbels, the Reich minister for public enlightenment and propaganda, played a big part in convincing Hitler of the publicity value of the Games. As a result, film-maker Leni Reifenstahl, a favourite of Hitler's, was commissioned to film events. Her film *Olympia* pioneered many of the techniques now commonplace to the filming of sports.

The video archives of the International Olympic Museum contain reams of footage that captured the Games in every dimension, both on and off the field. In the videos, Hitler and Nazi officials are featured as prominently as the athletes themselves. Wehrmacht soldiers and disciplined rows of volunteers form the backdrop to what German officials wanted to be remembered as the greatest Games ever. Signs stating 'Jews not wanted' and similar slogans were removed from main tourist attractions. Berlin was 'cleaned up' as the ministry of interior authorized the chief of Berlin Police to arrest all gypsies and relocate them to a special camp. All in all, the German government was believed to have spent the then-astronomical sum of about $30 million on an event that was meant to showcase the master

Aryan race, as Hitler believed the Germans to be, and suitably package a progressive and united image for the global audience.

It was to these Games that Dhyan Chand's hockey team – still a part of the British empire – was now headed. Interestingly, when the Indian team, twice Olympic champions by then, set sail from Bombay on what was perhaps the mission of their lives, there was barely anybody around to see them off. One of the team members recounted:

> Only the Bombay Customs players, Aslam, Feroze Khan, Jagat Singh and Brewin were with us, so were Behram Doctor and S.K. Mukherjee. The pier was crowded but none took notice of us world champions! Those of us who had been on tour before found this a new experience and not a pleasant one.

The first part of the journey was rough due to turbulent seas and all the players except C. Tapsell, E.J.C. Cullen and Assistant Manager Pankaj Gupta were seasick. While most of them recovered in a few days, Joe Phillips and Babu Nimal from Bombay repeatedly requested the team management to send them back. The team was beginning to worry about their lack of practice. The *Statesman* correspondent accompanying the hockey players noted that they were used to practising on deck but the rough seas precluded that possibility until the fifth day of the voyage, when they played hockey for an hour.

Only when the boat docked at Aden were the Indians able to practise full throttle. In Aden, the Indians had four hours on shore for which they kept themselves busy. The seriousness with which the hockey players were approaching their title defence was apparent from the fact that even on this small break in their voyage all they wanted to do was play. Soon after their arrival, the visitors went looking for a hockey ground and found the regimental training field of the 5/14 Punjab Regiment, which was then stationed in Aden. Members of the regiment, who had no prior knowledge of the arrival of the Indian Olympic team, were puzzled yet elated on suddenly seeing their countrymen. This episode was documented by one of the players in his diary:

> We left the boat with hockey sticks in hope that some hockey field or a plot of ground might be available where we could stretch our limbs.

We asked the bus driver to take us to a hockey ground and he took us to a sandy plot of land, level but full of pieces of bricks, which we afterwards found to be the regimental ground.

Once the nets were put up, the Indians asked the officer present if the ground could be used for practice. An unnamed Indian player later recounted to a newspaper reporter that at first, 'He hesitated but as soon as he discovered we were the All-India team and that Dhyan Chand was with us ... he allowed us to play.'[3]

Dhyan Chand's name worked like a charm and once the regiment learnt of the team's arrival, the call-in bugle was sounded; within five minutes the entire battalion had come out of its barracks to watch the players. It was a surprise gift for them and many of the subedars and privates who knew Dhyan Chand were pleased to see him there. They felt embarrassed because they had no prior knowledge of the team's arrival and hastily tried to put together a civic reception for the world champions.

GETTING GÖRING AND GOEBBELS' AUTOGRAPH: IN THE HEART OF THE THIRD REICH

For the Indian team, surviving as it was on a tight budget, the journey to Berlin was not the most comfortable. Having docked in Marseilles late on the night of 10 July, the Indians were to catch a connecting train to Paris en route to Berlin, which they missed. As Dhyan Chand explained: 'Dock workers there were on strike, and the passengers were put to great difficulty in getting their baggage through. It took us time to unload our luggage ourselves and get it through the Customs and other formalities, and the result was that we missed our train to Paris. We were lodged in an ordinary hotel in Marseilles for the night'. It was only on the morning of 11 July that the Indians boarded a train to Paris. There, the players spent a quiet day undisturbed by the city's sports media. As one of the players said ironically said, 'this was fame with a vengeance'.[4]

In sharp contrast to the luxuries afforded to many sportsmen today, the 1936 Olympic team arranged its own travel at the lowest cost. Dhyan Chand's recollection of this journey was written in his usual nonchalant tone in words that leap out of the mists of time: 'We took a night train to Berlin. It was a job even to secure the third class seats provided to us.

The night was cold and there was no sleeping accommodation. Cheerfully we forgot all these comforts. We were on a mission for our country'.

The Indians finally reached Berlin on 13 July and were accorded a splendid welcome at the Berlin station. They may not have received a send-off worthy of the Olympic champions in Bombay but in a country striving to put its best step forward, they were received as heroes. Dr Diem, chairman of the organizing committee of the Berlin Olympiad, welcomed the Indians. His speech was relayed through a microphone to a large waiting crowd. Our team was reminded that they were playing on behalf of the British-Indian empire when 'God Save the King' was played, after which a band escorted the Indians to a bus. They were driven through the streets of Berlin to the city hall, where the mayor of Berlin welcomed the Indians as per established Olympic tradition. Each member of the team was presented with an album containing pictures of Berlin and Dhyan Chand received a medal. His celebrity status had preceded him.

By all accounts, the Third Reich pulled out all stops in welcoming the Indians. Here, in the heart of Britain's greatest adversary, they were not just subjects of British colonialism but honoured guests. After the welcome ceremony, the Indians were motored to the Olympic Village twenty miles from the city. At the entrance to the Village, the commandant in charge of security received the team. 'God Save the King' was played once again and the Union Jack with the star of India was hoisted next to the Village gate. Eleven nations had already arrived and the band members escorted the Indians to their cottage towards the end of the Village. Unlike in 1932, when the team was quartered four men to a cottage, in Berlin the team stayed in one barrack containing eleven rooms and a common room.[5] This was five-star treatment by any standards. Dhyan Chand wrote:

> The cottage had 20 beds, a telephone and a refrigerator. Everything was kept spick and span, and every minute detail of our comforts had been attended to. Two stewards were there to look after us. One was Otto, an old-seasoned sailor who had visited India several times and spoke English well. The other was named Schmidt, and he spoke English haltingly.

In a reflection of the importance accorded to the Olympiad by the top brass of the Third Reich, the Village was often visited by top dignitaries. Hermann Göring, whose air force would launch the London Blitz just four years later, and Joseph Goebbels, who had orchestrated much of the propaganda for the Games, took a personal interest. A bemused Dhyan Chand noted, 'One day while we were in the dining hall, who should walk in but the burly Hermann Goering, clad in his military attire! We were after him in a trice to get his autograph. Later, some of us obtained Dr. Goebbel's autograph.'[6]

'THE SHOCK OF DEFEAT': THEY COULD BE BEATEN

Dhyan Chand's team had begun its tour preparations with a shocking defeat to a local team in Delhi. Now, in their first warm-up game on German soil, the team lost again. The Indians suffered a defeat against a German XI, losing 1–4. The Delhi defeat could have been dismissed as a one-off but it had already planted the seeds of doubt in Dhyan Chand's mind. This German blitzkrieg in Berlin was more serious and it served as the perfect wake-up call.

The Indians realized that they were not invincible and the Europeans had caught up. In retrospect, it served Dhyan Chand well because it led to a complete reappraisal of team strategy. Sixteen years later, the proud Indian captain wrote:

> As long as I live, I shall never forget this match or get over the shock of defeat which still rankles in me. Hitler's Germany had made great strides in their game ... The result of the play shocked us so much that we could not sleep that night. Some of us even did not have our dinner. At night Pankaj Gupta, Jaffar and myself went into a conference, in which Jagannath also joined. We were unanimous that a substitute be obtained in place of Masood. That same night Gupta rushed to Berlin and sent a cable to Kunwar Sir Jagdish Prasad, president of the IHF, asking him to send Dara, failing whom Frank Wells or Eric Henderson, and also Pinniger. We decided that if Pinniger was not available, Cullen of Madras should be posted as center-half and not Masood. This we did until Dara arrived just a day before we played France in the semi-finals.

Dara was a lance naik stationed at Jhelum and was familiar with Dhyan Chand's play as an inside forward. Money was short but such was the urgency that the federation tried to arrange Dara's passage by air so that he could reach Berlin before the Olympic matches began on 2 August. Despite the best efforts of the IHF, Dara had to wait in Karachi for nine days before he managed to secure a seat in an aircraft. He left by Imperial Airways, entrained in Brindisi, reached Rome, rested there for a day and finally reached Berlin by air to play in the semi-final against France the very next day. This was still considered quick work and the team thanked the federation for their admirable handling of Dara's last-minute inclusion.

The psychological impact of that early defeat was enormous and it set off a great deal of criticism. The *Statesman* correspondent devoted an entire special report titled 'Why SOS Cable was sent to India':

> Friends in India must have been startled by the cable which Professor Jagannath sent to the Indian Hockey Federation's President suggesting that Pinniger and an inside right should be sent to Berlin by air. Why this was thought necessary was explained to me by Mr Gupta, the assistant manager. It was felt that the team had no regular inside right and when they met at Bombay, Dhyan Chand at once suggested to the manager that Frank Wells should have been included in the team as Wells had proved a good partner to him in New Zealand. At Bombay, it was felt that with Emmett as inside right the team might shape up well.

This was no over-confident team. The Indians were well aware of the onerous nature of the task at hand. The team manager, Professor Jagannath, publicly declared that the standard of European hockey had improved considerably in the four years between 1932 and 1936. In the same interview, he sounded optimistic about India's chances of defending the title they had won in Amsterdam and defended with ease in Los Angeles. 'Our Indian team is a good blend of youth and experience and we shall do our best to maintain the high standard of Indian hockey. Dhyan Chand and R.J. Allen, center forward and goalkeeper, are the only members of the 1928 team, who have retained their places this year, but many of the others now with us were members of the 1932 team, which visited Europe after the Los Angeles Games.'

After the shock defeat in their first practice game, the Indians started playing every day but were still dissatisfied with some of their combinations. They went through rigorous physical drills every morning and in the afternoons divided themselves into two sides to practise match situations for more than an hour. The players had started to settle down and the thinking was that there was no cause for alarm, with six practice games yet to be played.

These practice games were not played in front of spectators. They were played on private grounds and the media wasn't permitted to cover them. The teams were allowed to make as many changes as they liked and none of the matches had an official status. In the second practice game, the Indians were back on song and won comfortably. This performance was a major confidence booster, as evident from the following recollection in the *Statesman*: 'Cullen played a very good game at center half and Jaffer [sic] was tried at inside right, where he was a success. If nobody arrives from India, I think Jaffer [sic] will be our inside right and Cullen centre half.'

The locals too were warming up to the Indians once they started winning and this became evident after the practice game in Stettin, which the Indians won 5–1. Interestingly, Dhyan Chand refereed the game. The visit to Stettin (100 miles from Berlin) reminded many team members of their visit to New Zealand when swarms of autograph hunters wouldn't let the players out of their sight. There were also a series of formal and informal functions organized by the locals to make the visitors feel at home.[7]

The shock defeat in the first practice game had prompted the team management to institute strict codes of discipline. As M.N. Masood writes, 'It was also decided that every member should go to bed at ten in the evening. However, Mr Jagannath, Mr Gupta, Dhyan Chand and Gurcharan Singh went to see Menaka's dancing the fourth day after this decision, and Mr Jagannath went again the following evening, returning at two in the morning.'[8]

Newspaper archives and contemporary reports haven't elaborated on the identity of the intriguing Ms Menaka, but it is clear that it wasn't all work for the Indians in Berlin; they were also having a good time. As Masood noted, 'the senior members seldom went to bed at the fixed hour, and as the days passed, no restriction in regard to bed hours appeared to bind anyone until abruptly the following notice was seen on 28th July: "It has been observed that the members of the hockey team are not keeping regular hours. In the interest of sound training and physical fitness, it is essential to observe regularity in meals, physical training and rest ..."""[9]

For many of India's competitors, beating Dhyan Chand's team would have been the greatest challenge. And it seemed that they would stop at nothing to make this happen. A controversy suddenly arose about the amateur status of the players and a question was raised with hockey's international administrators about how India's supposedly-amateur players could stay away from work for so long to play hockey. Of course, every other participating country could have been asked the same question. Dhyan Chand later narrated this distraction at length:

> While we were in Berlin, a point was raised before the International Hockey Federation (FIH) that the Indian team was not composed of all amateurs. They posed the question: How could a player be away from his country and place of work for more than five months at a stretch if he is an amateur? Were the players being reimbursed for the pecuniary losses they were supposed to suffer? They gave the example of our 1935 six-month tour of New Zealand. We succeeded in convincing the authorities that the players were on leave with or without pay, and that the IHF did not reimburse us in any way except meeting our normal expenses. According to my information, Mr G.D. Sondhi was responsible for convincing the FIH gods about the bona fides of our players.

The inimitable Mr Sondhi had worked his charm again.

A MARRIAGE PROCESSION OF RICH HINDU GENTLEMAN: HOW INDIA'S OLYMPIANS REFUSED TO SALUTE HITLER

The Berlin Olympics were declared open on 1 August 1936. M.N. Masood, a member of the team, left a minute-by-minute description of the opening ceremony that provides fascinating information. It was nothing less than a grand spectacle of Hitler's 'thousand-year Reich'. The Wermacht, as we have already noted, was fully mobilized in setting up the support infrastructure and the competitors were transported to the venue in army trucks. The Indians, with Dhyan Chand carrying the flag, were by far the most colourfully dressed of the contingents present. As Masood noted,

'With our golden "kullahs" and light blue turbans, our contingent appeared as members of a marriage procession of some rich Hindu gentleman, rather than competitors in the Olympic Games.'[10] But this was no ordinary 'marriage procession' – the members of the Indian team were about to make a huge political statement by becoming one of the only two contingents who refused to salute Adolf Hitler.

The opening ceremony of the Berlin Olympics was one of the great set-pieces of the Nazi era. As the giant zeppelin, the Hindenberg, circled majestically over the stadium, Hitler and his minister of interior arrived amid great fanfare to observe a military guard of honour.

M.N. Masood noted the fervour that the Führer generated:

> When the Führer neared the Stadium, a multitude of young boys who were watching the proceedings from outside, saw their idol approaching towards them. With one great cry, they shouted 'Heil, Hitler!' and broke the silence of the Maifield.[11]

In four years, that war cry would reverberate around the world but the panzer blitzkriegs and the horrors of the holocaust were still in the future. At the time, at least some Indians were impressed by this disciplined spectacle of the resurgent Third Reich.

As 'the hundred thousand Germans in the Stadium stood to their feet and sang with one voice' the two German national hymns – 'Deutschland' and 'Horst Wessel-Lied' – Masood writes that it 'made a strange impression' upon the Indian contingent and 'not an eye was left dry':

> India rose before our imagination ... somehow the spring of our national feelings was touched, and the unity and solidarity of the people in the Stadium made us look with shame and regret at our poverty, destitution and discord.[12]

But nationalist aspirations were not the same as sympathizing with the Nazi cause. What Masood does not mention in his elaborate description is the serious controversy the Indians created at the opening ceremony by not saluting Hitler during the march past. The Indians were the only contingent apart from the Americans to not perform the raised-arm salute as a mark of respect for the German chancellor.

British-loyalist newspapers like the *Statesman* were more focused on the defiant US contingent, making only a brief mention of what the Indians did. This was partly because of the dark cloud that hung over the participation of the US and the threat of a boycott by some of their athletes, with Jewish athletes Milton Green and Norman Canners staying true to their word. The high-profile American contingent, uncertain as to whether its participation might be interpreted as support for the Nazi regime and its anti-Semitic policies, had barely made it to Berlin after a narrowly won vote orchestrated by sports administrator and future IOC President Avery Brundage. But their contingent refused to dip its flag or 'doff its headgear' when passing the podium, eliciting 'a certain amount of whistling from a section of the crowd'. The Berlin Games are remembered mostly for the exploits of the African-American athlete Jesse Owens, whose triumph disproved Nazi theories of Aryan dominance. For most journalists, the Americans were the story of the Games.

Yet, the Indian decision not to salute Hitler was a grand gesture of defiance, totally in sync with the tenets of the dominant stream of Indian nationalism and the Congress Party. This was perhaps why loyalist newspapers in India chose not to play it up. The Calcutta *Statesman* chose to place its coverage of the Indian defiance on its political pages as opposed to the sports pages where all Olympic news was usually placed.[13]

It is important to note that G.D. Sondhi, one of the officials accompanying the Indian contingent, was deeply influenced by Nehruvian ideas. In the late 1940s, inspired by Nehru's internationalist ideals and the dream of pan-Asian unity, he single-handedly evolved and created the framework of the Asian Games. At a time when Britain was courting Hitler with its policy of appeasement – just two years after which the prime minister, Neville Chamberlain, was to triumphantly declare 'peace for our times' after the Munich conference – the Indian decision not to salute the Führer, it seems, stemmed ideologically from the anti-Nazi position taken by the Congress under Gandhi and Nehru. From the 1920s, the Congress had repeatedly opposed Britain in the event of a European war and regarded fascism and Nazism as forms of Western imperialism.

In 1936, the same year as the Indians were marching in Berlin, Nehru told the Lucknow session of the Congress that 'Capitalism in its difficulties took to Fascism' and 'fascism and imperialism ... stood out as the two faces of the now decaying capitalism'. It was as impossible for India to support

Britain's new opponents as it was to support Britain. From 1938 onwards, Gandhi began opposing Hitler in the pages of *Harijan*, at one point even sending him a letter to desist from violence. In 1939, the Congress resolved to 'keep aloof from both imperialism and fascism' in its session in Tripuri.

There is no evidence to show any direct linkage between the Congress and the athletes' decision to not salute Hitler in Berlin. But the fact remains that it was a political act, breathtaking in its audacity and in direct opposition to most other contingents at the Games, including the British. Managers like Sondhi were in all likelihood influenced by nationalist sentiment as articulated by the Congress leadership. The 'marriage procession' carried an underlying political message.

By the time the Games began, Indian fans at home were also fully geared for action. This is evident from the increased sales of Philips radio sets. The company had arranged for special coverage from Berlin, which was advertised aggressively:

> At a time like this news cannot travel quickly enough and it is with great interest that we are able to report that special arrangements have been made for broadcast commentaries from the Berlin stadium ... The world organization of Philips Radio with their two broadcasting stations are concentrating their resources for the benefit of Indian listeners. They have obtained information concerning these broadcasts and special plans have been made for reception of commentaries and eyewitness accounts from Berlin. Philips dealers in India's leading cities will be able to supply details of the programmes and the times when transmission will take place ... We would advise those readers without all wave sets or with obsolete models to go to a Philips dealer and hear the latest Philips all waves sets specially designed for reception in India ...

For the flag off of the special broadcasts, Philips had organized a talk titled 'All About the Olympiad, Berlin 1936' by Biren Roy, India's representative at the World Municipal Congress in Berlin, on 31 July 1936. The talk was broadcast between 9.05 p.m. and 9.24 p.m.[14] This was among the first radio programmes in India at a time when the medium was just starting to catch up. Although the first Indian radio stations (opened by the privately owned Indian Broadcasting Company in 1927) had been commercial ventures, they had failed and were taken over by a reluctant colonial regime in 1930. Radio became a government department and the state assumed a monopoly over all broadcasting. All India Radio was established in 1936 and the Olympic programme with Biren Roy was a major highlight.

'NOT AN INDIAN TO UPHOLD THE NAME': THE FAILURE IN OTHER SPORTS

By the time the hockey team started its title defence, most Indian athletes had already fallen by the wayside. While Rahim could not make it to the final round of the shot put competition, Raonak Singh, who competed in the 10,000 metres, dropped out at the end of 5,000 metres. He caused much amusement among the spectators because despite coming last almost throughout, he retired at the end of fifteen laps. G.P. Bhalla too failed to make it to the final of the 800 metres. He also finished last in the first heat of the 5,000 metres. In wrestling, Rashid in the welterweight and Rasul in the middleweight were eliminated in the first round.

India's poor performance was the subject of scornful reports back home. The correspondent for the *Statesman* wrote:

> There is the same old story to tell about Indian athletes and wrestlers at Olympic Games – failure and more failure. A wonderful country as ours, with a population of over 350 million and some of the finest specimens of manhood in the world. But our great country, with its vast resources, its princely patrons of sport and its wonderful climate cannot produce a single winner in the greatest of athletic festivals. Running, Walking, Swimming, Wrestling, Boxing, Rowing – the manliest of sports and not an Indian to uphold the name of his country.

He went on to suggest that the Indians would learn a lesson from their failures at Berlin and should seriously settle down to think about the next Games in Tokyo in 1940. Winning the hockey title isn't enough. 'Why should not India produce a winner in the marathon race in 1940?'

It is, however, naïve to blame the athletes for India's disastrous showing in Berlin. The team management was equally to blame. One of India's wrestlers, Karim, would have surely put up a creditable performance had he been allowed to fight in his weight category. Instead, when he reached Berlin, instructions from Sondhi demanded that Karim reduce his weight to appear in the welterweight class. As a result, for about fifteen days his coach kept him under such strict training that he lost several pounds and became much weaker.

Despite Sondhi's efforts, Karim could not make the desired weight class and was told a day before the competition that he would have to compete in his usual weight category. He was too weak to perform and was knocked out in the first round.

More shame awaited the Indians in the marathon. Swami finished thirty-seventh in three hours, eleven minutes and 47 4/10 seconds. By the end of the race, he was so exhausted that he had to be taken to the hospital where he needed to recuperate for the next two days.

One interesting sidelight of the Indian presence at the Berlin Games was the exhibition of traditional Indian games on the Olympic stage. A party of twenty-four athletes from the Hanuman Vyayamprasarak Mandoli, Amroti, had sailed for Berlin on 9 July by the *Conte Verde* to exhibit Indian games and exercises. The team was notably composed of Harijans, Brahmins and Mohammedans. Its organizers wanted to showcase an India that had overcome caste and religious divides and the participants from diverse social strata were chosen with care. Their exhibition in Berlin was a fascinating but forgotten interlude in the interplay between Indian nationalism and Olympism.[15]

'PAST HIS BEST DAYS': THE CARPING CRITICS AND DHYAN CHAND'S TITLE DEFENCE

HUNGARY, 4–0

In a marked improvement from Los Angeles, fourteen nations entered the Olympic hockey competition in Berlin. They were divided into three groups, which were as follows: Group I – India, USA, Yugoslavia, Czechoslovakia and Hungary; Group II – Germany, Afghanistan, Denmark and Japan; Group III – Holland, France, Belgium, Switzerland and Spain. It was announced that members of each group would play each other in a league format and India was slotted to open its campaign against the US on 2 August.

However, with only four days to go for the Games, Czechoslovakia and Yugoslavia withdrew from the competition. As both of these teams were in India's group, the organizers had to redo the groupings all over again. Afghanistan was moved to Group I, and Spain was moved to Group II. According to the new format, the winners of Group I were to play the runners-up of Group III and the winners of Group II were to play the winners of Group III in the semi-finals. Even this grouping had to be changed when on the eve of the competition, Spain withdrew citing political reasons. Eventually, the Indians were left with the US, Japan and Hungary in Group I.

They started their campaign well, defeating Hungary 4–0. The Indians scored twice in each half. Roop Singh scored three goals and Mohammad Jaffar, playing in a position he wasn't accustomed to, scored one. Though the win looked convincing on paper, the match demonstrated that the standard of hockey in Europe had advanced.

It was reported in the press back home that while the Indians were better than their opponents, their superiority was not as marked as on previous visits to Europe. One newspaper reported that the most disappointing revelation was that Dhyan Chand, undoubtedly the world's greatest centre forward, was past his best days. He showed much skill with the stick and excellent judgement in teaming up with his brother, but much of his wizardry had disappeared. At that point, he was no better than any forward on the side. It went on to suggest that Roop Singh, his younger brother, had become the cleverer player.

The correspondent went on to lament that India's display, startling enough for those seeing the team for the first time, was disappointing to those already familiar with the teams' previous accomplishments. He concluded by saying, 'The 1936 side is considered weaker than the side that played several matches in Germany in 1932 and cannot be compared to the 1928 side, which won the Olympic tournament at Amsterdam.'

From local reports on the game, it is evident that the only players who stood out were Roop Singh in the forward line and Tapsell in right back. The relatively mediocre performance of the Indians was partly ascribed to the poor weather conditions. It was a second-session match and kick-off was at 6 pm local time. The game started 'under a canopy of clouds and a cold icy wind was blowing across the ground'. Within five minutes of the match starting, it began to rain heavily and continued to pour till half-time. Moreover, the ground was very heavy and with thick grass on the field, it became impossible to play quality hockey. The local papers were full of praise for the Hungarian goalkeeper, who, it was argued, saved his team from a bigger defeat.[58]

Another match report, however, mentioned that the Indians had control over the game throughout. All through the match, the play was confined to the Hungarian twenty-five-yard line. Allen, the Indian goalkeeper, did not touch the ball even once. Only twice in each half did the Hungarians cross the Indian goal line.[59]

USA, 7–0

The Indians followed up the victory against Hungary by defeating the Americans 7–0. Roop Singh, Dhyan Chand and Jaffar each scored two goals while Cullen scored one. The Indians chose not to play their strongest side and rested three of their key players for the more strenuous engagements to follow. Even a 7–0 win failed to convince the scribes back home. The *Statesman* argued, 'The fact remains, however, that at Los Angeles four years ago India defeated USA by more than 20 goals scoring when and how they liked. The US have improved since then but their improvement does not represent the difference between 1932 and 1936, which goes to confirm that Indian hockey has gone back in four years and that the present team is by no means as strong as the two previous Olympic teams'.

The Indian team management also conceded that the US had made considerable strides in the four years since Los Angeles. This was especially noteworthy because the Americans had been playing professional hockey for only five years and there were only ten professional clubs in the US.

Even Dara's arrival to reinforce the team did not evoke enthusiasm. It was suggested that he had only a minor influence and it was foolish to think that he would be the difference between victory and defeat.

JAPAN, 9–0

Journalists covering the Games also thought India's hockey team was a victim of its past exploits. Despite the huge margins of victory, journalists already foresaw a tough contest with Germany for Dhyan Chand's team.

The negative tone of the reporting was not abated even as the Indians beat Japan 9–0 to top Group I. 'Germany has made tremendous strides and if the Indians are to win they will want to play even better than they did today, when they gave their best display up to date. Further they will need the same dry weather conditions as prevailed today. A record crowd of 16,000 including the Gaekwad and Maharani of Baroda watched the match.' The video archives of the IOC contain fascinating pictures of the Indian princely entourage among the sea of German spectators, resplendent in saris and jewels.

At the end of the group stage, the *Statesman* predicted:

> Here's a prophecy! We shall win the Olympic hockey championship again. If we are beaten, it will be by Germany, who have improved a hundred percent since we last met them. And if Germany win[s], it will be a lesson to India that she deserves, India has not improved a hundred percent – not on this team's showing. Perhaps it is because she has not sent her best team this time. This is the impression I have gained from conversations I have had with Professor Jagannath, manager of the team and Mr. Gupta, the popular assistant manager.

FRANCE, 10–0

It was only when the Indians trounced the French team 10–0 in the semifinal that the tenor of reporting improved. The *Statesman* correspondent, for example, mentioned in his match report that the Indian display, which was their best until then, aroused great enthusiasm among the fans. 'The Indians have become firm favourites for the championship. Germany, who will meet them in the final, have not the same speed and skill.' The local German press too, which had been overtly critical of the Indians to start with and had predicted a German gold in hockey, appeared restrained after India's semi-final win. This was reported in India with much glee. 'The forwards who had never before combined so effectively played sparkling hockey and German newspapers, who were ruthlessly criticizing the Indians stating they had little chance of winning, at once changed their views and commented in glowing terms on India's victory against the French.'[16]

Barefoot Dhyan Chand and those 'Flickering Sticks': The Hat-trick

Against all expectations of a resurgent German team, Dhyan Chand and his team crushed Germany 8–1 to win their third consecutive Olympic gold. Forced to swallow their dire predictions, the sportswriters once again wrote flowery paeans and the title defence was narrated in great detail. Triumphant subheadings in the *Statesman* summed up the mood of the match report: 'India's Triumph', 'Science Scores Over Force', and 'Dhyan Chand in Form'.

This report left little doubt about India's overwhelming supremacy: 'In the second half science triumphed over force and the skill of Indian forwards, assisted by a hardworking trio of halves brought goal after goal. The vast crowd rose as one man as the Indians made raid after raid, completely outwitting the home defence with their speed and stickwork and their uncanny accuracy of shooting.

Goal after goal was scored to the bewilderment of the German side and though they played with their greatest pluck and gameness and managed to score once, they were a well-beaten team.' It was in this game that Dhyan Chand truly came into his own in the Berlin Olympics.

Dhyan Chand had discarded his stockings and spiked shoes and wore rubber sole shoes, which increased his speed a great deal. That he was at his best is borne out by the handsome scoreline of 8–1. Dhyan Chand himself scored six goals. The German papers, which until then had been predicting a German gold, were full of praise for the Indians after the final. A correspondent for the *Morning Post* argued that Berlin would remember the Indian hockey team for long. 'These players, it is said, glided over turf as if it is a skating rink and their flickering sticks had the Japanese, normally so agile, mesmerized.' The reporter went on to conclude, 'Nature seems to have endowed Indians with a special aptitude for hockey'. The legend of Indian hockey and the Games' special affinity with what was still seen as the 'Orient' was embellished further.

It is a tenet of Indian sporting folklore that Hitler personally met Dhyan Chand and offered him an officer's commission in the Wermacht if he would play for Germany. This story is almost certainly apocryphal because none of the contemporary sources mention this incident and neither does Dhyan Chand in his autobiography.

Soon after the victory, the Viceroy congratulated the team on its record-breaking performance. The German consul general from India sent the following message to Sir Jagdish Prasad, president of the IHF: 'Please accept my heartiest congratulations on India's hockey team's remarkable performance at the Berlin Olympic Games. World's best team won the final'. Georg Evers, president of the Deutsch Hockey Bund and the International Hockey Federation, congratulated Dhyan Chand on his team's triumph: 'You and your boys have done wonderfully to foster the game of hockey in our country. I hope that you will return to Indian with good impressions and with the same feeling of friendship to the German hockey players as we feel towards you ... Tell them how much we all admired the skill and artful performance of the perfect hockey they have shown us'.[17]

On their way back from Berlin, the Indian team stopped in London. Lore has it that they met Douglas Jardine, already a star for his role in cricket's Bodyline controversy. It was reported in the press back home that Jardine stopped his car and posed for a picture with Dhyan Chand and Roop Singh. The team sailed back to India in the streamer *Strathmore*. Travelling with the team was the Nawab of Pataudi, the Maharajkumar of Vizianagaram and the governors of Bombay, Madras and Mysore.

However, the way the team was welcomed in India on its return was extremely disappointing. Similar to how it received no public send-off, there was no celebratory homecoming on their victorious return either. Masood later wrote a sombre recollection of the anti-climactic homecoming:

> Bombay received us at the Ballard Pier with only two of its representatives – Mr. Behram Doctor of the Bombay Hockey Association and Mr. Mukherjee of the Bombay Olympic Association. At the railway stations in Germany, we had to be escorted by cordons of volunteers for fear of being squeezed in by enthusiasts ... while in India, the land of our birth, we were welcomed by only two of her sons ... Rain came in big drops as we were landing as a benevolent gesture of welcome from the heavens, and also showing the citizens of Bombay the state of our feelings of being neglected.[18]

Modern Indian hockey players, neglected and forgotten in the passions due to cricket, would have found this relatable.

While the reception, or rather the lack thereof, accorded to the team on 29 September was shocking, the federation led by the president deserved praise for how it helped prepare the team for Berlin. As in the previous Olympics, the IHF was severely constrained for funds. In April 1936, the federation had a little more than Rs 6,600 left in its coffers. It needed Rs 40,000 to send the team to Berlin. Its financial troubles were compounded when the inter-provincial trials at Calcutta did not yield much by way of gate sales. Despite this, by the end of May, the federation had raised Rs 35,000 by way of contributions from princes, private individuals and several provincial hockey associations. The Nizam of Hyderabad contributed Rs 5,000 and the Gaekwad of Baroda £200.

The president and office-bearers of the association also made personal contributions to make the trip possible. Such was their contribution that even when it was known that the federation would incur an additional expense of Rs 1,700 in sending Dara to reinforce the team, it did not flinch.

The 1936 Olympic campaign finally put to rest any doubts regarding India's hockey supremacy. India had won all its matches in style, scoring thirty-eight goals in the process and conceding only one. Dhyan Chand, once discriminated against for his inferior social status, had consolidated his position as the darling of the Western world. A statue of his was erected in Vienna. Another statue erected later in Delhi's Dhyan Chand National Stadium remains the only sculpture dedicated to a hockey player in independent India.

His six goals against the Germans in the final were no less an achievement than Jesse Owen's four gold medals in track and field. As Gulu Ezekiel wrote, 'While on the track Jesse Owens exploded the many myths of Aryan superiority, which the Nazi forces had carefully propounded, on the hockey field Dhyan Chand created magic.' It was not without reason that the government of India issued a postage stamp in his honour and conferred on him one of India's highest civilian distinctions, the Padma Bhushan, in 1956.

After the Berlin Games, there was little doubt that the Indians would once again start their title defence as favourites in Tokyo four years later. Tokyo had won the vote to stage the Games of the twelfth Olympiad by a margin of 36–27 against Helsinki, a product of careful and calculated exertion of political influence on the members of the IOC. Eventually, however, the outbreak of World War II meant that there would be no Olympic Games until 1948 in London. There, the Indian hockey players presented their countrymen with a befitting gift for independence – yet another Olympic hockey gold, which was made sweeter by a 4–0 victory over England.

11

The 'National' Game
Hockey in the Early Life of Independent India

*When Nehru met me during the opening ceremony of the Bhakra Canal,
he asked me, 'Are you playing hockey? Do you play every day? Are your
other colleagues also playing seriously? Are they all well and happy?' He
had asked me so many questions in one breath that all I could answer
was 'Yes, sir.'*

—Balbir Singh Senior[1]

For a newly independent India, the London Olympic Games of 1948 were
more than a mere sporting event. The event served as a stage for a young
nation to cement for itself a place in the world parliament of successful
sporting nations. It was also a platform for an infant Indian nation state to
compete with its former master and give vent to years of frustration and
discontent.

The Indian hockey team satisfied this national yearning and won
its fourth straight Olympic gold in the process, having already won top
honours in Amsterdam in 1928, Los Angeles in 1932 and Berlin in 1936.
The golden journey did not stop in 1948 and continued until 1964, with a
brief silver interlude in 1960, when India had to cede the top spot to arch-
rivals Pakistan.

The 2018 Akshay Kumar starrer *Gold*, which dramatizes India's 1948
London hockey triumph, got a lot of historical details wrong, but it was
right on one count – when the Indian hockey team won gold at the 1948

London Olympics, defeating the English 4–0 in the final, much more than an Olympic victory was scripted.

It was a newly independent nation's declaration against the forces of colonialism, retribution for humiliation meted out by the English for almost 200 years and a statement to the world about the significance of sports in an era of decolonization. Sports had become a nationalist mirror in which communities were beginning to see themselves; at once a source of exhilaration, pride and national bonding for a young India.

Though claims of hockey as the 'national game' of the country trace back to the turn of the century and gathered momentum after the wins in Amsterdam, Los Angeles and Berlin, it was not until the London Games that hockey's supremacy became undeniable. Before 1948, both cricket and soccer enjoyed similar popularity and the question of which of the two would capture the Indian sporting heart in the immediate post-Independence context was still unanswered.

Compared to the Games of 1928, 1932 and 1936, the London Games offered a fundamentally different challenge for Indian hockey. The players, for the first time, weren't representing British India but were playing for their motherland. This was the first time India's team was representing the new tricolour and playing *against* the British, under whose imperial flag they had participated previously. The significance of this transition is best borne out by the legendary Dhyan Chand in his autobiography: 'I envy the 1948 Indian Olympic team to whom fell that honour (of meeting and defeating the English on the Olympic stage). How I wish I had at least been present to witness the historic occasion. But, like most of you, I was fated to be thousands of miles away at home listening to the radio and reading press reports.'[2]

The timing of the triumph was crucial. When the Indian hockey team was contesting for honours in London, the nation's borders were set alight by the first war with Pakistan and the 'unfinished agenda' of Partition, which would lead to more wars in 1965 and 1971 and continual tension since. Adding to the significance of the London Games was the prospect of the first India–Pakistan encounter. It was natural that the political arena would shift to the sporting field, providing symbolic battlegrounds for national supremacy. In George Orwell's words, 'Serious sport has nothing to do with fair play. It is bound up with hatred, jealousy, boastfulness, and disregard for all the rules.'

That Partition had changed the relationship between players who had once played on the same side is evident from the following recollection by Balbir Singh Senior, India's star performer at the London Games: 'It was at the London Olympics that Pakistan made their first appearance. The Indian and Pakistani teams were billeted at different places. We first met at Wembley Stadium during the ceremonial opening of the games. Niaz Khan, A.I.S. Dara, Shah Rukh, Mehmood and Aziz saw us, but I was surprised to see that our old friends were deliberately keeping a distance from us. The openness of old was gone.'[3]

VICTORIOUS IN ENGLAND: LONDON, 1948

Compared to other competing nations, the Indian hockey team arrived in London fairly late, on 14 July 1948. This was because they had been at a special training camp in Bombay, brushing up on their skills for the tough challenge that awaited them in London.[4] As part of their preparation, they played a series of practice games against leading domestic teams, which served as ideal training before the actual contest.

Dhyan Chand had retired and so had many of the stalwarts from Berlin. This was in many ways a new Indian team. It had retained some of the strengths from before but it also had some frailties, which meant that its success could not be taken for granted. In the first of the practice matches, the Indian Olympic side defeated the Best of Bombay 2–0, while in the second encounter it trounced a formidable Bombay XI 5–1. For the Olympic team, the star of the show was the vice captain, K.D. Singh Babu. The hockey correspondent of the *Times of India* wrote, 'It is tempting to write that Babu is as elusive as Dhyan Chand, India's Olympic wizard, but that would be an exaggeration. I am content to say that India is lucky to have such a brilliant forward in the team. If Babu could convince himself to part with the ball a little often, he would be a complete answer to any selector's prayer.'

This victory was followed up by a win against an Anglo-Indian team in Madras, the margin of victory being a comfortable four goals to two. Interestingly, the Anglo Indians led the Olympic team 1–0 at half-time. However, in the last ten minutes of the game, 'the Olympic side monopolized the play and registered three more goals, the goal getters being Glacken, Babu and Latif '. In the final preparatory match, the Olympic team got the better of a South Indian XI by four goals to one. Once again, the team, after being down 0–1 at half-time, staged a brilliant comeback to win the contest comfortably in the end.

In the run-up to the Games, India didn't leave anything to chance. Even before the team had reached London, Pankaj Gupta, the manager of the Indian Olympics squad, with the help of the secretary of the Indian Gymkhana, had reserved the number-one cricket ground of the Gymkhana in Osterley as the practice ground for the Indian team. The significance of this effort was recorded by the *Times of India*: 'Anybody who has knowledge of London and the Indian Gymkhana will realize that the No. 1 cricket ground at Osterley is a very good ground for hockey practice. (Here) the Indian hockey team will find everything laid on for them for their practice before the Olympic Games.'

Despite these efforts of professionalism by the Indian team management, the selection of the team wasn't free of the vices of regionalism. This explains the surprise omission of Leslie Woodcock, who was a strong contender for a berth, and Perumal, the brilliant Maharashtrian left-back, who had played very well in the trials.

The Indian squad flew to London by Air India's Mogul Princess on 13 July 1948 and was received at the London airport by the chef de mission of the Indian contingent, Moinul Haq. Soon after, they were taken to their designated quarters at a camp in Richmond (some miles from London), where they were thrilled to know that Indian food had been arranged for them. The *Times of India* reported the overall satisfaction of the Indian camp as follows: 'The Indians have been getting not only Indian food in all its courses, but in plenty. The waiters are all Indian and most of them come from Bengal. In the dining hall typical India prevails—everything is Indian; the usual talking and shouting and heaps of food, chapattis, dal, vegetable curry, meat curry, Indian sweets and so on and so forth and at the end of a long meal each boy gets a bottle of milk. What a contrast to the experience of previous Indian teams that had visited foreign countries on similar mission(s).'

However, it is important to note that Indian athletes weren't allowed to stay at the Richmond camp for the duration of their visit. A few days before the competition began, they were asked to move to an empty school in the north-west London suburb of Pinner. The Richmond camp, it was noted, was emptied to accommodate athletes from the advanced Western nations.

In an attempt to conceal such discriminatory treatment, the organizers declared, 'Many of the men moving out are feeling bitter but they should not. The position was explained to them when they came. Most of the accommodation was booked long in advance by countries whose teams are arriving only a week or so before the games begin.' The Indian officials mounted a protest against such discriminatory treatment, which in turn contributed to hardening the determination of the Indian hockey team.[5]

INDIAN 'SUNSHINE' IN LONDON: THE GREAT POST-COLONIAL SHOWDOWN

With Czechoslovakia, Poland and Hungary failing to submit their team entries to the Olympic Games Organizing Committee on time, a revised Olympic hockey itinerary was drawn up, with the participating teams divided into three pools. India was drawn in Pool A with Spain, Austria and Argentina. Great Britain was drawn in Pool B with Afghanistan, Switzerland and the US. Pool C consisted of Pakistan, Holland, France, Belgium and Denmark.

India started her campaign against Austria, winning comfortably by a margin of eight goals. Despite this, the quality of play wasn't of the highest standard as expected from the team. This was remedied in the next encounter against Argentina. Despite a relatively softer turf compared to the match against the Austrians, the Indian forwards put on an exemplary display and defeated the Argentines by nine goals. This was followed by a hard-fought two-goal victory against Spain, which propelled India to the semi-final. While India was due to play the Dutch in the semi-final, Pakistan had qualified from the other half of the draw and was to play the hosts, Great Britain. There had been a buzz about a possible India–Pakistan final even before the tournament started, but it was now starting to look like a real possibility.

Bruce Hamilton's piece for the *Times of India* on 8 August stated that experts who had seen the teams play in London had predicted an India–Pakistan final. He went on to suggest that India and Pakistan were the most outstanding teams of the competition, not only because of their high scoring and margins of victory but also due to their superior individual skills. 'No other team can match them for the spectacular way they carry the ball down the wings, dodging opponents and flicking it from one to another or seizing every chance they get in the scoring area.'

However, he went on to sound a note of caution, suggesting that the unpredictability of the weather could ruin the chances of an India–Pakistan final because the European teams were better equipped to handle the heavy turf: 'But there is one factor to be remembered – London's unpredictable weather. This weekend has been wet and miserable and the forecast is for continued unsettled weather. This may be decisive in tipping the scales in favour of Great Britain – at present the strongest challenger the Indian and Pakistani teams have.'

His analysis was based on India's lacklustre performance against Spain. Playing in wet, muddy conditions, the Indians found that their stickwork lacked the gloss from previous games on dry turf. Especially for those without long stud boots, the soft turf made it impossible to control the ball. Most of them slipped on the wet ground and their lightning speed of attack suffered in the process.

Hamilton mentioned that the wet conditions had not affected the Europeans' game as much as it had the men from the subcontinent: 'A heavier combination, relying more on team work than individual play and familiar with wet grounds, Great Britain may find that these conditions will suit them well.'

He was right. The British outclassed the Pakistanis, booking a date with India in the final. India, on the other hand, played a scratchy game to beat the Dutch.

The match report published in the *Times of India* was skeptical of India's chances in the final: 'India will meet Great Britain in the Olympic Hockey final on August 12 and unless the Indian players cut out their soft fancy stuff and adopt direct methods, India may find it difficult to retain the title ... These two matches (semi-finals) proved two things clearly. First, English and Continental hockey has improved immensely and their game is based on entirely different strategy and technique. Second, Indians and Pakistanis must learn to play in heavy boots, which give a better foothold on heavy turf.' The report concluded with words of caution for the Indians on the eve of the final: 'Finally, another thing was proved: namely, that to play against Britain a team must have sufficient vigour and stamina to last till the end. In today's match India's players were flat in the last ten minutes ...'

The stage was now set for a dream final: the defending champions from newly independent India taking on their former imperial masters, who had avoided playing Olympic hockey as long as India remained a colony. The Indian team was well aware of the extra connotations of the contest. In the words of Balbir Singh Senior, 'Britain had been Olympic hockey champions in the 1908 Games at London and in the 1920 Games at Antwerp. Once India made their entry in the 1928 Games at Amsterdam, they decided not to play. Britain never played an India XI as long as they remained our rulers. The 1948 Olympic hockey final was the first meeting between Britain and India'.

This was why, as Alex Valentine reported in the *Times of India* on 12 August, the Indians decided not to play any more practice matches and instead started a two-day 'armchair strategy' session in preparation for the final. 'The chief factor in Thursday's final, readily recognized by both sides, will be the weather. The Indians want hot sunshine for the next two days, the Britons want rain, or at least no heat.' That the weather had already tilted the balance in favour of the British was borne out when the groundsman in charge of the pitch declared in jest, 'A heat wave between now and the final will not leave the pitch much harder than what it is now.' When it poured on the eve of the final on 11 August, most of the Indian players decided to take the field in studded boots instead of playing barefoot.

The Indian team was embroiled in yet another controversy when the organizers decided to hold the third-place play-off between Holland and Pakistan before the final. Team India perceived this as a deliberate attempt at favouring the British. The ground, already soft because of the rain, would be further damaged by the play-off, seriously impacting the Indians' game. A.C. Chatterjee, manager of the Indian team, summed up the discontent in the Indian camp as follows: 'This in itself is enough to cut our chances by at least fifty percent, but instead of giving the finalists the advantage of the best possible ground under the conditions, the organizers have allowed the comparatively unimportant third place match to go on first. I shudder to think what the ground will look like when we take the field.'[6]

Anthony de Mello, commenting on the improved performances of the Europeans in London, observed, 'It seems to me that it is not at all too much to suggest that India's example of polish and skill at hockey in earlier years had inspired these other countries to play the game better and better. If this is so – and I am sure that it is – it means that India, despite the brevity of her international sporting career, has had something of real value to give to the rest of the world'.[7]

Despite the odds stacked firmly against them in the final, India won the battle in style, defeating the British 4–0. The overwhelming Indian superiority was borne out by the match report by Alex Valentine in the *Times of India*:

> India won the 1948 Olympic Hockey Championship in decisive fashion at the Wembley Stadium tonight, defeating Great Britain by four goals to nil. India's superiority was never in dispute. Despite the heavy, muddy turf and the light rain, which fell for considerable time during the game, the Indians outclassed the British team with their superb ball control, accurate passing and intelligent positional play. Long before half time it was evident that India should win comfortably. If England had had any other goalkeeper but Brodie, India might have doubled their score ... (By the middle of the second half) Britain had resigned to the fact that they had lost the game. But they were determined not to lose it by a greater margin. Whatever energies they had left they put into their defence. As the minutes dragged to the closing whistle, it was apparent the Indians were not going to get through the wall of British defenders. Full time came with yet another Indian attack on the British goal – and the match closed as it had opened. Only now the Indians were four ahead.

This British defeat on British soil unleashed some of the wildest celebrations Indian hockey has ever known. Today, many Indians are familiar with the television images of the delightful Indian invasion at Lord's after the victory at the 1983 cricket World Cup. The images of those celebrations, beamed live on television, are now etched forever in India's public memory. There were no live cameras to record the landmark hockey win in London for posterity, but contemporary press reports note that the few thousand Indian spectators present were delirious.

Amid spectacular scenes of jubilation, the Indian high commissioner and India's UK High Commissioner V.K. Krishna Menon ran on to the ground to join the celebrations. Reviled by Western – especially American – diplomats, even the stern Menon ('the devil incarnate', 'Mephistopheles in a Saville Row suite', 'the old snake charmer'), who was to later 'bore' the

United Nations with his seven-and-a-half-hour speech on Kashmir, let his hair down that day. As reminisced by Balbir Singh Senior:

> After the victory, V.K. Krishna Menon, free India's first high commissioner in London, came running to congratulate us. He joined us for a group photograph. Later, he also gave an official reception at India House, where a big gathering of sports lovers was present. The Olympics over, we went to the European mainland and visited France, Czechoslovakia and Switzerland. This brief tour, a fortnight in duration, was more of a goodwill nature, and earned India a great deal of fame. None of us had visited Europe before, and we were thrilled by the sights we saw.

On their return to India, a red carpet welcome was given to the team. The victory celebrations continued for several days and climaxed in Delhi where President Rajendra Prasad and Prime Minister Jawaharlal Nehru attended an exhibition match involving the Olympic team in a jam-packed National Stadium.[8] The victorious team of 1952 was to receive a similar welcome, but no celebration would match the London hockey victory until the national hysteria fueled by Ajit Wadekar's cricketers beating the English team in England in 1971. This was the true measure of what the hockey players had achieved a year after independence. The legacy of colonialism mattered deeply.

If sports are a metaphor for war, then hockey had proved to be India's most trusted weapon in the troubled years after Partition. In the complex post-Independence context, prowess in sports wasn't enough. Accomplishments had to be demonstrated in contests against the erstwhile colonizers, which would mark a symbolic victory against the former colonial state and satisfy the insatiable national thirst for equality and revenge.

To substantiate the point, even when India won gold medals in field hockey in the Olympic Games between 1928 and 1936, hockey could never outrank cricket or soccer in colonial India. This was because Britain refused to participate in Olympic hockey contests in those years, knowing that Team India would almost certainly win gold. This is especially interesting because Britain had won the Olympic gold in field hockey in 1904 and 1920, the only years hockey had been played before 1928, both of which India did not participate in. Team India's vanquishing of the British on the hockey pitch in 1948 helped consolidate the rise of hockey and cement it as India's national sport.

INDIA GOES TO FINLAND: HELSINKI, 1952

In Helsinki, the competition wasn't stiff enough to challenge the Indians. However, the internal politics that characterized Indian sports were gradually becoming apparent in hockey too. Even as the Olympic team was being finalized on 13 June 1952, power-hungry administrators were engaged in mini-battles of intrigue to push their 'favourites' into the team at the last minute.

The Uttar Pradesh and West Bengal associations were seeking the inclusion of an additional player and an unhealthy parochialism was evident in their choices. The *Times of India* reported, 'The effort to push Malhotra back into the team, who was originally selected and then dropped in favour of Jaswant and Gurung, smacked of provincialism'.

Even more worrisome was what followed. Telegrams were sent from Bombay to all the affiliated associations, requesting their consent to the inclusion of Malhotra from Uttar Pradesh as an additional half.

The telegram mentioned that Captain Digvijay Singh Babu and coaches Habul Mukherjee and Harbail Singh had stressed the need for Malhotra, especially in the event of an India–Pakistan final. The *Times of India* wrote that the 'latter portion of the plea struck several associations as very odd. They failed to understand how a player could be indispensable only for one game and could not be required for others.'

With Uttar Pradesh making a case for Malhotra, Bengal wasn't to be left behind. Soon after the first telegram had been sent from Bombay, a second telegram was sent from Calcutta. The contents of this telegram make for a fascinating read: 'As there are five halves already in the team the eighteenth player should be a forward and Bengal would be prepared to pay the expenses of C S Gurung, if selected.' Anticipating criticism, the telegram added that Gurung should be selected not because he was from Bengal but because he had performed well throughout the season. The *Times of India* made the following comment: 'The state of affairs is very illuminating and depressing, as these attempts to wangle in players come just on the eve of the team's departure. It may be mentioned that in 1948 also a similar selection of some Bengal players at a late hour had been allowed on the same condition – expenses borne by the Bengal Association.'

An important feature of Indian hockey at the time, evident from attempts to thrust players into the national team by agreeing to pay for their passage, was the poor financial state of the sport. The financial crisis was aggravated when the government decided to further reduce the subsidy allotted to the nation's premier Olympic sport. The IOC wasn't sure if it had the funds to send all or even most of the selected Indian athletes to Helsinki. The government of India had reduced its grant-in-aid from Rs 1,00,000 to Rs 70,000. State governments too weren't as forthcoming as in 1948 and some had removed sports from their immediate radar in favour of other, more pressing concerns. The *Times of India* reported, 'This has resulted in a large gap between expected income and anticipated expenditure.'

Despite hardship, the IOA finally managed to send the hockey team to Copenhagen, allowing them to acclimatize to the Scandinavian weather. Finally, the Indians started their title defence, defeating the Austrians 4–0. The performance, however, was at best scratchy and it was widely reported that the Indians had lost the edge that had won them four consecutive Olympic gold medals: 'The Champions won, as they were expected to, but they found the Austrians no easy obstacle on a pitch rendered slippery by rain.'[9] The sense of unease within the Indian camp was epitomized by the statements of Pankaj Gupta on the eve of the semi-final against the British: 'I want you boys to play your normal game; first-time clearances, short-passing and nippy thrusts. You know it too well, that's your natural style. No showmanship, mind you.'

In their semi-final against the British, the Indians were a transformed side. This is how Balbir Singh Senior, who scored a hat-trick (his second in Olympic hockey), described the performance against Britain: 'We were a completely changed lot in the semi-final against Britain. We moved swiftly and smoothly and scythed their defence with copy-book moves ... It was an accident that I got that goal. But I scored two more before the interval to get my second hat-trick in Olympic hockey – my first was in my maiden appearance in the London Olympics. Britain reduced the margin (1–3), but that was all they could do. India had reached the final.'[10]

Even after an improved performance, the final against Holland was expected to be a close affair. This was because of two reasons. First, the

rains had made the ground wet and slippery, conditions that were expected
to favour the Dutch. Second, the Indians appeared to be over-reliant on
Balbir Singh Senior, a point repeatedly emphasized by the *Times of India*:
'The Indians need to visit the practice grounds regularly to remedy defects
in their forward line, for it is too much to expect Punjab's twenty-eight-
year-old centre forward Balbir Singh to initiate and execute all his side's
attacks'.[11]

These predictions weren't accurate as the Indians retained the title fairly
convincingly, defeating Holland 6–1 in the final. Balbir Singh Senior was
once again the star, scoring his third Olympic hat-trick in style, having
scored nine of the thirteen goals in Helsinki. In his own words, 'I was in my
element that day and scored five of my team's six goals. The match gave me
another hat-trick, my third in Olympic hockey. Holland got a consolation
goal, but overall it was a one-sided final.'

On arriving home in India, the team was accorded a royal reception in
the capital. The number of functions far exceeded those in 1948 and the
celebrations continued for nearly a month. At the official function in Delhi,
the Olympic team played a match against a Rest of India XI in a packed
stadium. Present in the audience were President Rajendra Prasad and Prime
Minister Nehru.

Balbir Singh later recounted the overwhelming welcome the players
received on their return:

> The train in which we traveled was literally mobbed by enthusiastic
> hockey fans. People surged around our compartment and waited for
> our darshan. When we emerged from the train, they almost crushed
> us with bear hugs and shows of affection. We endured it all with a
> smile. The four Punjab Police players – Dharam, Udham, Raghbir
> and I – were taken in open jeeps in a huge procession in Jalandhar.
> Thousands of people lined the streets and cheered us from treetops
> and housetops. We were showered with small gifts, baskets of fruit
> and sweets and garlands – these constituted the people's simple way
> of showing their gratefulness.[12]

Balbir Singh had emerged a worthy successor to the mantle that Dhyan
Chand had left behind.

WINNING BY A 'SHORT WHISKER': MELBOURNE, 1956

Indian dominance at Olympic hockey would continue in Melbourne, where the team was to win its sixth consecutive gold medal. However, those in charge of Indian hockey were already worried about the warning signs that emerged in the Games. As Pankaj Gupta noted soon after the win:

> Yes, India maintained her supremacy in world hockey at Melbourne by a short whisker and this, I say, must make us pause. We can no longer take anything for granted. The standard of world hockey has improved and other nations like Holland, England, Germany and Pakistan have caught up with India in technique as well as in standard. Complacency must give way to genuine concern. We have an unparalleled wealth of hockey talent, which I regretfully consider, is not being fully exploited.[13]

The Indians were aware that Melbourne 1956 was a far tougher assignment compared to Helsinki 1952. This may have prompted them to appoint Balbir Singh Senior, the nation's leading star, as captain. Under him, now an Olympic veteran and winner of two gold medals, India started in style, humbling the Afghans 14–0 in their opening engagement at Melbourne Olympic Park.

Strangely, even this high margin of victory failed to satisfy the Indian scribes covering the tournament. Following the victory, the *Hindu* reported, 'It was one way traffic throughout but if we were represented by our 1932 or 1936 teams, we may have registered a cricket score.' This comment also shows the kind of aura surrounding Dhyan Chand and his teammates, and demonstrates the pressure the Indian team was under to stand up to its glorious past.

The high margin of victory was, however, soured due to an injury to Balbir Singh, who broke a finger and was out of action for the next few games. With India heavily reliant on his outstanding scoring abilities, this was seen as a major blow to the team's chances of retaining the gold. But even without Balbir in their ranks, the Indians bulldozed their way past the US 16–0 and beat Singapore 6–0.[14] The match against Singapore, however, brought out some of the weaknesses that were to hamper

India's chances in the semi-final against Germany. Without Balbir on the team and with the Singaporeans resorting to ultra-defensive tactics, the Indians found it extremely hard to score. Not until the twenty-third minute of the game were the Indians able to break the deadlock, a first for Indian hockey in the Olympics.[15] Though the Indians were all over their opponents in the second half and ended the group with the total tally of thirty-six goals to none scored against them, critics were sceptical of India's chances in the semi-final against Germany. This was best summed up by Pankaj Gupta:

> I happened to be at Melbourne, where there were occasions when I felt most uneasy at watching our hockey team in action. Our earlier matches against Afghanistan, USA and Singapore were no criterion but our main hurdles were Germany in the semi-final and Pakistan in the final. Our victories over Germany and Pakistan were both lucky and unimpressive.[16]

India's victory against Germany hadn't done much to silence critics, as evident in this report from the *Hindu:*

> The stock of hockey in the Indian sub-continent went down at the main stadium of the MCC cricket ground today when both India, reigning Olympic champions since 1928, and Pakistan qualified for the final beating Germany 1–0 and Great Britain 3–2 respectively. India's nine-man selection committee must seriously consider their next step in selecting India's national team in future. Never before in India's Olympic history has any nation provided such stiff opposition to India. Something has gone wrong somewhere, otherwise how we could win by the narrowest margin in the game in which we had been world beaters is difficult to appreciate ...[17]

'VICTORY CASTS ITS OWN SPELL': THE FIRST INDIA–PAKISTAN FACE-OFF

The final in Melbourne was India's first meeting against Pakistan on the Olympic stage. The Indians were under intense pressure on the eve of the final, a state of affairs palpable in the reminiscences of Balbir Singh Senior:

I could not sleep that night (on the eve of the final), and after tossing about restlessly for a while, I went out for a stroll. It was quite late in the night when someone called out my name. Turning, I saw Ashwini Kumar, his face creased with worry. Ashwini put his arm around my shoulder and guided me to my room. He talked cheerfully, gave me a tablet, made me lie down, and sat next to me.

The tension was greater for the Indians because they had more to lose than Pakistan had to gain. For Pakistan, a silver medal would be a triumph, whereas for India, anything but gold would be a disappointment. This explains the unrivalled scenes of jubilation following India's narrow 1–0 victory in the final. The celebrations were more in relief than anything else. India, despite all criticism, had managed to retain her crown. Balbir Singh Senior said:

> Victory casts its own spell; every nation rejoices in it, and we were no exception. There were the usual rounds of celebrations and hugging and kissing among players and officials. We were feted and felicitated and hunted down for autographs. I had been through this remarkable experience at London and Helsinki. But Melbourne was different. Our supporters, hundreds of them Australians and New Zealanders, were flushed with the thrill that India had beaten Pakistan in the Olympic final. Several hundred of enthusiastic friends we made on our 1955 New Zealand tour met us again in Melbourne. They were among our most vociferous fans ... That day when I led my team out to the victory rostrum, I swelled with pride. Sharing the rostrum on either side of me were the captains of Pakistan and Germany, the silver and the bronze medal winners. The crowd cheered us. It was a thrilling experience to acknowledge their applause. The National Anthem sounded sweet, and the tricolour, fluttering proudly in the stiff breeze, looked a grand sight.[18]

The celebrations, however, failed to conceal the fact that in Melbourne the Indians had lost more than they had gained. It was visible to all that India's supremacy was now a thing of the past and unless the Indians focused on improving their game, it would only be a matter of time before they would be humbled by the Pakistanis or the Europeans led by the Germans and the Dutch. Pankaj Gupta tried to sum up the grim situation:

I am going to stick my neck right out by saying that morally we lost the final against Pakistan whom we managed to beat by one goal thanks to a penalty conversion by Gentle. It was an even game up to a point but then Pakistan were all over us. Even before Gentle had scored the all important goal, shortly before the interval, Pakistan were awarded a penalty bully and according to my interpretation of the rules it should have been a goal but fortunately for us the Australian umpire ignored the infringement by Amir Kumar and we breathed again. If they had been a goal up things might have been a lot different.[19]

In another article, Gupta attempted to explain the reasons behind the decline:

The supremacy of a country in any game depends a lot on those who play the game, those who manage it and those who govern the country. We have indeed players of a caliber who can still hold their own in the international arena despite the fact that other nations have lately emerged as opponents truly worthy of our steel ... We have a great responsibility on our shoulders and we must see that the game does not suffer because of parochial interest, personal sentiment or administrative interference at Governmental level ... *We have wonderful players and if the right team and right skipper and manager are chosen there is no reason why we should not continue to remain world champions for a long time.*[20]

His last statement summed up the dangers that were eating into the foundations of Indian hockey. The words 'right skipper and right manager' smacked of the very provincialism that was corrupting Indian hockey and it was time for a reality check. And the 1960 Olympics in Rome was when this finally happened.

INDIA'S FIRST GREAT HOCKEY 'DEBACLE': ROME, 1960

From the very start, India's campaign in Rome appeared jinxed. Almost all the victories were by narrow margins and on more than a couple of occasions, they were plain lucky. Though the Indians started well by winning the opening match 10–0 against Denmark, the performance was far from satisfactory. Following this victory, the *Hindu* reported that the Indian forwards were yet to show thrust in attacking or teamwork in field combinations. If Prithpal Singh had not given them a three-goal lead within the first fifteen minutes, things might have been difficult, although Denmark was still no match for India. In the quarter-final against Australia, India won by the narrowest of margins (1–0), the winning goal scored at the last minute of the second extra period. Throughout the match, the Indians missed easy openings. Pankaj Gupta recorded, 'This match does not reflect credit to the world champions and I consider it a providential escape in this match.' Against New Zealand and Holland too the Indians gave an average performance and only Bhola among the forwards and Prithpal by virtue of his penalty corner conversion did justice to their pre-tournament billing.

Against Holland, the Indians were down a goal for most of the first half for the first time in Olympic history. The match was tied one apiece till the last seven minutes, when the Indians scored three quick goals. To Holland's credit, they had the better exchanges in the initial minutes and defended stubbornly in the beginning of the second half when the Indians went on an all-out attack. Even in the semi-final against Britain, the Indians were seen defending for most of the first half and when the British stepped up the pressure at the start of the second half looking for the equalizer, it was only goalkeeper Laxman's brilliance that saved India the blushes. He saved four strikes from Mayes and Hindle and with Prithpal playing a great game at the back, India scraped through to the final.

In the final, India was unable to assume the ascendancy that was expected from the world champions. In front of the biggest crowd ever assembled for a hockey match, telecast throughout western Europe via the Eurovision link up, the Pakistanis came out on top, though the match never reached the expected high standards because of the poor ground conditions.

Both sides were under intense pressure to win and the Indians lost the plot more than the Pakistanis, giving up their Olympic title in the process. At the interval, Pakistan was up by a goal, scored by Naseer in the eleventh minute of the match. Even when the Indians pressed for the equalizer towards the end, they failed to create any significant opening. With five minutes to go, the Pakistanis resorted to time-wasting tactics by hitting the ball out of play at every opportunity. The fairly large Indian section of the crowd jeered such conduct but it enabled Pakistan to hold on to their important one-goal lead.[21]

As soon as the match ended, the Pakistanis went berserk. Their players were seen running right across the pitch, embracing and shaking hands with each other and their fans celebrated way into the night. It was the first time in Olympic history that the Indian hockey team had been pushed to number two on the podium and Pakistan cherished its moment of glory.

The signs of India's impending decline had been evident since the early 1950s. Through it all, India was still winning. This defeat, that too at the hands of Pakistan, meant that Rome was seen as nothing short of a debacle in the annals of Indian hockey.[22]

The pages of IOC's official magazine during this period were full of heart-rending post-mortems and prescriptions for the regaining of lost glory. Two things stood out after the defeat: one, blame was heaped on the political rivalries of regional sporting satraps, which were seen to have damaged Indian hockey, and two, the debate between 'robust' (European) and 'skillful' (Indian) hockey.[23]

By the 1980s, most contemporary commentators would trace the decline of Indian hockey to the rise of astro-turf and India's failure to adapt to a more physically demanding form of the game. The records indicate, however, that the debate between the Indian and Western form of the game predated astro-turf. In 1962, S.M. Sait emphatically that 'we have to concede that our standard of hockey has deteriorated'. In his view, the Indians had erred in adopting foreign tactics:

> It is very strange that our players instead of continuing to play the old type of scientific and skilful hockey have made the mistake to take up [the] hard-hitting type of hockey which was almost alien to us. It was a delight in the past to watch our forwards indulge in quick short passing and skillful dribbling ... Now what we saw in Rome was a different picture altogether. Our players were trying to outdo our opponents in hard hitting and individual thrusts. It is needless to say that we failed miserably.[24]

It is telling that what Western commentators had long referred to as typical examples of 'magical' Indian stickwork was seen by Indian commentators as 'scientific' hockey. It was now felt that India's players were losing out in a bid to imitate the Western players.

But perhaps the deeper malaise was that of provincial rivalry, which was considered a huge problem by those who worked closely with Indian hockey after the 1950s. No one explained this better than Charanjit Rai, who in a prescient article in *Indian Olympic News* noted that the loudest voices of recrimination after the Rome defeat came not from former players but from 'those who had never achieved this distinction' and held positions of power at the state and national level in hockey's administrative structure.[25]

In an early precursor to former hockey captain Dhanraj Pillay's famous lament in the early 2000s against the czars of Indian hockey, Rai argued that the players would be affected 'unless treated fairly and sympathetically' off the field. Not mincing words about the politics of player selection that had already begun to haunt the game, Rai argued that the only way to regain the title in Tokyo was to 'select the team purely on merit … Even when ten players have been selected purely on merit and one position has been filled in with an undeserving player, this injustice has an adverse effect on the other ten. They may not express their resentment but subconsciously it finds it[s]outlet adversely affecting their performance on the field'.

Rai's analysis carried hints of 'injustices' and 'undeserving' players who were wrongly promoted. Regardless of the truth of this assertion, the fact that such talk was already becoming part of the public discourse about hockey is significant. He had touched upon the issues that were creeping into Indian hockey.

'Sweet Revenge' in Tokyo, 1964

The loss to Pakistan had a deep impact on Indian hockey and the next four years were dedicated to planning how to regain the title. As the Indians were about to embark on their journey of revenge, the sports media back home was optimistic about its chances of wresting the crown back from Pakistan in Tokyo. The scribes were beginning to suggest that if the team did manage to win, it would have performed a much greater task than the stalwarts of the golden age of Indian hockey. This was because in the

1930s and 1940s, India had the best players in every position and there was hardly any serious competition to pose a threat to its supremacy. However, by the 1950s, hockey had established firm roots in Europe and Southeast Asia and there was no question of an easy victory for either India or Pakistan.[26]

As far as preparations were concerned, the Indians did their best before Tokyo. The players came together for an intensive training session at a pre-Olympic camp and also toured New Zealand and Malaysia as part of their Olympic planning. Also, there didn't appear to be any major dissensions within the team and regionalism had not yet afflicted the Olympic preparations in the way it had in the lead-up to London, Helsinki and Melbourne.

However, India did have her task cut out for Tokyo, partly because some of the Indian players had helped train the Europeans and Southeast Asians. Former Indian greats like Penniger, Cullen, Gentle, Kishen Lal and Carr had accepted professional assignments in nations across the world. With the Indian diaspora gradually increasing, many Indians who could have donned Indian colours chose to go abroad and strengthen the teams of the countries they settled in. Finally, the Indians had also somewhat modified their earlier style of play and had resorted to power hockey, relying more on short corner and long corner conversions than field goals, allowing the Europeans the opportunity to catch up.

That the gap had indeed narrowed was evident in the first match itself when the Indians struggled to beat Belgium in a hard-fought encounter.[27] Things were even more difficult in the second engagement against Germany when the Indians struggled to hold the Germans to a 1–1 draw. When the Germans took the lead in the twentieth minute, it appeared that the match was beyond India. Thankfully, they managed to save the day via a penalty-corner conversion by Prithipal Singh. Things barely improved in the match against Spain when India was once again held to a one-all draw.

'Gone are the days', lamented the *Hindu*, 'when hockey fans all over the world were only concerned with the margins of India's victory. Today it has become a matter of survival and at the moment India is finding it difficult even to qualify for the semi-final … India is now occupying the third place in Pool B with Germany and Spain taking the first two places respectively. While Germany has five points, Spain and India have four each with Spain having the better goal average'.

Another factor that hadn't endeared the Indians to experts was their rough approach. Willic, a former German star, summed up the rising discontent against the Indian style of play:

> I have never known India playing the man instead of the ball and at this rate nobody will have any respect for India. What is more, the entire ground of Indian officials were mum and blind over this. You taught us and the world how to play, but now it is you who have forgotten how to play. From a player's point of view and now as a coach I appeal to you to put an end to this state of affairs.

Eventually, India managed to scrape through to the semi-final with a 2–1 win against Holland. T.D. Parthasarathy in his match report drew attention to what could have been a real tragedy:

> Making the semi-final grade was a real ordeal for India who had to thank providence that it managed to beat the Netherlands by the odd goal in three ... India was lucky to win because after Netherlands had leveled matters, the latter all but got the lead. The goal was, however, disallowed ... In the 20th minute the Dutchmen forced a short corner and following a melee in front of India's goal, the Netherlands inside left Van Hooft took everybody by surprise by scoring. This created a sensation among the Netherlands followers. The Dutch players threw their sticks up in the air in jubilation, but to the surprise of all, including many in the Indian camp the British umpire Kendrick Eaves disallowed the goal for offside. The decision came as a rude shock to the Netherlands, who seemed unable to recover from this.

In the semi-final against Australia, the Indians fared better, winning the contest 3–1 and as Parthasarathy said, 'All said and done the victory was well deserved, and fighting back to the wall, the Indian team did a grand job'.[28]

AVENGING PAKISTAN IN TOKYO

If hockey has any gods, then they could not have scripted a better final lineup than India vs Pakistan. Here was a wounded championship team striving to regain its lost title from the challenger. The off-field rivalry between the nations added an extra edge to the contest. In less than a year, both countries would be at war over the Rann of Kutch and the tensions were already building up. In modern terms, the only thing comparable to the emotionalism of this match was the incredibly tense India–Pakistan game in the cricket World Cup of 1999, at the height of the Kargil war. In 1964, the war was still months away, but India's hockey pride still had to be restored. This was 'war minus the shooting'.

Finally, India re-established its supremacy in world hockey by defeating Pakistan 1–0. Rene G. Frank, the secretary general of the FIH, left a moving description of this final and the emotions that moved both teams:

> The India–Pakistan final which was played in a highly-charged emotional atmosphere was really extraordinary. It was one of the best and probably the best of the matches which I have had opportunity to attend. Two fine teams of appreciably equal strength were each doing their utmost to win … If India finally proved a winner by a narrow margin, this was because in my personal opinion its players seemed to me to be inspired with a greater will than their opponents to carry off this victory which enabled them to regain the title of Olympic Champion which they had always held and which was wrested from them for the first time in 1960 by Pakistan.[29]

The performance of Indian goal-keeper Laxman stood out in the match. Most observers agreed that the result might have been different had it not been for his athletic defending.

The celebrations matched the occasion. The victory was followed by 'indescribable scenes of joy (which lasted) for many minutes'. That it meant so much to a troubled India, ravaged by a war against China in 1962, is evident in the way the press back home wrote about the victory: 'Eleven gallant men will import eleven pieces of gold into India next week and they will be allowed through the customs with smiles and congratulations. We never expected it to be an easy job but we worked for it most sincerely … We started shakily but as the tournament progressed we have gained strength and courage and we made it.'[30]

The golden glow of this victory was felt around the country. A paan shop in Delhi distributed soft drinks for free soon after the Indians regained the gold. A taxi driver, when interviewed, suggested that he had been waiting for that moment for four years. A number of college students said that the

victory would encourage many in the capital to take to hockey. The prime
minister, Lal Bahadur Shastri, and President Radhakrishnan expressed
delight and sent congratulatory cables to captain Charanjit Singh. The
news of India's victory was conveyed to Shastri when he was addressing a
public meeting in Khatauli village in UP. He immediately reacted by giving
his audience the news of the nation's triumph in Tokyo.

The Tokyo Games of 1964 became one of Indian hockey's finest
achievements. It was only after sixteen years, in Moscow in 1980, that the
Indians once again managed to finish ahead of the field. Despite winning
the 1975 World Cup in Kuala Lumpur, India's performance witnessed a
sharp decline at the Olympics. In Montreal in 1976, the team finished a
dismal seventh. Even within the country hockey had been thrown into
turmoil by the start of the 1970s, a story we recount in the next chapter.

While some critics rubbish India's victory in Moscow, pointing to a
depleted field due to a Cold War boycott by anti-Soviet Union countries,
there's little doubt that a performance that won the country another
Olympic gold medal will always rank as an important chapter in Indian
sports history.

THE 'RED' GOLD: MOSCOW, 1980

Given the absence of several leading hockey nations of the world, many
tend to undermine the value of India's performance in Moscow. While there
is some truth in this argument, because nations like Pakistan, Holland and
Germany stayed away due to the boycott, an Olympic gold will always
remain special. The boycott can hardly discredit athletes who won honours
at the Moscow Games in 1980 and Los Angeles in 1984.

India had prepared well for Moscow. To ensure they were well
acclimatized, the team was sent there before the rest of the contingent.
This gave the players time to get used to the polygrass surface being used
for the first and only time in Olympic history.[31] In fact, there was quite a
controversy over its use because a powerful lobby, led by the influential
president of the FIH, Rene Frank, was advocating the use of astro-turf.
Rumours in Moscow made it evident that the ageing FIH chief had insisted
at one stage that the Moscow tournament be played only on astro-turf.
However, the Russians, who had tackled the boycott so successfully and
ruthlessly, were not to be browbeaten. They made it known to Frank that

they could afford to run the Olympics minus the hockey tournament. As mentioned by the director of India's National Institute of Sports, R.L. Anand, 'Rene Frank got the message and gave in on the issue of the surface'.

India started the contest well, crushing the lowly ranked Tanzanians 18–0. K. Datta, covering the tournament for the *Times of India*, wrote in his match report, 'The score line seems to have been taken out a page [sic] from the history of Indian hockey. The matches were one sided then. It was also overwhelmingly one sided today at the Dynamo Stadium when our men opened the campaign in the 22nd Olympics.'

Balbir Singh Senior, who was in the audience, was happy at the performance and said it was refreshing to see Indian players strike rich form and score a haul of goals in their very first tie, though against feeble opposition.

The Indians were brought back to earth in their very next encounter against the Poles, managing a last-second equalizer to score a 2–2 draw. 'To say that Fernandes's goal in India's last gasp effort came as a great relief would be the understatement of the Olympic year.' It is worth mentioning that the Indians were left fuming at the end of this match due to some of the umpiring decisions that went against them. They were extremely critical of Dutch umpire Bob Davidson and blamed their inability to convert penalty corners on him.

However, as the *Times of India* reported, a very thin line divides a clean hit from a cut. It depended on what the umpire thought about it and 'it is better if our players get used to European umpiring rather than quibble about it. Most important they should be reminded of the old adage that it never pays to challenge the umpire or behave peevishly.'

In the following match against Spain, India snatched a last-minute equalizer to stay afloat in the competition. The Indians were once again upset with some of the umpiring decisions, though the manager of the team, Dayanand, ruled out any possibility of lodging a formal complaint with the organizers. What stood out in the match against Spain was the Indians' superior physical ability. As the *Times of India* reported, 'This Indian team in Moscow may not be the best to be sent out for an Olympic campaign, but it is fighting fit.'

India followed up the draw against Spain with a 13–0 victory over Cuba that ensured that a win against the Russians in the last group tie would propel them into the final.

Against the Soviets, the Indians displayed incredible skill and won a close contest 4–2. For a change, the umpiring worked in India's favour and the Russians were often left rueing their misfortune. The outstanding star in this match was Mohammed Shahid, who played an excellent match as game maker, setting up multiple openings for the forwards.[32] It was his form that gave the Indians hope for the final against Spain, a team whose penalty corner conversion record was much better than the Indians.

'THEY DO ALL SORTS OF THINGS WITH STICK AND BALL': GOLD AT LAST

India tasted gold in Moscow after sixteen years after beating Spain 4–3. K. Datta reported with relief in the *Times of India*: 'An Olympic hockey gold medal at last. But India should have won it by a more convincing margin. They played as they should have played till they led three-nil with twenty minutes to go. Then the defence began letting them down and when the end came the lead had thinned down to the barest minimum.' Congratulating the Indians on the victory, Horst Wein, the German coach of the Spanish team, said that the gold medal would help India return to the pole position in world hockey. According to him, the young team was the best India had sent to the Olympics for some time. The players were quick and fit. The team's ability to swiftly counter-attack and keep fighting until the end was something the European teams had to take note of.

The doubters, however, remained. Rene Frank, president of FIH, who had so movingly described the great Indian victory in Tokyo, now felt that the Moscow win was nothing but a flash in the pan. In an interview given to K. Datta for the *Times of India*, he stated that the standard of Indian hockey had gone down over time while the Europeans had improved considerably and that it had resulted in a levelling of standards: 'The Europeans first learnt the finer points from Indian hockey and then evolved tactics of their own. Indian hockey has evolved no new tactics. It is stagnant. It likes to live on old prestige … The organization of Indian hockey also is not what it should be.'

Vasudevan Bhaskaran, the coach of the Indian team in Moscow, was of a different opinion and suggested that there was no reason to undermine India's achievement in Moscow. He had high praise for the newcomers, fourteen of whom were playing in their first Olympics, and said he hadn't seen a more gifted player in India than Mohammed Shahid, who was naturally endowed with physical attributes that made for a talented inside forward. 'For years India should be able to depend on this versatile star,' he said.[33]

Back home, the hockey fraternity looked upon the victory as having heralded a renaissance in Indian hockey. Once again, there was hope all around that the golden run could be sustained. That such hope was overambitious became evident when the Indians were pushed to the fifth spot at the Los Angeles Games in 1984. Also, the infighting that had corrupted the edifice of Indian hockey continued unabated, resulting in a string of poor Olympic performances between 1984 and 2016.

12

'The Fall of Rome'

The Decline of Indian Hockey and the Green Shoots of Renewal

The future of Indian Hockey is indeed gloomy and the average Indian expects us to do everything possible to see that Indian Hockey is once again supreme in the world.

—Pankaj Gupta, Honourary Secretary, IOA, 1962[1]

Not only did artificial turf replace real sod, but also plastic balls replaced leather ones. A slow, analytical game gave way to one of nonstop, true-hop action. For India it was like starting over with all nations even in field hockey.

—Steve Ruskin, *Sports Illustrated*, 1996[2]

Indian hockey entered a dismal period from the late 1970s. As early as 1976, *World Hockey* magazine defined this decline in an article with the pathos-ridden headline, 'The Fall of Rome'.[3] The best that Indian hockey has done at the Olympics since 1980 has been a fifth-place position at the Los Angeles Games in 1984. It reached a nadir in 2008 when the men's team failed to qualify for the first time. Even though Indian hockey has significantly improved since – winning silver at the Hockey Champions Trophy in 2018, a third-place finish in the 2016–17 FIH World Leagues and a gold at the 2014 Asian Games – it has not been counted as a global leader in the sport for decades.

Since the late 1970s, hockey has languished in India, with only a few bright spots such as bronze Olympics medals in Mexico 1968 and Munich 1972, a World Championship win in Malaysia in 1975 and an Olympics gold in Moscow in 1980. It is hardly comparable to cricket in terms of popularity. With cricket reigning as the national passion, mass spectatorship of hockey in contemporary India has become a rarity. Television ratings show that the spectator base for hockey is only a fraction of those that watch cricket.

Indian hockey's failure to retain its earlier glory has been the primary reason for the game's decline in the popular imagination. While the glamour of cricket turned it into an aspirational sport, fully in tune with the consumer ethic of a globalizing society, hockey stagnated. In the past three decades, cricket has steadily expanded its catchment area, attracting talent from classes and areas not traditionally associated with the game – 'middle and rurbanized India'.[4] Hockey, on the other hand, languished, despite its traditionally larger base.

Administrative lethargy was a central reason for this decline. This became evident from the IHF's failure to protest field hockey's shift from grass to astro-turf in the mid-1970s.

The year astro-turf was introduced in 1975, India was a top hockey nation, having just won the World Cup in Malaysia. It changed the balance of the game globally thereafter. Yet, India's hockey administrators never officially opposed this move. In fact, they gave it tacit support.

Germany won the first international tournament ever played on the artificial surface. *World Hockey* magazine immediately understood the deeper importance of the victory, interpreting it as a sign of Europe bouncing back in 'the see-saw battle between Europe and Asia at the head of the world rankings'.[5] Field hockey was the only sport at which India could flex its muscles on the Olympic stage and the IHF and the IOA's lack of initiative to pre-empt the shift at the time is telling.

While the move to artificial turf had a serious impact, it was not the only reason for the decline of Indian hockey. Pakistan was worse off than India economically and had fewer artificial turfs, but still managed to do better at hockey for years. Though hockey in Pakistan has now declined, if it could do well for years, why couldn't India? Moreover, if India could be a hockey superpower despite even greater systemic hurdles in the colonial period, then why not in later years?

WHEN IT ALL WENT WRONG:
ASTRO-TURF AND THE 'NORTH-SOUTH' DIVIDE

Indian hockey in the 1970s fell prey to an unfortunate north–south divide. When it came to sports (and hockey), the south was still subservient to the stranglehold exerted by the north in sports management. As a result, southern sports administrators were determined to challenge the well-entrenched northern supremacy even if it damaged 'national interest' in the long run. In the fight over the control of Indian hockey, the southern bloc, led by M.A.M. Ramaswamy, enlisted the support of the FIH in the early 1970s.[6]

Evidence in the IOC's archives proves beyond doubt that the Ramaswamy faction won control and retained it despite severe opposition, only because of the legitimacy bestowed upon it by the international federation. This alliance pre-empted the possibilities of a strong Indian protest when the shift to artificial turf was proposed in the mid-1970s.

As a close ally of the FIH and its president, Rene Frank, Ramaswamy, having assumed presidency of the Indian federation, had little choice but to offer passive consent to the move to astro-turf.[7] The division is rooted in the fight for supremacy between the north and south blocs and proved central to the subsequent decline of India's leading Olympic sport. More than the shift to astro-turf, it was regional power play that resulted in the disappearance of hockey from its position of centrality in the Indian sporting landscape.

THE MYSTERIOUS SHIFT TO ARTIFICIAL TURF AND INDIA'S SILENCE

The shift to artificial turf was a chance development. In 1973, during a visit to Montreal (the venue of the 1976 Summer Olympics), the president of the FIH and other leading administrators realized the impossibility of organizing the Olympic hockey competition. Not a single ground picked as a potential venue for the proposed competition was up to the mark. Furthermore, it was apparent that the organizers weren't capable of making the grounds fit for play in the fickle Canadian climate. There wasn't adequate time between the end of winter and the start of the Summer Games for the pitches to be readied.[8]

Montreal's mayor, Jean Drapeau, and the vice president of the Montreal Olympics Organizing Committee came up with the idea of using an artificial turf pitch in place of the traditional grass surface for the competition. This, it was suggested, would enable the Olympic tournament to go on without hindrance. *World Hockey* magazine reported in October 1975: 'To show what could be done and to allow the FIH to judge whether such a surface was really suitable, a demonstration of hockey was laid on in Toronto in a stadium which normally was used for American football.'

The trial was successful and the people present in Toronto were profoundly impressed with the success of the experiment. The outcome was that the FIH, based on a highly favourable recommendation from its president, in a few months consented to the Montreal Olympic hockey tournament being played on artificial turf instead of grass. Soon after, an astro-turf constructed by the Monsanto company was sampled by some of the best European talents. A match was organized by the French Hockey Federation near Paris, followed by a magnificent dinner in honour of past international players. Most present were impressed with the turf and consented to the shift.

Interestingly, Asia, the traditional home of hockey, was not represented at these meetings.

A grand premiere on artificial turf took place in Montreal on 19 July, when an eight-nation Olympic preparatory tournament opened on what was later to be used as the surface for the Olympic Games. India pulled out of this tournament at the last minute and was not able to get a first-hand experience of playing on artificial turf. The Europeans, on the other hand, loved it. The *World Hockey* magazine reported:

> As soon as the first few matches had taken place, it was abundantly clear that playing hockey on artificial surface of this type produced enormous benefits ... artificial grass permits easier ball control and this in itself helps to reduce the number of infringements of the rules – which means less whistle and fewer stoppages. The game thus becomes easier to follow, as well as being a faster spectacle and much more interesting from a spectator point of view.

Another great advantage of playing on artificial turf, in the magazine's view, was the large number of games that could be completed in a single day on the same pitch, given that maintenance was simple and inexpensive. As per this school of thought, playing on an artificial surface greatly reduced the chances of injury compared to a conventional turf pitch. 'Despite the high initial cost, there is bound to be a considerable increase in the construction of artificial surfaces for hockey pitches. Here is a fundamental advance, which can only be to the benefit of our sport. Without any doubt the increased attraction for players and spectators opens up vast new horizons.'[9]

Ever since the 1976 Montreal Olympic Games, field hockey has been played exclusively on artificial turf. This was possible because India, where 'cows are sacred and fake grass an anathema', as one foreign scribe argued, did *not* raise even a feeble voice of protest.[10]

Whatever little protest was voiced came from the north lobby, which had been ousted from power by the faction led by M.A.M. Ramaswamy. Having succeeded in gaining control of the IHF with full support from the FIH, Ramaswamy was in no mood to oppose the move to astro-turf, even if it spelt doom for India.

When Indian star Ajit Singh argued that 'Astro-turf is a very costly affair', no one seemed to take notice. Singh, a veteran of three Olympics (1968, 1972 and 1976), pointed out that 'India, as late as 1996 could afford no more than 12 astro-turf fields, in sharp contrast to countries like Holland which had many more.'[11]

Yet, the IHF lent its full support to the FIH in consolidating the shift. For the historian, the Indian Federation's support for astro-turf is a telling clue to the politics that defined it.

'CONSIDERABLE TROUBLE BETWEEN THE NORTH AND THE SOUTH': HOCKEY'S TRAGEDY IN THE 1970s

Things had been going reasonably well for Indian hockey until 1973, when Ashwini Kumar, president of the IHF, was forced to step down from his post due to burgeoning opposition against him. His resignation was followed by a long spell of anarchy within the ranks of the IHF and conflict between the north and south blocs as P.N. Sahni from Punjab and the M.A.M. Ramaswamy from Madras engaged in a bitter struggle for the presidency.[12]

Rene Frank of the FIH saw this factional fight within Indian hockey as a purely regional dispute. Writing to the IOC President in 1978, he explained that 'the fight started in 1973/74 by some sports leaders of the North, having close links with the Sikh community, in order to avoid that the hockey leadership should go to the South.'[13] While Sahni had the backing of Kumar, Ramaswamy, an extremely influential businessman in Madras, had the support of figures in Delhi's central government, especially Union Minister Sikandar Bakht.

The feud turned murky when the group led by Sahni made every effort to stall Ramaswamy's assumption of the IHF presidency. This was an early example of the fights over control that have plagued Indian sporting federations. The government eventually had to step in and appoint a reputed supreme court judge to oversee the hockey federation's elections.[14] The dispute peaked in 1974 when the IOA revoked its recognition of the IHF and took over the administration of hockey in the country.

In the time-honoured tradition of Indian officialdom, Bhalindra Singh appealed to the IOC to intervene in his favour to 'nip the evil in the bud' and to pre-empt governmental intervention while hockey was suffering.[15] With the IOA appealing to the IOC for help, Ramaswamy enlisted the support of the FIH. Significantly, he argued that as a south Indian he was a victim of a northern conspiracy. It was an argument that appealed to Frank and he was to consistently back Ramaswamy thereafter.[16]

In the middle of all this, the Indian hockey team, still under the stewardship of the IOA, won the 1975 World Cup for the first and only time in Kuala Lumpur, under the coaching of Balbir Singh Junior.

So bad was the administrative situation by then that the coaching camp before the tournament and the tour itself had to be funded by the Punjab government in the absence of funding from a dysfunctional IHF. This had some unforeseen consequences. The camp, Balbir Singh wrote:

> ... was held on the campus of Punjab University, Chandigarh. A newly constructed girls' hostel was given as the residence for the trainees. This being in front of another girls' hostel across the road, some girls started making courtesy calls at our visitors' lounge. This was discouraged by having the front gate locked, and advising the girls to watch the players in action on the field. That prompted the players to give their best during practice sessions to impress the girls.[17]

On such vagaries is sporting success scripted!

Internal squabbling within the IHF seemed to come to an end temporarily in 1975, when Ramasamy won an acrimonious election against

Sahni and was duly recognized as president. But the losing side wasn't ready to back off. Numerous affiliated units were opposed to the move and therefore refused to participate in the activities of the IHF.[18]

Even Pakistan made an attempt to exploit the volatile situation in India. In a letter to the IOC president, Lord Killanin, the Pakistan Hockey Federation urged the IOC to institute a commission of inquiry into the affairs of Indian hockey to set an example 'for other countries in Asia who may be tempted to follow the example of India' and openly defy IOC rules prescribed in the Olympic charter.[19]

Indian sports were divided in a stalemate, with a northern faction controlling the IOA and a southern faction controlling hockey. In all this, the FIH's support for Ramaswamy was crucial. In 1978, for instance, Bhalindra Singh forwarded to the IOC a dossier of Rene Frank's latest correspondence with the north Indian faction, sarcastically noting: 'You can see from this whether Mr. Frank is determined to view this controversy from a very narrow angle, and will probably in the last analysis throw his weight with the Indian Hockey Federation rather than National Olympic Committee.'[20]

The fight between the IOA and the IHF flared up again in mid-1977. Air Vice Marshall C.L. Mehra, secretary general of the IOA, declared that the IHF was not interested in arriving at an amicable solution. After a flurry of letters between the two organizations, the IOA finally suspended the functioning of the IHF on four grounds:

1. The IHF had not paid its dues to the IOA, amounting to approximately Rs 45,000.

2. Non-implementation of the ruling announced by the IOA that each state or affiliated member should be represented by 'one unit only'. This resolution had been adopted to prevent the mushrooming of dissident groups and had been implemented by all other national federations/associations. The IHF's refusal to accede to the ruling was perceived as creating a dangerous precedent for other national federations.

3. Non-implementation of the assurance given by the president of the IHF, M.A.M. Ramaswamy, to give equitable representation to those associations/individuals absent when he was elected president.

4. The acceptance of interference from a member of the government in the selection of the Indian hockey team and in the management of day-to-day affairs of the federation.[21]

The charge of governmental interference had deep roots. It was specific to the moves made by then Union Minister for Works and Housing Sikandar Bakht. Only a week before the meeting of the IOA general assembly, Bakht had attended the probables camp at Patiala and made statements contesting the rights and jurisdiction of the IOA. First, he had unilaterally foiled attempts to reinstate the three dissident hockey stars, Surjit Singh, Virender Singh and Baldev Singh, declaring that 'discipline in sports is essential and there must be respectful distance between players and selectors'.

This once again foreshadowed many of the current debates in Indian sports on the role of government. The IOA insisted on keeping it out but Bakht was abrasive in declaring that the 'Government had every right to ensure that public funds were not misused by any sports body. In Socialist countries sports were totally run by the government and there was no objection to it'.

Governmental interference, of course, was complete anathema to the IOC. It held that amateurism was an article of faith. IOC President Lord Killanin, on his visit to India in December 1977, told the media that if any instance of willing submission by a national federation to government or outside dictates was brought before an international federation recognized by the IOC, that national federation could be suspended by the international federation concerned. He reiterated that the IOC had the right to authorize a national Olympic committee to run the affairs of any national federation in which an existing dispute was adversely affecting the interest of the sportsmen concerned.[22]

Bakht's interference in hockey team selection by now had become a political hot potato. Raja Bhalindra Singh wrote to the IOC:

Unfortunately a minister of government who has no direct connection with sports has been using his official position to interfere in the affairs of the Indian Hockey Federation, and has gone so far as to influence the selection of the national team. This has been resented and has attracted a lot of adverse public criticism both in Parliament and outside. The official government stand, that of the Ministry of Education and Sports, is one of unhappiness. However, the minister continues to interfere and the President of the IHF, whose own position is not too secure, continues to flout all norms of behaviour by seeking help from this extra constitutional authority, and in a most authoritarian way flout both the autonomy of his Federation as well as the spirit of the constitution of the National Olympic Committee. He refused to listen to the National Olympic Committee and has not even cared to be present in the various meetings convened to set matters right.[23]

The IHF responded by going to court and obtaining a temporary injunction from the Madras High Court on 18 January 1978 against the disqualification.[24]

When the IOA requested a meeting to resolve differences amicably, Ramaswamy refused.[25] He cited three reasons for why he couldn't attend a meeting:

1. 14 January is Pongal Day – one of the most important feast days for us in South India and I had to respect my revered father's wishes and participate in the religious ceremonies at home.

2. As chairman and senior steward of the Madras Race Club, I had to be present at the race course to officiate the running of the South India derby.

3. The first circular and second circular convening the IOA meeting did not include any item on hockey affairs.[26]

In this ongoing battle for control, Ramaswamy had the government of India's support. As he wrote to hockey's global bosses, sports in India were under the direct control of the union government and Prime Minister Morarji Desai had given Sikandar Bakht complete control over hockey. He also assured the president of the international federation that in the battle against the IOA, the IHF was assured of Bakht's support.

In the corridors of international sporting officialdom, the issues in Indian sports were seen as a conflict between north and south India. This was certainly how Rene Frank saw it when he joined hands with the IHF. The latest fight had been triggered by Ramaswamy dropping three Punjabi players. In Frank's view, the opposition lobby, which had failed to check

Ramaswamy's ascendancy to the IHF presidency, was using this as an excuse to fight a larger political battle. As he put it: 'It must be noted that players involved are most probably all Punjabis, three of them belonging to a team of which Kumar is the chief ... It must also be noted that all the people involved belong to the North.' The global hockey federation supported Ramaswamy because he was an eminent personality in south India, the director of a number of companies and had helped his association financially since becoming president.[27]

To no one's surprise, Frank's analysis of the infighting as a symptom of the north–south divide provoked a hostile reaction in the national media when his confidential letters found their way into Indian newspapers in June 1978. A good example of this was when veteran sportswriter Bobby Talyarkhan argued that Frank had overstepped his limits in declaring 'that the real trouble is between the north and the south of India'. Talyarkhan, who had earlier supported the IHF against the IOA and had been against the latter's takeover of the national federation during the 1975 World Cup, now pointed out:

> Frank has gone so far as to mention the Sikhs as an entity and I assert this is none of his business. By stating what he has done Rene Frank is merely adding fuel to fire ... Frank has no business to go into any details calculated to turn India's hockey control into a burning cauldron ... India's sport has enough internal squabbles for a foreigner to step in and add to the troubles.'[28]

Upset at the press leaks, IOA President and Air Chief Marshal O.P. Mehra specifically refuted the allegations of a north India bias in a rebuttal letter to Frank on 24 June 1978:

> ... the subject of North and South relations in India is a very sensitive one and if some of your friends in India have informed you that it provides a background to the present imbroglio in Indian Hockey, it is not true ... Raja Bhalindra Singh [Mehra's predecessor as IOA President] is a widely respected sports administrator in the country and uptil today no one has ever blamed him for any parochial feeling. Then again Mr. Ashwini Kumar when he left the Indian Hockey Federation, had more than a majority in the House.[29]

Mehra insisted that 'a paid employee' of the IHF had leaked the Frank letters containing the north–south references to the press. This, he argued, was a sure sign that Indian hockey was 'not in safe hands' and that 'a number of undesirable people' had found their way into it. Frank, he said, had 'hurt our national sentiments by giving a political slant to the dispute by referring to personal interests and North versus the rest of India as factor'.[30]

He also drew attention to Frank's silence over a similar tussle in Pakistan, arguing that the Pakistani government's takeover of the nation's hockey affairs by disbanding the hockey federation had far more serious consequences for the international sporting fraternity. In the four-cornered fight over Indian hockey, Mehra was hoping that the IOC would exert pressure and rein in Frank so as to balance the scales in the infighting between the IOA and the IHF.

Whether the north–south divide was genuine or merely a convenient platform to mask old-fashioned lust for power is debatable. In the meantime, the game continued to suffer.

The immutable fact is that vicious infighting was true of almost all Indian sports. International officials always saw it as a reflection of India's internal regional differences. IOC President Lord Killanin noted in 1978: 'Over my Olympic years, we have had considerable trouble between the North and the South and there was some opposition even to the election of Mr. Kumar, who is an excellent man, because both he and Bhalindra Singh come from the North ... Your federation is not the only one which has had trouble in India of a fairly similar nature.'[31]

If Indian sports were to have an epitaph, that would be it.

The tragedy of Indian hockey is that it has remained hostage to such politics off the field since the 1970s. Thirty years later, hockey star Dhanraj Pillay was to repeat the same accusations on Indian officialdom:

What I am saying is that the IHF just does not care. For them, the post and the aura of being IHF president are more important than anything else. Their ego is on a high such as you can never imagine. But we also have our egos. Don't you feel players like us have done something for the nation to take notice?[32]

Pillay had numerous public run-ins with hockey officials in his playing days and his distress was genuine and deep-seated. In his struggle lies the real tragedy of Indian sports, not just of Indian hockey.

The incident in 2008 when then-IHF Secretary K. Jyothikumaran was caught on tape accepting a bribe for team selection was certainly not the last tragedy to hit Indian hockey. It happened right after the Indian team had reached its lowest point, when it failed to qualify for the Beijing Olympics. It led to the IOA's suspension of the IHF and the removal of K.P.S. Gill as its chief after fourteen years.

TOKYO 2020: LIVING IN HOPE, WITH TEAM INDIA

Indian hockey did turn a new leaf with the 2010 Commonwealth Games in Delhi. The national team defeated Pakistan in a thrilling encounter in the pool stages and went on to beat Great Britain in the semi-final to set up a title clash with Australia. While the Australians were far superior in the gold medal contest, a silver medal at home in front of a buoyant crowd was a serious step up for India from failing to qualify for the Beijing Olympics just two years prior.

India had found a new star in drag-flicker Sandeep Singh and, all of a sudden, a good performance at the 2012 London Games was starting to look possible. Sandeep, a charming personality, became the poster boy of Indian hockey and sponsors began queuing up to support the young man from Punjab. 'Not many realized that this was the start of our problems,' recounted Michael Nobbs, the coach who delivered the Commonwealth Games medal against all odds. 'We could have done much better in London had the team been together. Many felt Sandeep's stardom was unfair. He was the sponsors' darling and was receiving a lot of media attention and money for he was the one scoring the goals. But in a team sport, it is often an issue with the others feeling left out and discriminated against.'

India eventually finished last at the London Games. This wasn't expected from a team that was on the rise and had a credible record going into the Olympics. Soon after, Nobbs conceded that 'The team was in disarray. There were multiple camps within it and "India" wasn't playing as a team. A few of the players were even planning to harm others thinking they were being given preference. As coach, I take responsibility for the failure but

I will also say that anyone in charge would have found such deep-rooted jealousy among the players impossible to deal with.'

Nobbs spilled the beans on the London campaign in a hard-hitting email to Hockey India a few years after his departure from the country:

> Let's look at the players, do you really think they are giving their best for India? It's a job and they will do anything to keep it including telling the coach how wonderful he is and that the other coaches were terrible. Butter the coach up and when the results aren't produced let's get rid of him, blame the coach and we will stay in the team longer. Gurbaj Singh is going to a disciplinary hearing today and this is because he is doing the same things he has always done. It's all about the money to him. Ask him why he refused to play at the London Olympics in a game against Germany. Are you representing India or yourself? Maybe that's why!!

Narendra Batra, who now heads the FIH and is the president of the IOA, was in charge of Hockey India in 2012 and was forced to make changes in the aftermath of London. Michael Nobbs gave way to a slew of coaches, including Terry Walsh, Paul Van Ass and Roelant Oltmans, to try and make amends in Rio.

Oltmans, a successful player in his day, emphasized a great deal on the need to improve fitness. The results between 2014 and 2015 indicated that things were starting to look up again for Indian hockey. An Asian Games gold in Incheon in 2014 ensured direct Olympic qualification for India, giving the team a full two years to get prepared for the 2016 Rio Olympics. Nobbs, who had left the system under rather unpleasant circumstances, wasn't too optimistic, however. As the team prepared for Rio, he tempered the medal hype by suggesting that a fourth- to sixth-place finish would be a more realistic assessment.

'The Asian Games win is a major achievement for the Indian team,' said Nobbs. 'However, I don't think India is yet ready to challenge the major powerhouses like Australia, Germany or Holland. A semi-final showing at Rio should be a legitimate aim and any placement between 4th to 6th will be a serious improvement for India at the Olympics. This is a young team and should become better in the next year and with a good coaching and support unit in place. However, what India needs to do right away is find a second goalkeeper after Sreejesh. Sreejesh is a brilliant athlete but if he gets injured all plans will go out of the window. You need a second goalkeeper who will be able to give Sreejesh the necessary breaks going into the Olympics.'

When we pressed him to tell us more, he added, 'The central problem in India is not the lack of facilities. There are adequate facilities in the country. What you need is to bring in more sports science and get the Indian coaches trained in the modern systems of coaching. This will mean that the youngsters in the age groups between fifteen and seventeen have already acquired the basic skills when they play for the senior national team. For the current set of boys, it has taken them three to four years – first under me and now under Terry and Roelant – to get used to the modern game. You need at least thirty boys who can all make the national team if you want to be a strong hockey nation. At the moment, the top twenty hockey players don't face serious challenges from the supply chain. That has to improve for India to get back their lost supremacy. And in doing so the central role has to be played by the academies by introducing modern scientific methods of coaching and training.'

When we visited the Indian training camp in Bengaluru ahead of the Olympics in May 2016, the mood was upbeat and positive. While Oltmans, who had by then replaced Terry Walsh as head coach and high-performance director, was keen on taking things one step at a time, the players did seem to be united and playing as a team. 'There is a lot of positive energy in the team,' said Oltmans before adding, 'Fitness is the key because if you see the track record of Indian hockey, we inevitably tend to concede goals in the last few minutes of a close game. It is about fitness and stamina. Compared to the European teams, India seemed to fall behind in stamina and weren't able to keep pace in the last few minutes. That's what we have worked to remedy in the last year and you should see results in Rio.'

To be fair to Oltmans and his boys, India did show glimpses of a turnaround in Rio. Not only did they win their first match against Ireland 3–2, but they also beat eventual winners Argentina and were up by a goal against Belgium in the quarter-final before losing 1–3. Had India not drawn 2–2 against Canada, the team may well have made the semi-final. 'We did 95 per cent of the things right', said Oltmans, 'but in an Olympics, it is the last 5 per cent that makes a difference. A few basic mistakes and we lost out on a possible medal.'

The campaign, however, was not devoid of drama. Soon after India's victory over Ireland, Boria went to a mall in Barra just a few minutes from the Olympic Village for an afternoon snack. Once he was done with eating, he walked into an Adidas store to look around and check on some Olympic stuff. Just then, Roelant Oltmans walked in and asked for hockey sticks and shoes.

Out of curiosity, Boria waited outside the store to see what the coach was up to. He came out about fifteen minutes later, his hands full with hockey sticks and shoe boxes. Slightly unnerved on seeing Boria there, Oltmans revealed that he had to buy equipment for the players for they were still having issues with their kit and gear. When Boria called Dr Batra back in India to check, he sent back a chain of internal emails, highlighting multiple issues the team was facing.

One of these emails, sent on 3 August from Oltmans to Hockey India, informed the administrators that the Indian team had still not 'receive[d] the right kit for Rio'. With just three days left for the matches to start, the team had only received one set. Oltmans told his bosses that it would be 'impossible' to manage with just that for the duration of the tournament. He was consequently left with no option but to go out and buy hockey sticks and shoes for the boys himself. Batra responded immediately by asking Hockey India CEO Elena Norman to 'sort it out on an urgent basis' herself. She was asked to send the kit by courier on an 'extremely urgent' footing since, in Batra's words, the 'Chef de Mission IOA will not do anything' about it.

But there was more. The Indian hockey team was also struggling to find TV sets to follow their competitors' games in Rio and didn't have enough chairs for the team to sit on during these viewing sessions. In an email to the Indian Chef de Mission on 1 August, Oltmans wrote that he had tried to rent television sets and more chairs but none were available in the Village. 'In the end we need proper furniture for all the players,' he wrote. 'Spending too much time in bean-chairs might occur [sic] back-injuries for the players.' He was seeking permission to buy three TV sets for both the men and women's teams as well as twenty-eight chairs to 'avoid injuries'. In an era where sports science is everything, the coach of the Indian hockey team was struggling for basic equipment when he should have just been focusing on his team's on-field strategy. Batra immediately requested the top Indian officials in Rio to provide an 'urgent solution' to these problems and ensure the well-being of the players.

This entire email correspondence is reproduced below for our readers:

Issue 2: On Kits for Team India

Dr Narinder Dhruv Batra <drkuku@batra.ind.in>
To:elena.norman@hockeyindia.org
Cc:mushtaque.secretarygeneral@hockeyindia.org,bihoa13@
gmail.com,nrami.nr@gmail.com,gupta.rakesh1952@gmail.
com,cdmrioolympics@gmail.com
4 Aug 2016 at 16:35
Please sort it out on urgent basis and send by courier. Chef De Mission IOA will not do anything, please sort it out yourself & confirm to me and treat it as extremely urgent.

Regards

----- Original Message -----
From: "Roelant Oltmans" <roelant.oltmans@hockeyindia.org>
To: "Elena Norman" <elena.norman@hockeyindia.org>
Cc: "Dr Narinder Dhruv Batra" <drkuku@batra.ind.in>; "Cdr R. K. Srivastava" <cdr.rks@hockeyindia.org>; "Matt Eyles" <Matt.Eyles@hockeyindia.org>; "Rakesh Gupta" <gupta.rakesh1952@gmail.com>
Sent: Wednesday, August 03, 2016 8:55 PM
Subject: Kit

Dear Elena,

Although we informed IOA and HI Matthew Eyles still didn't receive the right Kit for Rio.
We can only use 1 set.
As a Staff we're comon to wear the same kit but this will be impossible for the full 3 weeks. Chef de Mission told us he has informed IOA but still no feed back.
Please do the needful there are only 3 Days to go.
Thank you very much.
Kind regards,

Roelant Oltmans
Director High Performance
Hockey India

Issue 2: On injuries, TVs and Chairs

From: Dr Narinder Dhruv Batra <drkuku@batra.ind.
in<mailto:drkuku@batra.ind.in>>
Sent: Monday, 1 August 2016 08:59
To: N.Ramachandran; Rakesh Gupta; Rakesh Gupta CDM
Cc: Rajeev Mehta; Anil Khanna; V.D. NANAVATI; Elena
Norman; Rajiv Yadav; Injeti Srinivas; Injeti Srinivas; Mohd.
Mushtaque Ahmad; Mohd. Mushtaque Ahmad; Rajinder Singh;
Rajinder Singh; Mariamma Koshy; Mariamma Koshy; Roelant
Oltmans; Neil Hawgood
Subject: Fwd: Apartments in Rio

URGENT / IMPORTANT

Dear Sirs,

We request for urgent solution to the issues mentioned in trailing
mail of Mr Roelant Oltmans in interest of Fitness/Injuries and
performance of both Men & Women Hockey Teams.

Kindly revert and advice for solution.

Regards
[cid:image002.jpg@01D1EBFB.552D8420]

---------- Forwarded message ----------
From: Roelant Oltmans <roelant.oltmans@hockeyindia.
org<mailto:roelant.oltmans@hockeyindia.org>>
Date: Mon, Aug 1, 2016 at 7:42 AM
Subject: Re: Apartments in Rio
To: gupta.rakesh1952@gmail.com<mailto:gupta.rakesh1952@
gmail.com>

Cc: narayanan@olympic.ind.in<mailto:narayanan@
olympic.ind.in>, Dr Narinder Batra <drkuku@batra.ind.
in<mailto:drkuku@batra.ind.in>>, Elena Norman <elena.
norman@hockeyindia.org<mailto:elena.norman@hockeyindia.
org>>, "Cdr R. K. Srivastava" <cdr.rks@hockeyindia.
org<mailto:cdr.rks@hockeyindia.org>>
Dear Mr. Gupta,

Thank you very much to offer your TV to our team to be able to watch the Hockey matches during the Olympic Games.

As we discussed I've tried to rent more TV's but unfortunately they are sold out in the Village.

I would like to get permission to purchase 3 TV's to be able to follow the Hockey Competition in both the Staff Rooms and at least in one of the male and Female Apartments.

I also tried to rent more Chairs but at this moment there are no Chairs available in the Village.

Tuesday morning here might be a little chance but most likely there will be no Chairs.

We're pleased you've given us some Chairs but in the end we need proper furniture for all the Players.

Spending too much time in bean-chairs might occur back-injuries for the Players.

As mentioned in my earlier mail we need another 28 Chairs to avoid Injuries.

Please help us to fine a solution.

We all want our Hockey teams to perform weel but we need to support them as well with the right conditions.

kind regards,

[cid:image003.jpg@01D1EBFB.552D8420]

On 31-Jul-2016, at 11:27, Roelant Oltmans <roelant.oltmans@ hockeyindia.org <mailto:roelant.oltmans@hockeyindia.org>> wrote:

Dear Mr. Gupta,

As we discussed earlier today the Apartments of the Rio Olympics are no furnished properly.

For Athletes who have to perform at top-level during a longer period of the Olympics we need proper Chairs and Tables in the Apartments for 6 persons.

Actually there are only 2 Chairs in each apartment.

For men and Women we are using 9 apartments so there is a lack of 28 proper Chairs and for 7 Apartments we need at least one Table as well.

In the Staff Apartments we've managed to bring in some Tables.

You mentioned there is no possibility to arrange by IOA/Brasilian Organisers and there we need permission to purchase Chairs from the outside market to avoid Injuries during the Olympics.

During the Olympics we would like to give our Players the possibility to watch the Matches of our Competitors live on TV.

This will help the Players to prepare themselves for the upcoming Matches against these Opponents.

You allowed us already to contact Ren-COG to examine the possibility to rent TV's for the Men and Women and you're ready to pay for this rental service as well.

Thank you very much for your understanding.

Kind regards,

Roelant

In spite of these issues, Rio 2016 set up the road map for the years ahead. With proper mentoring under head coach Graham Reid, it should only be a matter of time before the Indians start delivering consistently on the world stage. 'India has beaten every major team in the last two years,' Narendra Batra told us. 'The fact that we have been able to host multiple world events in India has also helped, for it gives the players confidence. They are now exposed to the best facilities and no longer feel overawed when facing teams from the West. All we need now is confidence. We need to perform consistently at key tournaments and stop having intermittent bad days.'

Playing in the world league has helped and it can now be said with certainty that fitness is no longer an issue in the Indian team. The energy level of the players is consistent for the entire sixty minutes and they aren't apprehensive of facing any team in the world. Regular tours abroad have helped in giving them quality match practice. The 2020 Tokyo Olympics may very well be a game changer for Indian hockey.

Sreejesh, who continues to be the mainstay and is surely a contemporary great, alluded to this ahead of the series against Belgium in September 2019, which preceded the Olympic qualifiers: 'While we will be playing the qualifiers at home, there are always benefits that come with playing bigger teams like Belgium. It is the best preparation before an examination.'

'We have done everything we can to be Olympic ready,' said Batra. 'Now it will all boil down to how the boys handle the pressure and also an element of luck, which is essential in sports. If things start to go our way, there is no reason why the boys won't make the last four in Tokyo.'

While there is an outside chance of a medal in men's hockey, there is still some distance left to travel in the women's game. Qualifying for Rio was an achievement but it wasn't a surprise that the women struggled at the Olympics. While the current team has superstars like Rani Rampal, who is good enough to make any team in the world, the talent pool needs to be widened for the women's team to be consistently competitive at the global level. Under Harendra Singh and Sjoerd Marijne, two of the best coaches in India, there has been a significant improvement in the past few years. Yet, it's not enough to challenge the global superpowers of women's hockey. 'It is a process,' said Narendra Batra. 'We have committed a lot of resources to the women's game and it is now a matter of time before we see them making a real statement at the international level.'

TV AND MONEY

13

When Olympic Sports Lost Out

Cricket, Television and Globalization in India

One of the greatest tragedies of our hockey is that its most glorious phase preceded the era of live television in India.

—Shekhar Gupta, 2002[1]

Less than a week after India won the 2007 T20 World Cup in South Africa, news channels reported that four of India's hockey players and the assistant coach of the national team were going on a hunger strike.[2] The protesters, all from Karnataka, sat in a Gandhian protest outside the office of the chief minister of Karnataka to demand equal treatment as cricketers. This was triggered by the state government's decision to reward cricket player Robin Uthappa and then-national bowling coach Venkatesh Prasad with Rs 5 lakh each for their role in the T20 victory. The protesting hockey players also attacked the central government and state governments of Jharkhand, which had presented Mahendra Singh Dhoni, the cricket captain at the time, with a new luxury car. The governments of Haryana and Maharashtra were also criticized for showering their cricketers with similar gifts while ignoring the hockey players.

Justifying the strike, then national hockey coach Joaquim Carvalho pointed to the imbalance in the rewards for hockey players when they had won the Asia Cup shortly before the T20 win. During a live interview on Times Now, it became clear how offended he was:

We are not jealous of the cricket players. We are not against them
getting awards. We are also proud of them. We are simply saying that
hockey is the national game. Why do governments and politicians
not recognize our achievements? We just want the recognition we
deserve.[3]

Carvalho's point was underscored even further by the cynical response
of H.D. Kumaraswamy, the chief minister of Karnataka at the time, when
he declared that he would consider the hockey players for a reward only if
they won the World Cup![4]

There was a time when politicians would have been careful not to seem
callous towards Indian hockey. Now, there was not even a token statement
of support for the hockey players' predicament. It has become politically
beneficial to support cricket and not hockey.

It would have been unimaginable in the glorious days of Indian hockey
that cricket would supplant the game to such an extent in the national
imagination or that hockey players would be driven to desperate measures.

By 2019, India's hockey team and its support systems were significantly
better off than in 2007. Yet, there is no doubt that cricket rules the Indian
imagination. On every metric – popularity, prize monies and sponsorships
– there is a vast gulf between the overall status of cricket and other games.

The question is: why only cricket?

The Six Second Maharajah: When Cricket Was Not the Boss of Indian Sports

There is no evidence to show that cricket was any bigger in India than other
sports such as hockey and football before the 1980s.

In pre-Independence India, all three games became important playing
fields for the politics of identity and nationalist assertion. Some of the
greatest nationalist triumphs in colonial times came not in cricket but in
the other two games.

In football, the 1911 victory of the Calcutta-based Mohun Bagan Club
over the British East York Regiment was not just a sporting achievement
but also a nationalist milestone that spurred on the Swadeshi (indigenous)
movement. This is why contemporary commentaries on the victory focus
more on its social impact rather than the game itself. To cite one example,

Amrita Bazar Patrika pointed out that mental and physical strength was 'an integral quality of Bengalees' and urged Europeans not to consider them 'non-martial' any more.[5] Similarly, *The Mussalman* commented: 'The victory of Mohun Bagan ... has demonstrated that Indians are second to none in all manly games.'[6] But no one encapsulated the nationalist sentiment of the 1911 victory better than the *Nayak*, which pointed out that the victory would fill 'every Indian with joy and pride to know that rice-eating, malaria-ridden bare-footed Bengalis have got the better of beef-eating, Herculean, booted John Bull in that peculiarly English sport'.[7]

A measure of the centrality of football in the Bengali consciousness lies in Swami Vivekanand's oft-quoted remark, 'playing football rather than reciting the Gita will take one near to God'.[8] By the 1930s, the noted literary figure Sajani Kanta Das had noted that three things best described Bengali colonial identity: Mohun Bagan, Subhash Chandra Bose and New Theatres.[9] Until the time around Independence, football had a legitimate claim to be among the most popular spectator sports in India. As sports historian Mihir Bose has noted:

> While the Indians were fighting the British for their independence, one of the most popular games in the country was football. Logically after independence, football should have become India's number one sport. It is cheaper, it certainly permeated more layers of Indian society – even down to the semi rural areas – than cricket and as in other parts of the world, could have been a metaphor for nationalism.[10]

In sharp contrast to India's mid-2019 FIFA ranking of 103, the country began with a bang on the football field after Independence by winning gold at the first Asiad in 1951. India's barefoot players beat the booted Iranians in the final. Similarly, in the 1956 Olympics, India became the first Asian nation to enter the semi-final, eventually finishing fourth.

India's last great international football victory came in the 1962 Jakarta Asiad, when the team won gold, followed by a bronze at the Bangkok Asiad in 1970. Ever since, 'the unresolved dichotomy between the interest of the nation and club as well as the long-term failure of the AIFF/Sports ministry to appreciate the importance of professionalism and commercialism in Indian football' led to its terminal decline.[11] It is important to note that soccer always had a strong mass base in India – certainly no less than cricket – before television arrived and changed everything.

Similarly, the astonishing success rate of Indian hockey in the late colonial and early post-colonial period, when it won six successive gold medals at the Olympics between 1928 and 1956, turned the game into a symbol for Indian nationalism. This is clear from when the IOC toyed with the idea of dropping hockey as an event in the 1952 Helsinki Olympics and India went so far as to offer to host the hockey event separately in New Delhi.[12]

The success of the Indian hockey teams in beating Western teams demonstrated to the nationalists that Indians could compete on equal terms with the West. The success of Indian hockey was such that after Independence, the ministry of sports, not surprisingly, chose hockey as the official 'national game' of India.

The Board of Control for Cricket in India (BCCI) was only founded as late as 1928, a full four years after the formation of IHF. By this time, the hockey team had already won India its first Olympic gold. Anthony de Mello, one of the founders of the BCCI, pointed out that it was the pride of the Olympic gold that first ignited the desire to create an Indian 'national' cricket team:

Heightened by our hockey success at Amsterdam, our ambitions for Indian sport knew no bounds just then. We visualized our cricketers playing at the Oval, at Lord's ... and straightway was born in those of us connected with the game in India the determination, that sooner or later, it should happen.[13]

It was hockey that had initially caught the national imagination and it paved the way for cricket. Due to lack of popular support, 'cricket in India was far from being a flourishing national sport in the middle twenties.' With the exception of Calcutta, Madras and Bombay, there were few facilities for cricket across the country. Compared to other sports, cricket was still dominated by royalty, the British or by the elites.[14]

This is not to say that cricket was not popular. Ramachandra Guha and Mihir Bose, among others, have demonstrated the role cricket played in galvanizing nationalist sentiment from the 1880s onwards.[15] In the early twentieth century, the Bombay Pentangular tournament, for instance, was a huge commercial and popular success until it was shut down in the 1940s.

Yet, cricket was not the pre-eminent Indian sport that it has become today. Cricket in the late 1920s was more of a 'healthy cheerful adult' than a fully grown adult.[16]

Railways and Sports

Complete concentration and perfect coordination are the primary requisites of all sports. The Railways also call for the utmost concentration from every one of their workers and perfect coordination between them. The Railways and sports both bring together thousands of people from various regions and states and both forge links of friendship and brotherhood between people. The Railways and sports both have built up age-old traditions and both have become deservedly popular. Both aim at building a strong and robust nation.

Tie of Kinship

The playground is a nursery of inter-state fraternity. And it is h that a sense of kinsh springs up between the players and the spectators. Regional differences are no ba this emotional affinit is the Railway's huml but proud role to bri people together in fraternal association.

Even a pioneer of Indian cricket like Anthony de Mello saw the future of hockey and football as being much brighter than cricket until well after independence. In 1959, he observed that hockey and football, unlike cricket, were both mass sports:

> Soccer in India, like hockey, is a poor man's game. It is a game which most boys around the country play at one time or another – at school or in the maidan ... Thus there is a nationwide understanding of, and liking for, soccer, stronger than that for cricket, which has till now tended to be more a game for the rich man ...

Well into the 1960s, contemporary observers agreed that cricket certainly always had the 'glamour' due to its aristocratic roots, but its popular appeal in India was never more than that of hockey and football.17

Popular advertisements of the era serve as a great example for illustrating this point. From Air India to the Indian Railways, most public sector units until the 1960s used sporting metaphors in their print advertisements. Unlike the near-total saturation of cricket in sports-related advertising after the 1990s, the iconography of these advertisements of the 1960s largely focused on hockey, football or athletics.

For instance, an Eastern Railways advertisement extolling its role in building 'ties of kinship' and 'fraternal association' across regional divides drew parallels with how the playground was a 'nursery of inter-state fraternity'. The designers of this particular advertisement chose to put the image of a footballer in the foreground in front of a vast multitude of people.[18] Similarly, another Railways ad, on its role in promoting sports, noted:

> The Railways and sports bring together thousands of people from various regions and states and forge links of friendship and brotherhood between people ... Both (Railways and sport) aim to build a robust nation.[19]

The iconography of this particular advertisement gave as much space to hockey, football, tennis, athletics and boxing as it did to cricket. Even the famous Air India Maharajah, the airline's mascot since 1946, featured in advertisements in the 1960s that showed him as an Olympic athlete, running the mile in 'six seconds'.[20] If that same ad were to be produced today, it would be fair to guess that its copywriters would convert the six-second Maharajah into a six-hitting Virat Kohli.

The fact that advertisers could use the imagery of sports other than cricket to sell popular products is a significant marker of how different sports were perceived by Indians. Cricket wasn't in first place until television changed the very nature of Indian sports and nationalism.

THE INCREDIBLE STORY OF THE JWALAMUKHI 'MILLION': THE FORGOTTEN HISTORY OF HOW INDIA ONCE RECREATED OLYMPIA

Hidden amid the IOC archives in Lausanne is the intriguing story of the attempt to create an Indian equivalent of Olympia, in the town of Jwalamukhi. An Olympic torch is carried from Olympia to each venue of the Olympics every four years. Indian sports administrators emulated this practice for the XIX National Games of 1960 from the Jogmaya temple in the holy town of Jwalamukhi, near Hoshiarpur in Punjab.

The Greek ceremony was given an Indian twist with high priests chanting Sanskrit shlokas and lighting the flame from the temple's sacrificial fire. This was a deliberate strategy by the organizers to build local interest. Such was the popular interest in the event that the IOA's chronicler noted: 'As the torch emerged from the temple, there was a tremendous ovation from the crowd of 10,000 that had collected outside the temple.'

About 1,500 torchbearers carried the flame for the 350 kilometres from Jwalamukhi to Delhi over ten days. As many as a million people turned up to see them along the way.

The Jogmaya connection had given the Indian equivalent of the Olympic flame a kind of religious sanctity that fuelled the fervour. At Jullunder, for instance, the town hall, where the torch was kept for the night, became a 'virtual mandir' and thousands filed past the flame and 'made their offering'. In Ludhiana, on 18 February, as many as 50,000 people lined up on both sides of the Grand Trunk Road as the torchbearers made their way into the city. Such was the frenzy that policemen and soldiers 'found it difficult to control the rush of people who wanted to pay their homage to the flame'. When the torch reached Patiala, the effusive chronicler noted:

> ... almost the entire population of Patiala came out to give an unprecedented reception to the torch on February 20. The main bazaars wore a festive appearance unknown in the recorded history of that city ... at various corners in the city people distributed sweets. Milk, fruits and flowers were offered to the runners. Thousands of men and women filed past the torch at Yadavindra Stadium where it was kept for the night. [21]

Similarly, at Ambala city and Cantonment, 'all arrangements to control the crowds broke down' as the thousands gathered far exceeded the expectations of the organizers. From Panipat to Delhi, the Grand Trunk Road was lined with thousands as they came to get a glimpse of the holy torch that was to start the National Games.

Part of the fervour was certainly stoked by the sanctity attached to the Jogmaya Temple of Jwalamukhi, but no one doubted the sporting nature of the event. The ritual of the Olympic flame relay had been Indianized and the breathtaking response was a measure of the support that the National Games and Olympic sports had at the time, at least in north India.

CRICKET, INDIAN-NESS AND TELEVISION

The rise of cricket as the pre-eminent Indian game can be dated back almost precisely to when television began expanding. Television became a mass medium in India only during the 1980s. There were three intersecting factors that contributed to this: the creation of a national network of transmitters linked with satellite technology; Doordarshan's commercialization and resultant focus on entertainment; and economic reforms that made television sets cheaper.

Until the 1982 Asiad, Indians had never seen sporting events on television. The only way to follow any game had been via radio commentary. Now, for the first time, they could see their sporting heroes in colour. It changed everything.

India's dominance in hockey had been on a decline since the late 1960s. The first time the majority of the Indian audience watched the hockey team in action was when they lost 7–1 to Pakistan at the 1982 Delhi Asiad and the camerawork certainly didn't help the situation. For instance, Mir Ranjan Negi, the hapless goalkeeper on that day, later complained that the inexperienced Doordarshan cameramen never showed how he charged at Pakistan's defenders. The camera would only cut to the empty goal after he had been beaten in his charge and television viewers only saw an undefended goal post that seemed wide open to Pakistan's roving forwards. Negi never played a game for India after that day and for years was hounded as a 'traitor' who had 'sold out'. It got to the point where someone even cut the electricity at his wedding function.[22]

His story has since been picturized in the 2007 Bollywood blockbuster *Chak De! India*. The loss to Pakistan on television, watched for the first time by a national Indian audience, did irreparable damage to the image of Indian hockey across the nation. The tragedy of Indian hockey, as Shekhar Gupta points out, was that while television expanded, Indian hockey declined:

> Our last championship victory, the Kuala Lumpur World Cup in 1975, was telecast live but then all of India had no more than a thousand television sets, all black and white, and in the metros. Hardly anybody, therefore, would have seen the stirring image of Aslam Sher Khan, brought in as a desperate last-minute substitute to take a penalty corner, kissing his amulet before banging in the hit that took India into the final ... A sporting 'product' was needed to sell those wares, to consume the sponsors' and the advertisers' money, and hockey did not make the grade.[23]

A detailed breakdown of Indian hockey's performances supports our analysis. India lost only two games in the first three Hockey World Cups. Between 1986 and 1990, it won only one game. While the team has performed consistently at the Asian Games, it has languished at the Olympics and in World Cup hockey.

Table 13.1
Indian Performance at Hockey World Cups, 1980–2019

Year	Venue	Position
1982	Mumbai	5
1986	London	12
1990	Lahore	10
1994	Sydney	5
1998	Utrecht	9
2002	Kuala Lumpur	10
2006	Mönchengladbach	11
2010	Delhi	8
2014	The Hague	5
2018	Bhubaneswar	6

Table 13.2
Indian Performance at Asian Games 1980–2019

Year	Venue	Position
1982	Delhi	Silver
1986	Seoul	Bronze
1990	Beijing	Silver
1994	Hiroshima	Silver
1998	Bangkok	Gold
2002	Busan	Silver
2006	Doha	5th
2010	Guangzhou	Bronze
2014	Incheon	Gold
2018	Jakarta	Bronze

Table 13.3

Indian Performance at Olympic hockey, 1980–2006

Year	Venue	Position
1980	Moscow	Gold
1984	Los Angeles	5th
1988	Seoul	6th
1992	Barcelona	7th
1996	Atlanta	8th
2000	Sydney	7th
2004	Athens	7th
2008	Beijing	Did not qualify
2016	Rio	8

The decline in hockey standards began to turn spectators away at a time when television was providing opportunities for building an entirely new support base. In this context, Ramachandra Guha has argued that interest in football too began to wane after the telecast of the 1982 World Cup.

This was the first World Cup telecast live in India; alerted to the gap between their own local heroes and the great international stars, men in Calcutta began to turn away from their clubs. The slide continued; twenty years later, soccer ranks a poor second to cricket in the sporting passions of Bengal.[24]

The creation of a national network for the Asian Games coincided with India's epochal Cricket World Cup win in 1983. This, however, was not Indian cricket's first great win. The 1971 victory of Ajit Wadekar's team against England *in* England perhaps ranks higher strictly in terms of the sport. Wadekar's team was welcomed back with extravagant street parades in Bombay even though no one had actually seen them play.

The 1983 World Cup was different. Unheralded, inexperienced in the one-day format and led by a new young captain, Kapil Dev, the team, which became known as 'Kapil's Devils', was viewed by millions of Indians through their journey to winning the Cup. It is not surprising that this victory was followed by political felicitations that Wadekar's team and even the hockey players of an earlier era had never received.

The 1983 victory was followed by another victory in 1985 in the Benson and Hedges Champion of Champions Trophy in Australia. Again, television was the conduit, and for the first time, Indians saw the Australian tournament live and in colour. Interestingly, one can precisely map the rise of cricket with the increase in television penetration in the country. From 1983, the expansion of the television network became a key governmental priority. Between July and October 1984, for instance, practically one TV transmitter a day was commissioned.[25] As Fig. 14.4 demonstrates, starting from just one transmitter in 1971, eighteen had been set up by 1980. The graph leaps spectacularly in the early 1980s, with the total number of transmitters going up to 172 in 1985 and 698 in 1995. This expansion was accompanied by a simultaneous increase in the sale of TV sets. In the first decade of television, the number of TV sets increased from forty-one to 24,838. It took another twelve years for this number to cross the two million mark, but from the mid-1980s, the graph suddenly shot up and the makings of a mass medium become evident. By 1986, three million TV sets were being produced in India, including seven lakh colour sets and by 1992 the figure had reached thirty-four million.[26] 1992 was a watershed because that was the year when private satellite television first made its appearance.

It is no coincidence that the cricketers of this era, while not necessarily more talented than those of earlier generations, became the first brand names among Indian sportsmen. As television advertising expanded, companies were in search of heroes and found them in the national cricket team. Kapil Dev, Sunil Gavaskar, Ravi Shastri and Dilip Vengsarkar were hired to model for a whole range of consumer products, from shaving cream and toothpaste to clothing and English language guides.

Advertising was first allowed on television in 1976 but it only really took off in the 1980s with the growth of a national audience. The decision to allow advertising, the push to create a nationwide television network and the spread of colour television after 1982 all combined to create a new consumer spectacle. The rise of commercial television formed the basis 'for a new notion of collectivity, expressed as "the middle class" and based on the "idea of the democratization of aspiration"'.[27]

Figure 13.4 Growth of T.V. Transmitters[28]

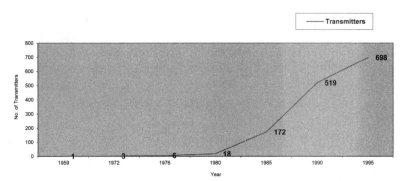

Television meant a turn for the new consumer economy. Ahmad Khan, head of advertising for Enterprise Nexus Lowe, said the following:

> ...what television did was that it opened, for a few million people, *whole new worlds* which they never knew existed. And it made them want and need things which they never bought before. So from just saving money for the sake of saving money, I think for the first time people said, 'Oh, I make money so that I can do things with it.' And this is something which I think happened for the first time in our history. I think that's what television did.[29]

Television enabled the circulation of commodity images on a national scale in a way that simply wasn't possible before. Cricket and cricketers played a key role in commodifying these images. It is no accident that the historical lineage of the Indian middle class as a political category can be traced back to 1985. That was the year Mani Shankar Aiyar, then a joint secretary in the prime minister's office, told the *Washington Post* that India had a middle class of one hundred million people and that they looked up to Rajiv Gandhi.[31] It was the first political articulation of the middle class as a social and political category and this was only possible in the context of a newly created national television network with an overt middle-class agenda, subsuming within it the state's lofty developmental objectives. This perception, in turn, fuelled television advertising and the focus on cricketers as the new heroes of the nation.

Fig. 13.5: TV Sets in India (1959–1992)[30]

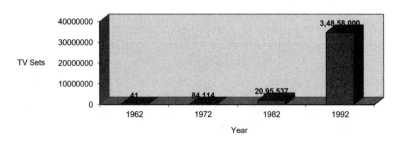

By the 1986 Asian Games, cricket had become so popular that a reader wrote to the *Indian Express*:

> The disgraceful performance of the 400-strong Asian contingent ... is not surprising when the nation's main sport is following the cricket score on radio and television. The result is that city children take to breaking window panes and noses ... Village children also have now taken to the Englishmen's game and dropped fast the Indian games ... Unless cricket is banished from this country, the rest of the sports would not get any encouragement, people would not do honest work in their work places and youth would not get adequate exercise.[32]

As cricket embraced the new charms of television, hockey, with a combination of bad performances, lack of administrative foresight and short-sighted planning continued to languish until cricket supplanted it. As Harsha Bhogle once said, 'Television is the seed that breeds sponsorships, ignites passions and carries sport across boundaries. Formula One has shown that. A seemingly monotonous sport with invisible drivers thrives solely due to brilliant television. Hockey can do more, much more, if it chooses to.'[33]

Globalization and the new economy were embraced by cricket while hockey administrators remained mired in old ways. The few times that Indian hockey did well, like at the Bangkok Asiad, its success was followed by administrative wrangling and internal discord.

Half the team in Bangkok, for instance, was sacked soon after it won gold because of differences between the players and the IHF. Hockey administrators have made belated attempts to embrace television, like with the National Hockey League on ESPN Star. However, as Rohit Brijnath put it, 'Cricket has settled on the mind and leaves little place and time for other pursuits. As a nation we are (now) guilty of a one-track mind.'[34]

'THE BATTERING RAM': SATELLITE TELEVISION AND THE CENTRALITY OF CRICKET

From 1991 onwards, satellite technology allowed private broadcasters to bypass the shackles of state control and their monopoly over television. Like elsewhere in the world, when global media corporations like News Corporation's Star TV arrived in India, they banked on sports to gain control over the local television market. And given the events of the 1980s, by sports it meant cricket. News Corp founder Rupert Murdoch had first demonstrated the immense commercial power of sports when he turned around the ailing Sky TV's fortunes in the United Kingdom by buying telecast rights for the English Premier League in 1992.[35] News Corp's various entities have consistently followed this strategy ever since – from buying television rights to Major League Baseball and American football to rugby league and union rights in England. In a speech to shareholders, soon after News Corp acquired Star TV, Murdoch outlined the importance of sports in his business plans for expanding into Asia:

> We have the long-term rights in most countries to major sporting events and we will be doing in Asia what we intend to do elsewhere in the world, using *sports as a battering ram* and a lead offering in all our pay-television operations. Sport absolutely overpowers film and everything else in the entertainment genre.[36]

Accordingly, News Corp chose cricket as the lynchpin of its strategy in India and ESPN announced its entry into the Indian market in 1993 by acquiring the exclusive rights to telecast the sport for five years for $30 million.[37]

This is a lesson that all major Indian broadcasters have learnt as well. Since the mid-1990s, the expansion of the Indian broadcast industry has been characterized by vicious wars over cricket telecast rights. India's well-documented transformation into the 'spiritual and financial heart of world cricket' during the same period was intrinsically linked to the infusion of television money.

CONFUSION AND THE SUPREME COURT: THE CRICKET TEST

As the torchbearer of satellite television, cricket has played a major role in the history of Indian broadcast reform and was the catalyst for the landmark supreme court judgement of 1995 that deprived the state of its legal monopoly over the airwaves.[38] That judgement, in one stroke, provided a legal basis for the burgeoning new economy of satellite television. All of this stemmed from a dispute over cricket.

The state's monopoly over broadcasting accrued from the colonial Indian Telegraph Act of 1885, which gave the central government 'the exclusive privilege' of establishing, maintaining and working telegraphs as well as the right to grant licences. Until 1993, Indian cricket had always been covered by Doordarshan. The crisis occurred when the Cricket Association of Bengal (CAB) sold the telecast rights of the five-nation Hero Cup to the multinational television company TWI. Doordarshan had failed to match TWI's bid and refused to allow the foreign broadcaster to uplink from Indian soil.

Claiming an exclusive right to do so under the Telegraph Act of 1885, Doordarshan accused the BCCI and CAB of being 'anti-national'. The Ministry of Information and Broadcasting condemned it as 'a diabolical move to violate the law of the land'. Soon after, customs authorities in Mumbai, under governmental instructions, confiscated TWI's broadcasting equipment.[39] Some media commentators immediately linked this to a larger crisis of the reform process itself:

> CAB will be bludgeoned into submission and somehow Doordarshan and the government will have their pound of flesh ... the next time Mr. Narasimha Rao (then-prime minister) and Mr. Jyoti Basu (then-West Bengal chief minister) go round the world seeking investments and much else besides, they must expect to be asked some searching questions.[40]

With TWI's equipment in the custody of customs officials, CAB appealed to the Supreme Court of India. In an important ruling on 15 November 1993, the court overruled the government and allowed TWI to generate its own broadcasts.[41] The case was urgent because its significance extended far beyond the game of cricket – the crisis of the Hero Cup seemed to jeopardize the 1996 World Cup, which was to be co-hosted by India, Pakistan and Sri Lanka. The South Africa Cricket Board had threatened to withdraw South Africa's support for the subcontinent hosting the tournament unless the wrangle over telecast rights was sorted out immediately. Following this, foreign broadcasting corporations were already demanding their money back from WorldTel, which held the World Cup telecast rights.[42] The issue of telecast rights threatened the loss of foreign investment and was at the heart of economic liberalization itself.

The supreme court's 1993 ruling, however, was limited to the Hero Cup. It did not solve the basic dichotomy of satellite broadcasters challenging Doordarshan's legal monopoly. Consequently, Doordarshan and the BCCI locked horns again in 1994 when the latter granted ESPN the rights to telecast India's series with the West Indies as part of a $30 million deal, which gave ESPN the exclusive rights to telecast cricket in India for five years.

Again, the BCCI appealed to the supreme court, which in an epochal judgement on 9 February 1995 ruled that the airwaves couldn't be a state monopoly as they constituted public property.

The court made it clear that it was the state's duty to see that airwaves were utilized to advance the fundamental right of free speech, which could not be done in a monopoly. The court said that the broadcast media 'should be under the control of the public as distinct from Government. This is the command implicit in Article 19(1)(a). It should be operated by a public statutory corporation or corporations ...' The judges further added that the fundamental right to freedom of speech and expression included the right to communicate effectively, including through the electronic media.

Ruling that the Indian Telegraph Act of 1885 was totally inadequate, 'intended for an altogether different purpose when it was enacted', the judges ordered the government 'to take immediate steps to establish an autonomous public authority ... to control and regulate the use of the airwaves'.[42] Thus ended the first Indian battle over broadcast reform. Cricket was the catalyst and the state lost its monopoly on television.

NATIONAL INTEREST: CRICKET AND THE LAST BROADCAST LAW

Cricket has become so central to Indian television that it was also at the heart of the second broadcasting law that India passed. This was the 2007 law on mandatory sharing of sports feeds. This is the only law pertaining to broadcasting that has been passed in Parliament in over a decade. On at least eight occasions since the mid-1990s, successive ministers of information and broadcasting who tried to bring in new broadcast laws had to take a step back in the face of strong opposition. Cricket, however, united parliamentarians like no other.

Its roots can be traced back to the 2004 India–Pakistan cricket series, when the ministry first forced Ten Sports, which had the broadcast rights, to share its live telecast of matches with Doordarshan to benefit non-satellite watchers. This seemed like a popular cause to espouse, but apart from acquiring these sports broadcasts ostensibly in the 'public interest', Doordarshan also wanted to make money by selling advertising spots. This was a serious threat to Ten Sport's advertising revenues and so its parent company Taj TV protested in a bitterly contested case in the supreme court.

The ministry countered in late 2005 through new downlinking guidelines that made it mandatory for private sports channels to share feeds of all major sports events of 'national and international importance' in the larger 'public interest'.[43] These guidelines directly affected free market considerations, and private sports broadcasters who had paid large sums of money to acquire the broadcast rights repeatedly challenged their legal validity in various courts through 2006 and early 2007. On at least three occasions, judicial rulings restrained the central government from interfering with their rights. In August 2006, for example, the supreme court ruled in favour of Ten Sports, which contended that it would lose Rs 80 million a day in advertising (for the July tri-series involving Sri Lanka, India and South Africa) if it was forced to share its signals with Doordarshan.[44] ESPN Star, which had exclusive rights for India's tour of South Africa in late 2006, also received protection from the supreme court for refusing to share its signals.[45]

By early 2007, the dispute between private sports broadcasters and the ministry had reached its boiling point. The immense confusion over legal structures meant that virtually every cricket series involving India was preceded by bitter court battles and tremendous uncertainty for viewers. In January 2007, Nimbus's initial refusal to share broadcasts with Prasar Bharati led to many cricket watchers missing the first few games of the India–West Indies series. Apprehending the anger of the average cricket fan, the central government, on 3 February 2007, promulgated an ordinance that turned its mandatory fee-sharing guidelines into a law. This became the Sports Broadcasting Signals (Mandatory Sharing with Prasar Bharati) Act that was passed by Parliament on 9 March. It stipulated a 75:25 revenue split between the rights holder and Doordarshan.[46]

The parliamentary debate over the bill reflected two things: the serious concern in the government over the legal challenges to its guidelines and the immense potential of cricket for building public and political opinion. Harnessing political support for an overall law on broadcasting was difficult, but when it came to cricket, things were easier. When questioned about the infringement on the private market, Information and Broadcasting Minister Priya Ranjan Dasmunshi repeatedly pointed to the public's right to watch cricket, though the bill itself was not cricket-specific:

> Cricket is a popular game of the masses ... A long battle continued in court to get the terrestrial rights. Fifty million TV homes depend on terrestrial television in the villages, semi-urban areas, even in the rural areas to watch the matches ... It was, therefore, a bounden duty of the Government to think [of] something which can justify the cause of the people in the greater public interest. We had to bring the Ordinance keeping in view that the World Cup Cricket is coming up ... one should also appreciate that out of the total fund generated through tickets in the whole world, more than 75 per cent is generated from the Indian market alone. But, the tragedy is that the Indian common viewers cannot see the match.[47]

The appeal to the rights of the cricket-watching public found favour with most parliamentarians, cutting across party lines. The response of Dasmunshi's predecessor, the BJP's Ravishankar Prasad, was typical:

> Cricket, today, is not only a game, but it is almost a passion in India ... We are one with you that the ordinary people of the country, who have got a simple antenna of the terrestrial [sic] should have the right to see the cricket matches because cricket, today, is not only an elitist game, but it has reached in rural areas also ... If there are 4.5 crores of terrestrial homes in the country, the people must have the right to view the games ... So, many litigations are going on. Therefore, in that way, our party appreciate(s) your concerns through this legislation. We are with you.[48]

The bill raised serious issues that were worthy of debate: the myth of Prasar Bharati's autonomy and its commercial advantages through state patronage, deeper questions about the validity of the state's right to rule on what constituted a sporting event of 'national importance' and the rights of private operators who had paid large amounts of money for broadcast rights through open market bidding. Nimbus, for instance, claimed it would lose 12 per cent of the projected earnings from its $612 million contract to broadcast Indian cricket over the next four years. But there was hardly a dissenting voice in the parliamentary debate as speaker after speaker reiterated cricket's 'uniting' potential and the 'rights of the common man' to watch the game.[49]

'MATCH KE MUJRIM' AND CRICKET AS A METAPHOR FOR LIFE

India's biggest sports broadcaster, Star India, currently pays Rs 60.1 crore per match to the BCCI for broadcasting matches of the Indian team played at home. It is part of a five-year Rs 6,138.1 crore deal the network won in a bidding contest in 2018. This is over and above the Rs 16,347.5 crore deal it won for IPL rights in 2017. Star has invested in other sports too – badminton, kabaddi and hockey – but nothing matches the pulling power of cricket. The success of its HotStar app, for example, accrues a great deal to cricket streaming rights.

The unrelenting drive to construct and capture a national market for maximizing profits led television producers to turn to cricket as the lowest common dominator of what might be termed 'Indian-ness'. But television's unrelenting focus, by its very nature, substantially redefined and re-enforced these linkages. In the days before digital apps, the narrow base of television ratings defined programming and cricket emerged as an easy option for success.

Cricket, along with Bollywood, has a pan-Indian appeal across socio-economic and regional categories. News of a small-town crime in Mathura may not interest anybody in Kerala but news of the Indian cricket team interests people in every region of India. Star India chairman and President of Disney Asia Uday Shankar draws a deep connection between cricket and national identity to explain its emergence as a prime attraction on television, even more so than Bollywood:

I think as far as Indian identity is concerned, cricket overtakes even Bollywood. While Bollywood is a big source of entertainment, its conscious articulation as an Indian medium by the common people is not so pronounced.

But cricket is perhaps consciously the most nationalistic activity that Indians indulge in. So to that extent, there is no cricket minus India. Every time that you watch cricket you are sub-consciously or consciously reminded of the Indian identity ... Now in terms of importance, cricket has left Bollywood far behind. It is next only to big political stories and really big economic stories ... And very often it overtakes political and economic stories as well.[50]

Shankar's comparison of cricket with Indian nationalism is revealing. This is a link that sociologists and historians have stressed ever since C.L.R. James inaugurated the discipline of sports history with the statement, 'What do they know of cricket who only cricket know?'

There is no doubt that cricket's hegemony on television is tied to nationalism, and television, for its own purposes, has played a big role. Arjun Appadurai noted:

...television has now completely transformed cricket culture in India. As several commentators have pointed out, cricket is perfectly suited for television, with its many pauses, its spatial concentration of action, and its extended format. For audiences as well as advertisers it is the perfect television sport.[51]

Cricket's sheer length and complexity make it one of the most tele-friendly games on the planet. For instance, a TAM study in 2002 found that in comparison to football, cricket offered far greater and more effective opportunities for advertisers, in the stadium as well as on television.[52] For television in general, cricket is a predictable news event, for which advertising can be bought and sold well in advance. The focus of television on cricket as a spectacle has reinforced the link between cricket and what Appadurai calls the 'erotics of nationhood':

...cricket, through the enormous convergence of state, media, and private-sector interests, has come to be identified with 'India', with

'Indian' skill, 'Indian' guts, 'Indian' team spirit, and 'Indian' victories, the bodily pleasure that is at the core of the male viewing experience is simultaneously part of the erotics of nationhood. This erotics, particularly for working-class and lumpen male youth throughout India, is connected deeply to violence, not just because all agonistic sport taps the inclination to aggressiveness but because the divisive demands of class, ethnicity, language, and region in fact make the nation a profoundly contested community. The erotic pleasure of watching cricket for Indian male subjects is the *pleasure of agency* in an imagined community, which in many other arenas is violently contested.[53]

Long before Star's 'Mauka' series of ads, which began during the 2015 Cricket World Cup, Star News started a programme called 'Match ke Mujrim' (Criminals of the Match).

Set up like a court trial, the show was telecast on the evening of every match and featured a 'trial' of four Indian players who did not perform well on the day. It was performed in front of a live audience and featured a prosecution attorney, former Indian captain Bishen Singh Bedi and another former cricketer as the defence lawyer. The two would present their case and ask viewers to vote on which Indian player was the villain of the day through SMS. Despite vehement criticism in the media, the show generated a tremendous response for Star News. On the day India lost the Bangalore test match against Pakistan, it was staged live out of a public park in the city and more than 10,000 people turned up at the venue. This was in addition to the twenty million or so viewers Star News claimed to have access to. For the Star News CEO who initiated this programme, the justification was simple:

For an average Indian cricket lover, a player doing something that costs India the match is the closest thing that comes to treason on a daily basis ...

When people are let down then, unlike in the case of politicians, who still people feel they can fix when someday the guy comes to seek their votes ... With cricketers they have no such comforts ... because cricketers in this country make so much money ... people feel the guy can still get out to a very casual shot and there is nothing I can do about it …We have channelized that popular anger in a very democratic forum…We felt it would be [a] good idea to give people a forum to vent their anger and their point of view …

The kind of interventions we make in other activities like politics, civic and municipal administration, economics … we have started doing that in cricket. In the same way that I would look at who's responsible for misery during Bombay floods … who is responsible for this goof-up in administration … Here we look at who is the culprit in the match.[54]

Indian news television is constantly searching for a national 'public' while attempting to create a national 'market'. 'Match ke Mujrim' encapsulated this process. It extends the link between cricket and nationalism to a seemingly logical conclusion – players are gladiators for the nation; if they lose, they are traitors.

The first non-sport channel to get into cricket was Sony's India arm, which in 2000 bought the telecast rights for all ICC-designated-one-day cricket for seven years. Sony, which until then ran a single entertainment channel in India, launched a second channel, SET Max, specifically to broadcast cricket. Having spent $255 million on the rights, Sony officials re-designed the network's entire branding around cricket. Kapil Dev was hired as brand ambassador, a series of cricket-related programmes were created around him and the network head made it clear that he expected Kapil to 'do for Sony Entertainment what Amitabh Bachchan did for Star'. A key aim of this strategy was to build programming that would draw in non-sports-watching viewers, with a special focus on families and women.[55]

Sony hired women presenters for its 2003 World Cup coverage, who were specifically told to avoid cricket jargon and 'be the voice of the cricket-widows' by asking commentators basic question about the rules of cricket. Cricket magazines railed against what they called the 'invasion of the dumb belles', but by the end of the World Cup, Sony's managers themselves were surprised by the ratings.[56] By the second week of the World Cup, 36.5 million women were estimated to have tuned in, nearly 46 per cent of the total viewership.[57]

The Sahara Group took the same route with the telecast of the 2006 India-England cricket series. With Sahara One, the group's flagship entertainment channel doing badly on the ratings, Sahara bought the television rights for the series, hoping cricket would encourage non-Sahara viewers to sample it. The network built a synergy between its entertainment programming and cricket by getting the lead actors of all its soap operas to talk about the cricket series during their shows. Sahara One's CEO explained:

> The ingredients of cricket are quite similar to that of a show on a general entertainment channel. There is drama, there is entertainment, anger and cheerfulness in cricket, which is there in all our soaps, too. Therefore, there is bound to be a great synergy.[58]

Sahara One's advertisement line, 'Television *ke begum aur* cricket *ke badshah ek hee* channel *pe*,' summed up this philosophy. (The queens of television and the kings of cricket, all on one channel.) Kerry Packer's 1977 World Series had initiated the process of converting cricket into a television spectacle, but in India this process has evolved more than anywhere else with television networks turning cricket into a continuing soap opera – a spectacle far beyond the game itself.

Cricket is now central to the idea of India and Indian-ness. This version of cricket, however, is very different from the gentlemanly imperial sport that the British had in mind when they first introduced it in India. India has appropriated and Indianized the sport. As the sociologist Ashis Nandy said, 'Cricket is an Indian game, accidently discovered by the British.'[59]

Pride plays a big part in the fierce competitive spirit that exists in the Services. Regiments and divisions have gloriously old battle honours and this is an incentive for proud rivalry, which cannot be matched on the 'civvy street'.[32]

Ambitious young commanders never overlooked this aspect. In a fighting force where pride and tradition dictated identity, defeat on the sporting field was always looked upon as a slur on a regiment's reputation, linked to notions of honour and never to be tolerated.

It is instructive that in his foreword to Dhyan Chand's memoirs, Major General A.A. Rudra chose to highlight what the hockey legend meant for his regiment. His brief note on a career that was characterized by breathtaking games for clubs and his country, mentioned only one game played for the regiment. Once, when playing in the final of the Punjab Indian Infantry tournament in Jhelum, Dhyan Chand's side was down by two goals to nil with only four minutes to go. Just then, his commanding officer called out, '*Aage bado jawan, kuch toh karo* Dhyan!' (Go forward soldier! Do something about it, Dhyan)

Dhyan Chand responded with three goals in four minutes to lead his team to victory. While the goals were a tribute to Dhyan Chand's own abilities, the incident also reveals the fierce competitive spirit of inter-regimental sport.[33] Dhyan Chand himself emphasized that annual tournaments were 'eagerly competed for' and that 'our officers felt very proud'.

Historians of the British Indian Army have documented that loyalty often accrued from personal ties in the feudal mode that were not necessarily based on the rank of the officer in question alone, but also his personal attributes. Respect had to be won and once given it was almost always undisputed. The independent Indian Army continued this tradition. In that sense, the use of the sporting field was more than just about the sport itself. It was a management tool. The Duke of Wellington, who attributed his victory at Waterloo to the 'playing fields of Eton', would have understood.

In a world before the evolution of the hi-tech battlefield, soldierly loyalties grew from elemental passions. A telling anecdote from an air defence regiment illustrates this beautifully. Brigadier Mehta recounts that while he was out on a war game, a non-commissioned officer (NCO) asked a young major where to place the anti-aircraft gun. The major wanted to sit in the shade so he simply ordered for it to be placed under a tree, conveniently forgetting the sheer uselessness of such a position for a gun that was supposed to shoot into the sky. When the NCO objected for perfectly valid military reasons, the major, also a burly competitive wrestler, simply responded: 'Don't talk too much with me. If you don't like it, let's wrestle and he who wins will put the gun where he wants.' That was the end of the argument. The gun remained under the tree and the major, whose conduct could justifiably be termed unprofessional, became the toast of the soldiers' barracks for his 'manliness'. On such talk are soldierly loyalties and ties of brotherhood sometimes built.

The Indian Army is by no means unique in its focus on sports. Between 1917 and 1919, the US armed forces too made sports and athletics central components of military life. Millions of enlisted men participated in organized sports at domestic training camps and behind the frontlines in France. So intense was this focus that one writer observed that 'Uncle Sam has created not only an army of soldiers', but 'an army of athletes'.[34] In the case of the US, the connection between sports and the military was a new one – after the Spanish–American war, a reformist generation of officers used sports as a means to combat 'desertion, alcohol and the lure of prostitution'. As one officer put it, 'There is no better way to make a good sailor and at the same time a loyal and true man to ship and country, than (through) these athletics contests.'[35] Accordingly, in this view:

> Civilian military officials embraced sport and athletics as the most efficient means to cultivate national vitality, citizenship and the martial spirit. Military training, infused with a heavy dose of sports and athletics, would not only train American men in the 'soldierly values' of obedience, citizenship, and combat, but would also usefully repair class schisms and restore social order and patriotism to the nation.[36]

The Americans were learning what the Indian Army had always known. The success of military sports during WWI surpassed all expectations and 'accelerated the development of a national sports culture'[37] in the US. Sports became an essential element of military training on the lines, suggested by planners since the beginning of the twentieth century. As early as 1906, one writer suggested that 'Uncle Sam has not encouraged athletics for amusement' but for the way in which it produced esprit de corps among

SPORTING SOLDIERS

14

The Army, Indian-ness and Sports
The Nation in the Olympic Ideal

THE INDIAN ARMY AND ITS 'MISSION OLYMPICS'

For years after he won a silver and India's only medal at the Athens Olympics in 2004, Colonel Rajyavardhan Singh Rathore remained a recruitment poster boy for the Indian Army. Right until 2008, his visage decorated a huge, virtually permanent Army hoarding at the entry to Delhi Cantonment, as one drove into the city from the international airport. The photograph on the hoarding captured Rathore's face in a moment of pure ecstasy as he kissed his silver medal, with the ceremonial olive wreath on his head. A caption below the photograph stated the following: 'Join the Indian Army, Be a Winner for Life'.

This was understandable, given that Rathore, who later got elected as a BJP Lok Sabha MP from Jaipur and served as sports minister in the first Narendra Modi government, spent years as a professional soldier in the Indian Army. What merits closer attention though is the discourse about the Army, the Olympics and Indian nationalism that followed India's failure to win more medals at the Athens Games in 2004.

Speaking at a public function in 2004, then-President A.P.J. Abdul Kalam tapped into popular sentiment about the continuing Olympic failures when he asked the Army to come to the rescue: '"Why are we not winning Olympic medals" is working on your mind. It is working on my mind also! ... Some countries use armed forces. If our army decides to use one brigade only for sports, we will have arrived in the international sports scene.'[1]

The Army responded by publicizing its commitment to a new programme called 'Mission Olympics'. This included recruiting young and talented sportsmen from around the country, giving them an army rank without involving them in military work and training them for the 2008 Olympics.

As far back as July 2001, after a similar debacle at Sydney, the Army created a sports academy – the Army Sports Institute (ASI) – in Pune with the funding of Rs 60 crore from the defence ministry's annual budget. The ministry's official website made the aims of this project clear: 'To restore national pride in the hearts of our fellow countrymen and to project a winning image of the Army, the Chief of Army Staff has availed of the opportunity to meet the challenge of the Olympics.'[2]

These moves came at a time of great hand-wringing in the mainstream media about India's 'humiliation' at the Olympics. In a comment typical of the media discourse in 2004, Chandigarh's *Tribune* bemoaned the lack of sporting success, equating it with national failure: 'A country of a billion people, but India is left to bite the dust even when facing competitions from countries like Moldova or Ethiopia at international arenas. Lack of proper training, infrastructure, planning and crass callousness of those at the helm have combined to ensure lackluster performance by Indians in the competitions as competitive as Olympics [sic].'[3]

Simultaneously, the Army's Mission Olympics was received by the press with virtually universal acclaim and praise that tapped into its credentials as a respected bulwark of the nation itself. A writer from the *Tribune*'s argued: 'If determination, dedication and discipline are the pre-requisites of success, the Indian Army has these in abundance. Besides, the Army has the advantage of accountability. So faith will not be misplaced if it is reposed in the Indian Army to win Olympic medals for the country.'[4]

In other words, this discourse believed that India's Olympic efforts had failed because of poor sports management and only the Army was capable of turning things around. A typical view expressed on an online discussion group run by a news website on the topic illustrated this point: 'I do expect a lot from the Army. It will be all the more better if the Indian Olympic

Association and its representatives are taken over by the Army. No one wants to see politicians involved in anything constructive'.[5]

This raises three issues about India's sporting discourse. First, the Olympics is clearly seen as a barometer of national pride and therefore viewed through a nationalist gaze. Second, Olympic failures are blamed on sports management bodies, which are seen as parochial and only interested in politics. Third, the Indian Army, perceived as an apolitical edifice of the nation, was seen by many as the last resort, capable of salvaging India's dream of winning Olympic medals. As such, India's engagement with Olympism is a useful entry point to understanding changing notions of Indian nationalism as well as the role of the Indian Army in a democratic Indian state.

What has been the Indian Army's role in India's Olympic movement and why has it become so central to it? The answer to these queries shed light on other crucial issues: Why are the Olympics so important to Indian nationalism? To what extent are differences in internal regional identities responsible for India's Olympic failures and why have nationalist sentiments not overcome these?

By fleshing out the history of the Indian Army's sporting engagement, this chapter provides a new understanding on the developing notions of Indian-ness, the constant struggle with centrifugal regional identities, the politics of identity in British India and the Army's transition from an imperial to a nationalist, apolitical force in independent India.

At its core, Indian Olympic sports are also a stage where competing Indian identities grapple with each other to impose their own hegemony. By focusing on the Army, we have a fresh lens through which we can look at existing debates about the 'the idea of India' itself and questions about how many Indias there are within the Indian nation-state.

SEPOYS ON THE PLAYING FIELD: 'THE PRINCIPAL SOURCE OF SPORTING INSPIRATION'

Most sports historians of India acknowledge the British Indian Army's role in inculcating the practice of modern sports in the furthermost corners of the subcontinent. Writing in 1959, pioneering sports administrator Anthony de Mello was unambiguous on this score:

The principal source in the history of modern India is the British Army, whose members, for so long stationed in our country, had introduced most of the games we play ... The inspiration for most of our sports came, as I have said, from the British Army.[6]

This claim was by no means an exaggeration. In the nineteenth century, at a time when virtually all Western sporting disciplines were being standardized into their present form, troops belonging first to the East India Company and then the British Army carried these forms wherever they went. This is true of virtually all modern sports associated with Britain, with the exception of rugby (India's hard grounds precluding that possibility). Sports and what became known as the 'games ethic' was a way of life and its cultural dispersion was inevitable.

The Army was its greatest conduit, simply by virtue of being the British organization with the greatest spread across the country. For instance, in the case of cricket, while most historians have traditionally attributed its organized rise in India to the Parsis of Bombay in the 1840s, there is now new evidence to show that the first Indians who took it up were sepoys of the East India Company. News reports published in the *Sporting Intelligence Magazine* brought out by the editor of the *Englishman* newspaper in 1833–50 document cricket matches played by Indian sepoys in places as far apart as Cuttack, Silchar, Barrackpore, Dum Dum, Agra, Cuttack, Midnapore and Sylhet.[7] These reports show that cricket was well established in the Indian heartland through the agency of the Army, well before Bombay's Parsi elites adopted it.

The early popularity of cricket among the sepoys was ascribed to the game's potential to bridge the differences between the European and the natives. A contemporary magazine report drew attention to this aspect of the sport, noting: 'Cricket is essential in improving one of the great defects, so often complained of, the distance of the Europeans in the intercourse with the native.' It goes on to suggest that European officers, from the senior to the junior, encouraged the game either as spectators or players. 'Were they not to do so ... I fear the sepoys would not long continue to play.'[8]

But once introduced, every cultural form assumes a life of its own. It is equally true that the sepoys in many cases were matching their English counterparts on the playing field. Contemporary descriptions of cricket in the East India Company Army maidans indicate that matches that pitted the native sepoys against European officers can also be seen as early historical prototypes of the fictional nationalist playing field depicted in the film *Lagaan*. As we have speculated elsewhere, 'It may be a mere coincidence that the cities and towns where sepoy cricket was fairly well developed were those which were prominent in the sepoy uprising of 1857.'[9]

Similarly, modern observers attribute the early spread of hockey to the British Army. While hockey, loosely defined, has historic antecedents going back to the stick games played by the ancient Greeks, it was invented in its modern form on the playing fields of imperial England. In his short account of the history of hockey, Chris Moore emphasizes that it was adopted in the empire:

> ... Mainly, it must be said because of the British Army which, in those imperial days, traveled widely in order to keep a watchful eye on all those red bits on the map. Wherever the army went they tended to take the British way of life with them. Including hockey. And that is how the game invented on the English cricket field came to be played the world over ... At that time the British Army was everywhere, looking after the far flung domains of the Widow of Windsor. Notably, of course, in India.[10]

It is no accident that the great Dhyan Chand learnt all his hockey skills on regimental hockey fields. Both Chand and his brother Roop Singh, who also served India with distinction, were soldiers. Dhyan Chand's father, Subedar Sameshwar Dutt Singh, also played hockey in the Army and had grown up in a martial ambience where physical activity was valued.

Dhyan Chand joined the First Brahmin Regiment in 1922, later transferring to the Punjab Regiment, and his real training began only after he put on the uniform. As he put it, 'I do not remember whether I played any hockey worth mentioning before I joined the Army.' His description of how he learnt the craft of the game illustrates the role of the Army in developing Indian sports:

> I shall tell you when I first started playing hockey. It was just an accident how it came about. When I joined the First Brahmin Regiment, we had a *Subedar-Major* by the name of Bale Tiwari who was a keen hockey enthusiast and a very fine player. He took a fancy to me.

DREAMS OF A BILLION

> My regiment was well-known in hockey circles, and hockey
> was the only outdoor game to which the regiment devoted most of its
> sporting attention. Bale Tiwari initiated me into this game and gave
> me my first lessons. He was my guru. We had no fixed times at the
> Cantonment to play hockey. We indulged in it at all hours of the day.[11]

The indulgence in sports stemmed from two reasons. At one level, it
was simply a consequence of British troops carrying their own culture with
them. However, it is equally true that the British Indian Army purposely
adopted sports as a means of inculcating esprit de corps among its troops,
native and European. In the case of hockey, one observer humorously noted
that part of its appeal was 'the wondrous chance it gave to privates and
lance corporals to hit the colonel indiscriminately while pretending to aim
the ball'.[12]

Whether the colonels were hit or not, there is no doubt that team sports
were seen by them as essential tools to develop bonds among men who
were expected to fight shoulder to shoulder, besides serving the purpose of
keeping them usefully occupied in peacetime.

In a colonial force where notions of kinship and izzat (honour) were the
key to inter-personal bonding, sports were, in modern parlance, a useful
management tool. In that sense, sports fulfilled a deeper social purpose
specific to the martial traditions of the Army.

So pervasive was the Army's influence on hockey that the Army Sports
Control Board virtually controlled Indian hockey affairs until at least 1928.
As Dhyan Chand was to record:

> … the IHF in those days was largely conducted by Army men; in fact
> the president of the IHF was Major Burn-Murdoch.
>
> There is a feeling in some ill-informed quarters that Englishmen
> did not do much for hockey in India. This is not quite true. For my
> hockey I am gratefully indebted to British Army Officers who not
> only took great interest in this game, but also played with us on all
> occasions forgetting their official rank and status.[13]

Dhyan Chand was not an exception as a successful soldier-sportsman
in colonial India. It is no coincidence that Sansarpur, a tiny village on the
outskirts of Jalandhar cantonment, produced as many great hockey players

as it did. When the British Indian Army took over the entire agricultural land of the village for building the new Jalandhar cantonment, it was thought prudent to not only introduce hockey as a means of keeping the village youth occupied but also to provide a source for fresh, physically fit recruits. Sansarpur emerged not only as a major breeding ground for the Army but also produced fourteen Olympians and perhaps 'the world's highest per capita of Olympic medals'.[14]

As late as 1996, when a *Sports Illustrated* reporter visited the village, he noted that the Army's legacy had deep roots. As a local told the magazine reporter, 'British Army brought hockey here at the turn of the century … The village's first Olympian was Colonel Singh in 1932.'[15] It would not be an exaggeration to say that the early rise of Punjab as the cradle of Indian hockey and the centrality of Punjabis in the Indian Army's recruitment after the 1857 Mutiny are not entirely unconnected.

While the pre-eminence of hockey in colonial Punjab is also linked to the patronage of the house of Patiala and the complex interplay of princely politics, in a state where virtually every village boasted of serving or retired soldiers, social conditions enabled the game's players to acquire a pedigree and a skill set that was passed on from generation to generation in the early years.

The story of Indian football is also similar, with the Army leaving a deep imprint in the early years. While it is impossible to ascertain when the game was first played in India, it is reasonably clear that it came with the East India Company. Football's early pioneers were 'officers and men of Trading Farms and Regimental Battalions', besides naval officers who used to play at ports of call like Calcutta, Bombay, Madras and Karachi.[16]

This is not to suggest that sport remained a preserve only of soldiers and men-in-arms. It is true though that the institutional foundation of football in India was laid by the defence-services-led Dalhousie Club in 1878, acknowledged as the oldest football club in India.[17] There were no organized tournaments until the Dalhousie Club showed the way in 1889. The club raised subscriptions from commercial houses and started the Trades Cup in that year. For four years, the tournament was the biggest event in the football calendar until the IFA Shield became the most prestigious tournament from 1893 onwards.

A little later, the Calcutta-based Indian Football Association (IFA) was affiliated to the English Football Association and it was only then that

Indian football found another home.[18] Yet, a deeper analysis of the politics of Indian football until independence reveals that while the IFA was now the nodal body, the British-controlled Army Sports Control Board continued to hold the balance of power in the management of the sport.

ATHLETES IN OLIVE GREEN: THE ARMY AND SPORTS IN INDEPENDENT INDIA

After Independence, the Army continued to play an important role in Indian sports, although its position in the post-colonial setting had changed. It was now an apolitical institution. The Congress nationalist elite that came to power in 1947 had always been suspicious of the Army's steadfast loyalty to the British during the years of the Independence movement and the Army was gradually weaned away from the pre-eminence it had hitherto enjoyed in the structures of power in New Delhi. At one level, this tendency was impeded by the sudden eruption of multiple threats from Pakistan in the years following the 1948 war over Kashmir, but the overall tenor of the time was to reduce the Army's perceived potential to intervene in politics.

As the Army was downgraded, the first three defence ministers – Baldev Singh, Gopalaswamy Ayyangar and Kailash Nath Katju – also became comparatively less influential with Nehru as compared to other powerful cabinet ministers like Maulana Azad and Govind Ballabh Pant. When Nehru's close confidante Krishna Menon was appointed defence minister in 1956, it did increase the ministry's profile but for all the wrong reasons. The Army top brass was so upset with his disdain for them that General Thimayya resigned as Army chief. It wasn't just about differences in perception and personal animosities. In real terms too, the Army found that Indian defence expenditure averaged a low 2 per cent of the GNP yearly, until the rude shock of the 1962 war with China.[19]

Be that as it may, sports continued to be central to day-to-day life in regimental maidans across the country. At least until the early 1970s, this ensured that the Army remained the dominant force in national competitions in most sporting disciplines.

As it turned from being imperial arbiter to national protector, its sporting activities too became very much an extension of its new role as defender of the nation. While it was no longer to play a direct role in the politics of sports per se, the Indian sporting arena itself could not have survived without the Army's quiet lifeline of talent and expertise.

The Army was so pre-eminent in Indian sports during the early years of Independence that in 1962, a piece in the IOA's official journal declared unambiguously:

> Little research is necessary to establish the fact that Services are today the backbone of the country's sporting endeavour. No fewer than nine of the major national championships in various branches of sport are held by Services teams or individuals today. Though still far from world standards the gap is gradually being narrowed.[20]

A roll call of the defence services' dominance in national sports in the first decade and a half of Independence proves this point. At least until 1962, the services held complete sway over national athletic competitions.

Milkha Singh, the greatest male athlete India has ever known, began his career as a cook in the Army and it was from there that he rose to the heights of the Rome Olympics. From 1956–57 onwards, the services dominated swimming as well. Services teams held the national basketball title for five consecutive years between 1957 and 1962 and the national boxing title between 1956 and 1962. In those early years, soldiers held the gymnastics title seven times and featured on the honours roll of hockey four times. They also achieved great success in golf, squash, volleyball, wrestling, football and cycling, winning a total of fifty-six national titles across all sports until 1962.[21]

Soldiers in Indian sports were so dominant that when the Sino-Indian war broke out in 1962, India was forced to withdraw from the Empire and Commonwealth Games in Perth that year. On its own, this was entirely understandable, given the great shock and humiliation that the country was reeling from at the time. But there was another reason for the withdrawal. As the IOA noted:

> Two reasons that must have swayed the Government were the release of foreign exchange and the fact that a great number of Servicemen would be on 'sports duty'. The composition of the team would have amounted to more than 50% of the contingent at Perth being athletes from the Services.[22]

Simply put, without the soldiers, there was hardly a national team. This is the true measure of what the services meant for Indian sports.

This is partly why in the national catharsis that followed the humiliation on the Chinese border, sportsmen from other professions were at the forefront of the effort to contribute to the emergency National Defence Fund created by the finance minister. Their efforts could not have matched those of the big business houses, but they still carried great symbolism: Balbir Singh, the 1956 Olympic hockey captain, donated all three of his Olympic golds; K.D. Singh 'Babu' offered to donate his 1948 gold from the London Olympics; P.K. Banerjee, India's 1960 Olympic football captain, gave away three of his gold medals from national competitions; Keshav Datt, who had played hockey for India in London and Helsinki, gave away his Olympic medals too; and S.K. Chatterjee, of the historic 1911 Mohun Bagan team which beat the East Yorkshire team to win the IFA Shield, gave away his gold medal from the club.[23]

The donations spree was not just restricted to Olympians: Sandhya Chandra, the national swimming champion, gave away her two national golds; Dilip Bose donated the Asian Tennis Championship trophy; Bengal's film stars organized a special cricket match for Indian cricketers to raise money for the war effort.[24] The likes of Uttam Kumar and Mala Sinha rubbed shoulders with Lala Amarnath in Calcutta to add impetus to the fund-raising drive.[25]

In addition, the pages of the official IOA journal were filled with fervent appeals for all sportsmen to invest in Defence Deposit Certificates – 'Lend to Defend' was the catchphrase. The IOA appealed to all sports associations across the country to hold special events to collect money for the Defence Fund, arguing that sport was 'the most popular form of entertainment in the country' and urging its members to tap into its monetary potential by showcasing top stars in special events.[26]

It is not known how much money was generated through this appeal, but there is no doubt that India's sporting community did its utmost to pay its debt to the Army in a time of national crisis. K.D. Singh 'Babu' once said, 'Since I won this gold medal for the country, I think its best utilization would be none other than the cause of the country at a time when the enemy is knocking on our door.'[27]

'ARMY OF ATHLETES': SPORTS, THE PSYCHOLOGY OF SOLDIERS AND THE MILITARY IDEAL

The Indian Army's evolution from a colonial force to the silent vanguard of the nationalist ideal in independent India is one reason for the stability of the modern Indian nation-state. Stephen Cohen, for instance, has shown that though the Army was never in any sense a major instrument for the liberation of the subcontinent, it nevertheless continues to have a profound influence on the polity.[28] More recently, Ramachandra Guha, among others, has identified the Army's steadfast professionalism and its divorce from overt politics as one of the reasons why Indian democracy endures, in sharp contrast to virtually every other post-colonial state.[29] The Army's cultural influence as a pan-Indian, disciplined and secular force has made it one of the staunchest pillars of modern India.

Its influence on Indian sports derives from the nature of the military force itself and the structures of governance that it has followed. After independence, these colonial traditions were re-labelled with the new aims of modern Indian nationalism. Yet, the Army's imprint on the sporting arena has so far been a forgotten footnote in studies of the Army and its wider role in the nation.

After Independence, the Indian Army continued its intense focus on sporting activity that it had inherited from the British. The Army's dominance in sports was not simply a function of its large numbers and facilities. The reasons for this are rooted in the sociological imperatives of creating a disciplined military force. Trained in the ways of dominant British culture, the Army's Indian officers after Independence continued in the British tradition of the 'games ethic' that saw sporting achievement as a form of character building and teamwork. There was something in the way of life of the Services that produced the kind of results that the Army's sportsmen delivered in the early years.

In the 'gentlemanly' world of the Army's elite, sports were seen as a form of social mobility. They were a means of inculcating regimental bonding among men whose fighting potential was supposed to depend on such fraternal ties. One IOA report noted:

After a hard day's work (life can be tough in the Services) the men let off steam in some sporting activity. The big advantage is that officers in charge of sport in battalions and regiments have a solid technical background. This means that novices are taught on correct lines. A promising sportsman is encouraged to specialize and in a few months a new champion is in the making.[30]

Sports were so important that they often became a key barometer of a regiment's izzat, a tool for building fierce pride among soldiers and the competitive spirit that was seen as a tool to weld diverse groups of men into cohesive units. The playing field offered officers a useful arena to bond with the men they commanded and to build ties of kinship. Obedience flowed from respect, and what better way to build respect than by rubbing shoulders with subordinates as equals on the field?

In a profession where following orders could sometimes mean certain death on the battlefield, astute commanders knew that the rigid bonds of army discipline needed the glue of personal bonding. This was particularly important for young officers who were expected to lead soldiers directly in battle. Brigadier (retd.) Rakesh Mehta, who captained the services' cross country team in the 1970s, said:

Men always look up to their commander. A hierarchy of kinship exists in the Army and this is strengthened in the sports field, especially if commanders play with the troops. It's the best place to get to know your men intimately. This is why there was always an emphasis on sports and particularly on youngsters. Your personality got built up on the sports field, in the eyes of the men and half your life as a youngster was spent on the playing grounds.[31]

Brigadier Mehta remembers that when he was commissioned into the Army in 1970 in the 144 AD Regiment, the respect and esteem of a fighting unit in soldierly canteens and barracks depended on its sporting prowess. Commanding officers saw the success of their regiments in sporting competitions as a way of raising their own profile and focused intensely on training athletes. In a martial world, 'manly' achievements on the playing field were highly valued and he remembers that in his regiment, virtually every officer, including the commanding officer, played in some team or the other. One of the key markers of regimental izzat was the laurels won in inter-regimental competitions. Another observer stated the following:

Pride plays a big part in the fierce competitive spirit that exists in the Services. Regiments and divisions have gloriously old battle honours and this is an incentive for proud rivalry, which cannot be matched on the 'civvy street'.[32]

Ambitious young commanders never overlooked this aspect. In a fighting force where pride and tradition dictated identity, defeat on the sporting field was always looked upon as a slur on a regiment's reputation, linked to notions of honour and never to be tolerated.

It is instructive that in his foreword to Dhyan Chand's memoirs, Major General A.A. Rudra chose to highlight what the hockey legend meant for his regiment. His brief note on a career that was characterized by breathtaking games for clubs and his country, mentioned only one game played for the regiment. Once, when playing in the final of the Punjab Indian Infantry tournament in Jhelum, Dhyan Chand's side was down by two goals to nil with only four minutes to go. Just then, his commanding officer called out, '*Aage bado jawan, kuch toh karo* Dhyan!' (Go forward soldier! Do something about it, Dhyan)

Dhyan Chand responded with three goals in four minutes to lead his team to victory. While the goals were a tribute to Dhyan Chand's own abilities, the incident also reveals the fierce competitive spirit of inter-regimental sport.[33] Dhyan Chand himself emphasized that annual tournaments were 'eagerly competed for' and that 'our officers felt very proud'.

Historians of the British Indian Army have documented that loyalty often accrued from personal ties in the feudal mode that were not necessarily based on the rank of the officer in question alone, but also his personal attributes. Respect had to be won and once given it was almost always undisputed. The independent Indian Army continued this tradition. In that sense, the use of the sporting field was more than just about the sport itself. It was a management tool. The Duke of Wellington, who attributed his victory at Waterloo to the 'playing fields of Eton', would have understood.

In a world before the evolution of the hi-tech battlefield, soldierly loyalties grew from elemental passions. A telling anecdote from an air defence regiment illustrates this beautifully. Brigadier Mehta recounts that while he was out on a war game, a non-commissioned officer (NCO) asked a young major where to place the anti-aircraft gun. The major wanted to sit in the shade so he simply ordered for it to be placed under a tree, conveniently forgetting the sheer uselessness of such a position for a gun that was supposed to shoot into the sky. When the NCO objected for perfectly valid military reasons, the major, also a burly competitive wrestler, simply responded: 'Don't talk too much with me. If you don't like it, let's wrestle and he who wins will put the gun where he wants.' That was the end of the argument. The gun remained under the tree and the major, whose conduct could justifiably be termed unprofessional, became the toast of the soldiers' barracks for his 'manliness'. On such talk are soldierly loyalties and ties of brotherhood sometimes built.

The Indian Army is by no means unique in its focus on sports. Between 1917 and 1919, the US armed forces too made sports and athletics central components of military life. Millions of enlisted men participated in organized sports at domestic training camps and behind the frontlines in France. So intense was this focus that one writer observed that 'Uncle Sam has created not only an army of soldiers', but 'an army of athletes'.[34] In the case of the US, the connection between sports and the military was a new one – after the Spanish–American war, a reformist generation of officers used sports as a means to combat 'desertion, alcohol and the lure of prostitution'. As one officer put it, 'There is no better way to make a good sailor and at the same time a loyal and true man to ship and country, than (through) these athletics contests.'[35] Accordingly, in this view:

> Civilian military officials embraced sport and athletics as the most efficient means to cultivate national vitality, citizenship and the martial spirit. Military training, infused with a heavy dose of sports and athletics, would not only train American men in the 'soldierly values' of obedience, citizenship, and combat, but would also usefully repair class schisms and restore social order and patriotism to the nation.[36]

The Americans were learning what the Indian Army had always known. The success of military sports during WWI surpassed all expectations and 'accelerated the development of a national sports culture'[37] in the US. Sports became an essential element of military training on the lines, suggested by planners since the beginning of the twentieth century. As early as 1906, one writer suggested that 'Uncle Sam has not encouraged athletics for amusement' but for the way in which it produced esprit de corps among both officers and enlisted men – 'a rebuilding process which begins when the soldier puts on the blue or khakhi'.[38] This is precisely the planning principle that is at the heart of life in the Indian defence services.

'SCRAPE THE BOTTOM OF THE BARREL': A CREAKING ARMY AND THE DECLINE OF SPORTS (1989–2019)

When the 436 Air Defence Missile Regiment was raised in 1985, the first task its commanding officer Colonel V.B. Mohan faced was to establish its reputation in a brigade full of illustrious old regiments. He responded by identifying good sportsmen among his new recruits and putting them into training. Within a year, these new sportsmen were winning inter-regimental tournaments, heralding 436's arrival in a pantheon of old regiments. Brigadier Mehta, who was one of Colonel Mohan's battery commanders, explained to us that the sportsmen became the 'pride of the regiment'. Competitive sports, as he put is, were 'a way of projecting the CO and the Regiment's personality in the Army.'

All this changed drastically in the late 1980s. Since then, the Indian Army has seen an unprecedented level of troop commitment. Up to four divisions were deployed in Sri Lanka from 1987 until their withdrawal in 1990. The north-eastern insurgencies required even greater troop deployment and so did Punjab until 1993, with Operation Rakshak. But the greatest challenge came from the militancy in Kashmir from 1989 onwards. A large number of troops are always actively deployed in Kashmir – on the Line of Control, in Siachen and in counter-insurgency operations. Then there are the 67,000 or so troops of the Rashtriya Rifles, the specialist counter-insurgency force raised in 1990 under the home ministry. It was raised to reduce the internal policing burden on the Army but has ended up being composed predominantly of Army officers and soldiers on deputation.

Since the mid-1990s, in order to ease the burden on infantry units, it has been mandatory for every young officer in the support services like the Army Supply Corps, Signals and Ordnance to serve a term in the Rashtriya Rifles. Furthermore, several thousand troops remained actively involved in counter-insurgency operations in the north-eastern states for years. Most observers agree that the heavy payload of internal security duties has meant that the 'Indian Army had to scrape the bottom of the barrel to meet this sudden rise in military commitments'.[39] In the words of a former general:

The Army rose to the challenge magnificently in this period of turbulence. But, it did not remain unscathed. Prolonged operational deployments in the most adverse conditions took a heavy toll. Not merely in morale and well being of the Force, but also in its effort at modernization ... There continued to be a clamour for more troops. Not only from the military commanders, but also from political leaders from the regions, who saw the Army as the first as well as the last resort when everything else seemed to fail.[40]

The extra burden has been compounded with other sociological and economic developments that have led to a severe shortage of officers. The shortage went up from 17.31 per cent in 1986 to 28.18 per cent in 2000 (12,883 officers) because young men did not see it as a lucrative career anymore.[41] By 2019, as Defence Minister Rajnath Singh informed Parliament, the Army was short of 7,399 officers (over 14 per cent of its sanctioned strength) and 38, 235 other ranks. With the liberalization of the economy opening up lucrative options, the Army, which had always attracted 'gentlemanly elites' until well into the 1970s, didn't seem to be attracting enough Indians at the officer levels.[42]

In an institution stretched to the limit by its professional demands, sports have had to take a backseat. The Army's dominance in Indian sports gradually declined from the 1980s as a direct function of its own changing profile and its growing entanglement in internal security duties.

An anecdote from 31 Armoured Division tellingly illustrates this point. When Major General G.D. Singh took command, he issued orders for a new inter-regimental sporting competition within the division. This was a departure from the usual inter-brigade competitions at the division level. As part of his efforts to build fraternal ties across his command, even a ladies' sports meet for army wives was organized in Jhansi. But the sting was in the tail. Orders were issued that regiments not taking part in the competition would have to pay a monetary fine that would go into the division's private discretionary fund. The order reflected the apprehension of regimental teams simply not turning up. Sporting competition once helped define regimental pride but now the threat of fines was needed to ensure participation. It is not that commanding officers did not want to participate. They simply did not have enough resources, time or men to spare for regular training. For example, regiments that had been operating with fifty to sixty officers each in the 1970s were now operating with only fifteen or sixteen. Where was the time for specialized sports? But orders had been passed, so some regiments simply scraped together a team as a formality.[43]

The professional landscape for the average Army officer has changed drastically. If Colonel V.B. Mohan had raised a regiment in the 2000s, he would not have had the time or the personnel to focus on sporting glory.

The Army's changing orientation has had a drastic impact on its sporting achievements. In the 1960s and 1970s for instance, teams like the Signals, ASC and the Guards were prominent contenders in national hockey. In recent years, however, services teams have not been the dominant force they once were in national sports. The Army continues to play sports but the exigencies of its professional pressures mean that specialization and the competitive edge at the national level have gone down. Competitive sports demands time, dedication and specialized training. Earlier, commanding officers could encourage and cajole their men to indulge in it. In peacetime, professional reputations, after all, were built on such men.

Now, though the pride and the intent remain (witness the special celebrations in Colonel Rajyavardhan Singh Rathore or Vijay Kumar's regiments when they won Olympic silver medals in 2004 and 2012 respectively), professional reputations increasingly depend on the battlefield, even in the peacetime.

Hard-pressed and undermanned commanding officers, having to choose between soldiers who fight and soldiers who play, are loath to let their men off for training. Budding Army sportsmen often have to make the difficult choice between a military career and sporting success.

COLONEL RATHORE, HONORARY CAPTAIN VIJAY KUMAR AND MISSION OLYMPICS

When Colonel (then Major) Rajyavardhan Singh Rathore won the silver in the double trap event in Athens, finishing behind the UAE's Sheikh Ahmed Al-Maktoum, his success brought to everyone's attention the silent role of the Army in India's sporting endeavors more than ever before. In a nation starved of Olympic success, Rathore, in his first triumphant comments, touched upon a theme that was to become the staple feature of the discourse around the Army and sports in days to come: 'That is what we army officers

are there for – to make our country proud.'[44] A closer analysis shows that
Rathore is as much an example of what is right with the Army's sports as
what is wrong with it.

Rathore, a graduate of the 77th NDA course, passed out with a sword
of honour from the Indian Military Academy before being commissioned
into 9 Grenadiers.[45] Military training gave him his first lessons in shooting
and he served with the Grenadiers in 1994–96 in the volatile Baramulla
and Kupwara regions of Kashmir.[46] The demands of military service meant
that he did not take up competitive shooting until 1998. In the selection
trials for the Mavalankar competition, he participated in double trap, trap
and skeet and won two gold and one silver medal. He was then advised
to concentrate on double trap. 'Initially, there was no one to help him and
he would watch seniors shoot and try to rectify his faults and mistakes.'[47]
While honing his skills at the Army Marksman's Unit in Mhow, Rathore
asked for a posting in Delhi.[48] His mother, Manu Rathore, hints at the
difficult choice the young major had to make at that early stage of his
shooting career:

> He chose to be posted at Delhi so that he could train without
> interruptions. *He did not even bother about his promotions.* All this while,
> Gayatri (his wife) has been with him, providing him support and
> comfort. She has been his pillar of strength, sharing his problems and
> calming him when the going got tough. She has been managing his
> schedule, booking his tickets and hotel rooms. In Italy, she would sit
> in the basement with the machine, pulling targets and assisting him.[49]

No sportsman can be a stranger to personal tales of sacrifice and hardship.
But Rathore's tale holds a lesson in the strengths and the limitations of the
Army's potential for creating world-class champions.

The Army did support Rathore and its facilities provided him the
bedrock for his early grooming. But to go beyond that and compete with
the best global sportsmen, you need wider exposure and the opportunity
to train with the best. Rathore succeeded on the strength of his own drive
but he was later to gently mention the kind of expert help that was sorely
needed for Indian sportsmen in government service:

> ...there should be a set of people who should be entirely coordinating
> with these top few shooters where they want to train, how they want

to train, with whom they want to train, which competitions they must shoot as training and which competitions they must shoot to win.

If they are having problems at home those problems must be sorted out, because sportsmen, especially shooters, would not be able to concentrate if he has got a family problem. If there are any administrative problems, then the government can easily solve them.

For example, it could be related to somebody's posting. An athlete may not be happy at the Railways; then move him to where he wants, because this is for a national cause. This is just giving an example of how the government can come forward and help.[50]

Long before he won the Olympic medal and became a national hero, Rathore had already won gold at the 2003 World Cup in Sydney. Yet, it took a full year even after Athens for Rathore to get the Army's permission to sign up for the endorsement contracts that were coming his way. In a world where sporting success is based on specialized training, the Army's seclusion from the wider global structures of sports was jarring. The best training facilities abroad cost money, which could come in by way of endorsements. As advertisers lined up outside his door, Rathore had to wait for the defence ministry's approval.[51] He could have chosen to leave the Army but he did not. When the permission came, he chose to share his money with the Army:

> Fifty percent of my endorsement money goes to the Indian Army. It'll use it to promote sport. I have great regard for General Joginder Singh, who stood up to this changed environment, thought out of the box and has set a healthy precedent.[52]

Conditioned to working in splendid isolation, a tradition-bound Army moved slowly towards embracing the new global reality of sports as a commercial enterprise. Even though Rathore was all praise for the Army's support, the fact is that even a national hero like him had to wait his turn. Imagine the challenges faced by lesser-known sportsmen. Soon after winning his Olympic medal, and long before he became sports minister, Rathore expounded on this theme:

> I have always stated that the entire Olympic movement in India is alive because of government support, and that stands true … a

lot that I have achieved is courtesy to the funding provided by the government.

Yet, a lot needs to be done to improve not only the sport of shooting, but other Olympic sports also. *The progress towards improvement is slow and at this speed it will take us ages to win the number of medals that India should actually be winning.* A lot of things need to be done, and need to be done faster. There are a lot of policies, a lot of directions, which are in place, but the execution is lacking.[53]

The permission for Rathore to cash in on his brand image came partly due to the ministry of defence's realization that Rathore could be used to show the Indian Army in a 'positive light'. Therefore, he was to only take up endorsements that would project 'the image of the nation and image of the Army in good light'.[54] This explains the Army billboards of Rathore at the time and his projection in the recruitment drive for officers.

Compare this to the experience of Honorary Captain and Subedar Major Vijay Kumar, who also trained at the Army Marksmanship Unit (AMU) at Mhow, before winning a silver in the individual 25 metre rapid fire pistol event at the London Olympics in 2012. He joined the Army's Dogra Regiment as a soldier in 2001 and was attached with the AMU from 2003 onwards, where he was coached by Russian Pavel Smirnov for some time.

When we asked him about how he became a shooter, Vijay's response was unequivocal: 'The Army made a great contribution. When I went for Army training, the instructors there chose me for sports. I had never done shooting before. When I first fired with a service gun, as we were all made to do, they told me that I was a little better than the others. And they chose me specifically for sports. They picked me out and that is how I started out my sports career. I was selected on the basis of my shooting with a service gun and then shifted to sports guns. This was all done by the Army. As you rise up the ladder, they provide what you need: guns, coaches, better facilities. It all depends on your achievement and your growing speed. You look at the number of players over the years in any discipline – hockey, athletics, horse riding, rowing, shooting – and there is no other organization that compares with the Army, which does so much for sports.'

By the time Vijay started shooting for India, Rathore had won his silver in Athens. That had a big impact on him. He said, 'It was the first time we got to know that there was an Olympics as well. Otherwise, you don't get to know about possibilities of higher achievements. When you see one of your own winning, you think, "yes, we can also win it." Before this, there was no Olympic medal in shooting. There was one in tennis by Leander that I knew of. Rathore's medal showed us the possibility. When you meet a person who has won like that, you think that he is like you; that he is not extraordinary. The only thing is that he worked hard. When you get friendly with a person like that, your own confidence builds up.'

That training took him to the Olympics podium but eventually also exhausted the limits of what the Army could offer. He told reporters a week after he won his Olympic medal in 2012: 'Indian army helped me in shooting by giving me coaching facilities and providing me with pistol and ammunition but I need money for my daily needs … Since 2006 I won many national and international medals that includes 2010 Commonwealth Games' three gold and one silver medal. But I have not been recommended by my seniors. I have not been given any promotion or honorary award or any other kind of facility.'[55]

We asked Vijay in 2019 about his seeming post-2012 dissatisfaction with the Army and if he wanted to quit soldiering after London, as several media articles had indicated at the time. No, he had never wanted to resign, he clarified. 'The point was that I was asking and requesting why the Army should not promote a person who had won at the Olympics? When other organizations or states promote their own players to higher ranks, why can't this be done in the Army also? I was expecting that they would do it the same way. But people started saying that I want to quit. I wasn't willing to quit. I was only asking. Maybe they should have done it without asking. That was my point. But some people started taking it wrong way. I told them about this the moment I landed back in Delhi and went back to my unit. They asked me, "you want to quit?" I said no, I was only suggesting that based on what I had achieved, I should get what others were getting.'

Vijay was eventually promoted to the rank of subedar major and honorary captain. He also won a Padma Sri and a Rajiv Gandhi Khel Ratna award before finally retiring from the Army at the age of thirty-two in 2017. Two years later he was given a job as a deputy superintendent of police by his home state of Himachal Pradesh. 'My file was pending for two years and after a two-month foundation course in Shimla, I am training now in Palampur,' he told us on the phone in August 2019, while he was still at his police training. His journey encapsulated both the possibilities and the limitations of professional sportsmen within the Army's structures.

Rathore and Vijay Kumar's success came soon after the Army's widely publicized plan for creating Olympic champions was put into practice. In 2001, then-Army Chief Gen S. Padmanabhan, concerned about the lack of Olympic success, set up the ASI in Pune under Colonel Naik, a former Asian Games gold medallist in rowing. Naik visited sport institutes across the country to study their shortcomings and set about creating a sporting academy of international standards. Key sports disciplines were identified and his officers then recruited budding youngsters from across the country. The idea was to find talented elite sportsmen from within the Army as well as getting in younger children between the ages of eight and fourteen years who had excelled at the sub-junior and junior levels. They were offered positions as cadets to train in specially designated Boys Sports Companies.

Their living costs – travel, clothes, food and other essentials – became the responsibility of the ASI, which was run on a Rs 60 crore allocation from the defence ministry. According to Naik, the training had one aim: 'We want them to remember at all times that they are here to get India an Olympic medal'.[56]

By itself, such an academy is not novel. The Chinese have had such training mechanisms aimed at Olympic glory for a while now, as have the Australians. What is unique about India is that the Indian Army that took the lead here, in consonance with its wider objective of safeguarding national notions of pride and honour. The move was greeted with widespread media approval, with one reporter calling it 'an emergency rescue act by the Army'.[57] According to the Army, 'The potential candidates are selected primarily based on performance in a structured selection process, without any reservation/quotas of any kind'.[58]

In some ways, the new Olympic mission of the Army was built on a long-standing tradition of sporting talent at various regimental training centres. For instance, the Punjab Regiment artillery and engineers had always followed the practice of hiring talented children from their recruiting bases under special Boys Sports Companies with a view to building their own talent pool. They were later recruited as soldiers. The ASI simply borrowed this template. The difference was that this time, the Olympics was the explicit goal, not just regimental glory.

By mid-2019, over 300 athletes and 1,200 cadets in Boys Sports Companies were training in the Army's various establishments nationwide. Its Mission Olympics Wing has five nodes. These include the ASI in Pune (athletics, archery, boxing, diving, fencing, weightlifting and wrestling), Army Marksmanship Unit in Mhow, Army Yatching Node at Mumbai for sailing, Army Rowing Node in Pune and the Army Equestrian Node in Meerut. Four ASI athletes – the archers Subedar Tarundeep Rai and Havildar Pravin Jadhav, the walker Havildar Irfan (20 km walk) and the para-athlete Anandan G. – qualified for the Tokyo Olympics by September 2019. Boxers like Amit Pangal are also expected to carry Indian hopes. While the Army doesn't have a specific budget for Tokyo 2020 in particular, it allots approximately Rs 15-20 crore each year for these sporting facilities.

There are three weaknesses to this system. First, the Mission Olympic Wing has no outside non-defence sportspersons training with it, apart from 100 cadets funded through the government's Khelo India initiative.

Second, sports requires specialization and domain experts who work with systems. But under the Army's tenure policy, officers keep getting posted elsewhere. One senior Army sports administrator told us: 'They don't realize that all those things work for routine army work, but when it comes to specialization in sports, it may not work that way. The new guys come in as a routine and may not have the clarity for a specific assignment. So, a lot of good officers moved on and that is how the sports program can suffer or lose focus because officers also have to look at their careers.'

Third, a lot of new talent has stopped coming in because several states now offer a lot of incentives if you are a sportsperson. A senior officer told us, 'In Haryana if you win a medal, you could become a Deputy Superintendent of Police to start with. You saw Vijay Kumar's case where he saw the promotions others were getting. Similarly, a lot of good boxers skip the Army now to join Haryana Police. To retain and groom talent, we have to take a holistic view. This includes promotion avenues so we can see if these are on par with the civilian set-up or with opportunities outside. A lot of this depends on the leadership.'

While the Army's overall sporting effort is admirable, the drawback is that it remains largely closed to outsiders or outside influences. Its facilities are largely restricted to Army men and women alone.

This begs the question: would it not make a big difference if civilian medal hopefuls were also given the opportunity to use the facilities and the equipment at the Army's excellent shooting ranges if an appropriate cost-sharing system was worked out? In 2007, for example, National Cadet Corps (NCC) cadets stood second in the junior shooting national championship, second only to the Army, winning thirty-four medals in various categories.[59] Many of its young shooters beat Army marksmen, but there was no institutionalized mechanism to adopt them for further training in either the armed forces, the para-military forces or the state police forces. Most of these NCC shooters came from low-income backgrounds and without institutional support, much of their talent was lost to India.

This is crucial, given the breeding ground the Army continues to provide for Indian sport. Sixteen per cent (eleven of sixty-six) of Indian medals at the 2018 Asian Games, for example, came from Army soldiers. The ASI itself enabled participation of two Indian Olympians in 2004 in Athens, one in the 2008 Beijing Olympics, eight at the 2012 London Olympics and nine at the 2016 Rio Games.

Of these, Subedar L. Debendro Singh finished closest to an Olympic medal in 2012 when he stood fifth position in Boxing (49 kg). In the last two decades, the ASI claims to have won 937 international medals and 4,544 national medals.

Greater coordination between sports associations, the government machinery and the Army is a must. Sports minister Kiren Rijiju said while visiting the ASI in July 2019, 'I have tried to pick up some of those institutes and centres where we have the best potential and where we can get immediate results from. These are those low-lying fruits that we need to pick. The ASI is well known and has given us results also. I am impressed with the way the Army has managed and given all kind of support to produce world-class athletes. We will see what we can do with the ministry and the Army to improve the centre further ... This is one of the few centres in India which we are dependent on for medals at international meets.' He was spot on.

While the Army remains a national asset, following its highest traditions in matters of sports, it could perhaps also do with a refreshing air of openness. It has created a robust sporting bedrock, but a few creative and holistic tweaks to it may make the task of winning Olympic medals easier.

INDIAN HEROS

15

Torchbearers of a Billion

Indian Legends and Some Forgotten Stories
From the Olympic Games

Until recently, success stories in Indian sports were few and far between. Hence, stories of near-finishes became even more poignant in our collective imaginations. Because we grew up with accounts of failure far outnumbering standout Indian performances, most of our national sporting memories from the Olympics were about tales of rued chances and ruminations on counterfactuals.

What would have happened had Henry Rebello's hamstring muscle not snapped during the final of the triple jump event in London in 1948? What would have happened had Milkha Singh not lost pace in the final stretch of the 400 metres final in Rome in 1960? He could well have added an Olympic medal to his already impressive career record: four Asian Games gold medals, a gold at the Commonwealth Games in 1958, victory in seventy-seven of the eighty races he ran in his career, and the Helms World trophy in 1959 given by the United States Athletics Federation to the best 400 metres runner in the world. What would have happened had P.T. Usha thrust herself forward a millimetre, enough to nudge ahead of the Romanian Cristina Cojecaru, who caused national heartbreak after the results of the 400 metre hurdles were announced at the Los Angeles Games in 1984? What would have happened had the floor under Abhinav Bindra's feet not been loose during the final in Athens after he qualified for the ultimate round in third place?

There are other heartrending stories of men and women who missed the grade narrowly and, in so doing, lost their place in the country's sporting pantheon. Not many remember freestyle wrestler Sudesh Kumar, who in 1972 had come tantalizingly close to winning an Olympic gold medal.

Notions of sporting stardom have also changed in India. For example, wrestler K.D. Jadhav's bronze in Helsinki in 1952 was independent India's first individual Olympics medal. Yet, his achievement did not get a first-page mention in the country's leading newspapers. The celebrations were muted and restricted to the sports pages. Only the men of his native village, who escorted him with a cavalcade of over 150 cows, gave him a memorable reception. In contrast, tennis player Leander Paes's bronze-medal in 1996 was perceived as a national triumph, celebrated nationwide amidst all classes and vocations.

In terms of significance, an individual Olympic medal by the 1990s appeared to matter much more than in the 1950s. By way of contrast, there were a series of celebrations countrywide when the 1952 hockey team returned with a gold. Yet, K.D. Jadhav's efforts in the same Olympiad were hardly given due acknowledgement. The political class, which celebrated hockey as a potent symbol of nationalism, did not treat Jadhav with similar respect. Jadhav had to wait until 2001 to posthumously receive the Arjuna Award for lifetime contribution to Indian sports. Even after winning his medal, he managed to build himself a rather modest cottage only after selling his wife's jewellery.

Hockey's lasting nationalist significance since the 1920s was the principal reason behind such differential treatment. Politicians and sports administrators all wanted to join the hockey bandwagon, similar to how people are today with cricket.

THE EARLY HEROES

At the Helsinki Gams in 1952, K.D. Jadhav started the wrestling competition in terrific form, winning all his early bouts. Such was his performance that he was assured of a medal even before he fought his last two fights on 22 July. Whether or not complacency had crept in, we will never know.

This is how the *Times of India* celebrated his achievement: 'History was created here today when India, who has been competing in the Olympic Games since 1924 gained a place in the individual honours list for the first time through K.D. Jadhav, the bantamweight wrestler, who won a bronze medal. Although Jadhav was today beaten by Russia's Roshind Mahmed Bekov (gold medal) and Japan's Shihii in a points decision (silver medal) he gained his place with a series of brilliant bouts during the last week.'[1] The newspaper went on to describe Jadhav's bout against the Russian in detail:

> Although Jadhav was aggressive and a good trier, able to equal the formidable Russian's skill he was unable to match his strength and this weighed the scales against him. The Russian won all three periods. In the first Jadhav jerked him down but was himself twisted over in falling and narrowly escaped a fall. Bekov had the Indian in difficulties after that but Jadhav always wriggled clear.

What made Jadhav's performance all the more significant was that the rules at international contests were different from the rules followed in India.

While Indian wrestlers were used to winning simply by putting their opponents flat on their backs, international rules specified that the opponent had to be pinned for two seconds on the canvas with their shoulders touching the mat before a fall verdict could be declared. Jadhav had learnt of this rule at the London Olympics of 1948 four years earlier when Reese Garder, the US lightweight champion who had trained the Indian wrestlers for a week before the Games, coached him. In London, Jadhav had finished sixth in a field of forty-two.

Jadhav is now a forgotten man in the annals of Indian sports but his story is one of true grit and resilience. The manner in which he made it to Helsinki is nothing short of thrilling. Gulu Ezekiel describes it thus:

> Jadhav's berth to Helsinki was sought to be sabotaged by officials who placed him second in the nationals at Madras. But Jadhav fought the system by writing a protest letter to the Maharaja of Patiala who intervened on his behalf.
>
> Back then, those representing the country in most sports had to fend for themselves and arrange their own funding. Friends and

neigbhours helped out with the shopkeepers of Karad arranging to buy his kit. It was the remarkable sacrifice of the principal of Raja Ram College, Mr Khardekar who sold his house to get the funds needed for the trip, that finally saw Jadhav on his way to Helsinki.[2]

Another Indian wrestler who distinguished himself in Helsinki was K.D. Mangave, who eventually finished fourth in the featherweight category. Mangave bowed out of medal contention in the fifth round when Josiah Henson of the US beat him.[3]

While Jadhav had a medal to show for his performances, Henry Rebello was distinctly unlucky at the London Games of 1948. A young nineteen-year-old triple jumper, Rebello was a favourite to clinch gold, having shown exemplary promise in meets preceding the Games and consistently jumping over 50 metres, a distance covered by the eventual gold-medal winner in London.[4]

Rated very high by experts, Rebello had qualified for the final with ease with a jump of 49 feet, easily clearing the cut-off of 48 feet and 6 inches. But as luck would have it, he tore a muscle during his first jump in the final and had to be carried off the field in pain in one of the worst tragedies in India's athletic history. This is how he later described his fate:

> We were huddled in our tracksuits and under blankets to keep ourselves warm. I was training with Ruhi Sarialp of Turkey when it was time for my turn. I was wondering how to approach the event. Should I go for a big jump in my first effort or keep it till the third or fourth attempt? I took off the track suit and was getting ready when an official suddenly stopped me as a prize distribution ceremony was about to commence near the jumping pit.[5]

When he was asked to commence his jump fifteen minutes later, Rebello committed two follies that transformed his life:

> I was just 19-and-a-half and inexperienced. I should have insisted on some time for warming up. That was my first mistake – not to warm-up. My second was to go flat out on my first jump. We had a total of six and I should have taken things easy at the start ... I approached the takeoff board at considerable speed. I got my takeoff foot on the

board and started to take off for the first phase of the triple jump – the hop. Then, suddenly, I felt a sharp pain in my right hamstring muscle and heard a sort of 'thwack' like the snapping of a bowstring. My right hamstring muscle had ruptured. I was thrown off balance completely and landed with a tumble in the pit.

Rebello, as Gulu Ezekiel wrote, 'was carried off a on stretcher in agony. His hopes and dreams had been crushed'.[6]

Others who did well in the early years after Independence were Lavy Pinto and Nilima Ghosh. They performed better at the Helsinki Games of 1952 than they had ever done at home . Pinto ran his 200 metres in a time of 21.5 seconds – his best ever. Commenting on Pinto, the *Times of India* noted, 'India's ace sprinter Lavy Pinto, the fastest man in Asia after a slow beginning, finished with an electrifying burst of speed to nose out France's Bonino for second place in the eleventh heat of the 100 meters and so make the second round ...'[7]

If Helsinki was an Olympiad where India's individual contestants fared well, Melbourne 1956 will forever be remembered as the finest hour for Indian football. This was the only time in India's football history that the team made the Olympic semi-final, defeating hosts Australia 4–2. Commenting on the performance, the *Hindu* saw in it the start of a glorious Indian innings in the global game: 'Indian football made new history this afternoon when she scored a deserving 4–2 victory over Australia ... N.D. Souza was in grand form to secure a hat-trick ... India richly deserved her victory. This should take her a long way in international football ...' [8]

Even in the semi-final against Yugoslavia, which India lost 1–4, the team was not disgraced. In fact, the *Hindu* hailed India's performance against the fancied Yugoslavs in glowing terms: 'The stock of Indian soccer shot high up today when India met Yugoslavia in the semi-final of the Olympic soccer tournament in spite of the fact that India lost four goals to one. After the conclusion of the match the President of the International Football Federation Mr J. McGuire accompanied by FIFA Secretary Kurt Gassman and Sir Stanley Rous came to the Indian dressing room and warmly congratulated the Indian team on its fine performance. Sir Stanley further conveyed the Duke of Edinburgh's congratulations who asked Sir Stanley to convey the Duke's felicitations to the Indian team. The Duke was an interested spectator throughout.'[9]

In the semi-final, the Indians had managed to hold the Yugoslavs at bay in the first half and had taken the lead in the fifth minute of the second half. Had P.K. Banerjee not left the field with an injury in the second half, the result may well have been different. This is something Banerjee talks about with passion: 'It was certainly our highest hour. We had a great tournament and I personally was in the best form of my life. Against Yugoslavia I had to leave the field and that's when things turned against us. Though we did not win a medal, I'll always remember with great fondness our performance at Melbourne.'[10]

Few remember that the Indians also played quality football when they got their first taste of international competition at the London Olympics of 1948. India matched a far superior French side, although it ultimately lost the game 1–2. The barefoot display of quality football impressed many. In fact, India had also qualified for the World Cup in 1950 to be held in Brazil. Despite having a rich band of footballers, however, it could not take part in the only World Cup it qualified for.

The most commonly ascribed reasons for this withdrawal are the lack of foreign reserves, the barefoot style of play, the long sea journey and apprehensions about India's chances against the world's top teams. On the Asian circuit, India began with a bang. It clinched the gold medal in the first Asian Games football competition in 1951, beating a booted Iranian side in the final by a solitary goal. After the Melbourne Olympics, however, Indian football started wilting.

OH MILKHA! THE FIRST NATIONAL HEARTBREAK

Even a week before the start of the 1960 Rome Olympics, Milkha Singh was considered to be the favourite for the 400 metres gold. Vince Reel, the American assistant coach to the Indian track team, was confident that Singh would win a medal, maybe even gold. Such hope was based on the fact that Milkha was in peak physical condition in Rome. His training was described by the *Hindu* in some detail: 'India's great hope has been devoting between an hour and an hour and a half to training every day since his arrival in Rome. He is cutting the distances to sprints of about 150 yards with the object of speeding up.' 'If he has not the stamina now, he will never have it', said Vince Reel, explaining the reason for reducing the distances.[11]

What was expected to work in his favour in Rome was the tremendous heat which, Milkha Singh was confident, was sure to bother the others in the fray. Christopher Brasher, steeplechase winner at the Melbourne Games, also felt that Milkha Singh had a great chance of a podium finish for two reasons: his form and, more importantly, the schedule, which ensured that the semi-final and final were run on consecutive days and not on the same day as had been past practice. This was expected to help Milkha more than some of the other competitors.

Eventually, Milkha Singh finished fourth despite having broken the Olympic record in the process with a time of 45.6 seconds. This was a rare race where the first four finishers broke the existing world record. Hailed as the best ever, the race was covered in detail by the *Hindu*:

> The quarter mile event for men was the best ever seen in the recent track meet with America's 28 year old Otis Davis cracking the world record by 3/10 of a second to claim the first place nosing out Germany's Kauffman at the tape. South Africa's Spence was third in 45.5 seconds and India's Milkha Singh was placed fourth in 45.6 seconds ... There was nothing for the Indians to be upset by this result as Milkha Singh was caught among the top notchers of the world in peak form. The race was a feast to the eyes with all six setting terrific pace right from the start to finish. In fact, Milkha Singh ran the best ever in his life since his previous best was 45.8 seconds set up recently in Paris when he beat Abdul Seye of France ... Milkha Singh drew his best lane and everything was in his favour to produce his best. The finalists took an excellent start and it was Milkha Singh and Kinder who led first. Nearing the finish Davis overtook all with Kauffman close on his heels. Milkha Singh was then lying fourth behind Spence. Between Milkha Singh and Spence there was hardly a foot difference and had Milkha Singh run a well judged race instead of bursting out from the start he might have clinched the bronze medal.[12]

Like P.T. Usha two and a half decades later, the disappointing loss of Milkha Singh was to turn into an enduring legend of Indian sports. The loss still rankles and he remembers each second of the race. He describes it as the best and also the worst moment of his life:

Going into the stadium for the final, I was relaxed and confident about my chances. But when I saw my competitors, tension within me mounted. And with each passing minute it increased. I drew lane five with South African Malcolm Spence to my left and the German Manfred Kinder on my right. As the race was a photofinish, the announcements were held up. The suspense was excruciating. I knew that I had made a fatal error. This may have been because I was all keyed up for the race and was extremely confident of winning a medal. After running furiously fast in lane five for the first 250 meters I slowed down a fraction. At that point I even looked back or maybe it was just a side-glance. But that fraction of a second decided my fate allowing others to overtake me. I could not cover the lost ground after that and that one mistake cost me the race and also the medal.[13]

'After the death of my parents, that is my worst memory,' said Singh, one of the most respected Indian athletes of all time. When pressed about his feelings after the race, he seemed to go back almost fifty years. 'I kept crying for days,' was his first reaction.

A true sportsman, he had chosen to stay for the medal ceremony to congratulate Davis, Kaufmann and Spence. 'But to tell you honestly, I hated doing it. If I had my way I would have snatched the medals off their hands and run away.'[14] He was acutely distraught after the Games and made up his mind to give up sport. It was after much persuasion that he began running again.

Milkha Singh had first established himself as an athlete of prowess in 1956 at the National Games in Patiala and two years later broke the 200 and 400 metre record at the National Games in Cuttack. In the 1958 Tokyo Asiad, Singh continued to amaze, winning both the 200 and 400 metre races. In the 1958 Commonwealth Games in Cardiff, he won the 400 metre race, beating South African sprinter Malcolm Spence. Spence, however, had the last laugh when he beat Singh in Rome for the bronze medal.

There's little doubt that Singh is the greatest male athlete India has ever produced. Despite losing his parents in the bloody aftermath of Partition, Milkha went on to earn the title of 'The Flying Sikh'. His career was a fascinating prototype of P.T. Usha's – he ruled the Asian tracks in his heyday while facing heartbreak at the Olympics.

In 1947, Milkha Singh was among the millions of refugees of Partition, escaping to India by hanging from the footboard of a crowded train. Interestingly, when he went back to Pakistan later in his career, he was mobbed by fans and admirers on several occasions, a sign of the respect he had earned for himself across the subcontinent.

RANDHAWA, SRIRAM AND SOME FORGOTTEN STARS OF INDIAN SPORTS

The other Sikh who almost made the Olympic stage his own was 110-metre hurdler Gurbachan Singh Randhawa. He made it to the semi-final of his favourite event in Tokyo as the lucky loser and eventually finished a credible fifth in the final with a timing of 14.0 seconds. Bruce Kidd, who represented Canada in the same Olympics, remembers his interaction with Randhawa in Tokyo:

> He was a talented youngster. He was full of life and verve and when I congratulated him on entering the final, he was a little stunned. He had not expected a Canadian athlete to congratulate him for having made the final. In the final, he ran a good race and may well have made the podium had he done a few things better. In fact, had he started well he would surely have been in the first three. It was a standout performance for India had hardly ever produced an Olympic league sprinter.[15]

This is how Randhawa remembers the event:

> Tokyo in October had a fair amount of rain. We were praying for good weather as the track was of cinder. But despite the heavy downpour, it remained firm...Because of my lack of basic speed I was not good at starts. I took off rather slowly. But my hard training in different events had given me a lot of endurance and staying power. That came in handy. I covered a lot of ground between the fifth and eighth hurdles and almost caught up with the American Hayes Jones and Frenchman Marcel Duriez. I finished fourth in 14.3 seconds. But my painful wait was over when it was announced that I had qualified for the semi-finals as the fastest loser.[16]

In the semi-final, Ezekiel wrote, Randhawa was pitted against the unified team of Germany's John Heinrich, Duriez, Anatoly Mikhailov (USSR), Giorgio Mazza (Italy), Lazaro Betancourt (Cuba), Davenport (US) and Valentine Chistyakov (USSR). Chistyakov had two false starts and was disqualified. As Randhawa remembers, 'It was a tough race. My joy knew no bounds when I looked at the giant scoreboard to see that I had finished second in a personal best of 14 seconds which was also the national record.'[17] He thus described the final:

> Once off to the start, everything was forgotten. Again I had a slow start but I surged smoothly ahead of Duriez. Up front, the Italians Giorgio Mazza and Giovanni Cornacchia were struggling. Duriez tripped on the final hurdle and that gave me a slight advantage, allowing me to catch up with him at the tape...I had barely recovered from the effort when I saw the scoreboard. Light flashed on it, but soon they were put off. When they came on again, my name was at the fourth spot. But they went off again. When the lights returned I was in the fifth spot. The timing was 14 seconds ... I have no regrets. Maybe I should have broken the 14 second barrier. I have had my share of bad luck in life. But I must tell you that I was lucky at Tokyo to get into the semis as the fastest loser.[18]

While Randhawa is still hailed as one of the best sprint hurdlers the country has ever produced, the men who are almost forgotten in India's sporting annals are the wrestlers Sudesh Kumar and Prem Nath. Both of them came close to winning medals in the freestyle competition of the tainted Munich Games in August 1972. In fact, on 31 August 1972, the *Times of India* reported that India could hope for its first gold in Olympic wrestling if Kumar beat the Japanese Kiyomi Kato. Kumar had moved into contention by defeating Henrik Gal of Hungary in three minutes and seventeen seconds, using his pet hold of 'nikaal'. In the 52 kg class, six wrestlers remained in the fray for the three medals, giving Kumar a great chance for a podium finish. Sushil Jain described his bout against Gal in detail in the *Times of India*:

> In the opening second Hungarian Gal applied 'dhobi paat' to floor Sudesh but Sudesh was very swift to take a turn. Both wrestlers were

on equal terms with two points each. In the second round Sudesh did not wait for Gal's attack. It soon was very difficult for Gal to counter Sudesh's hold. Sudesh gave no chance to Gal, lifted him and put him on the floor very neatly.[19]

And just like Rebello, fate was against Kumar in his bout against the Japanese. In this bout, which he eventually lost on points, a string of refereeing decisions went against him, decisively influencing the course of the contest. Sudesh was on level terms with his opponent in the first round, with a point each. 'An undue warning to Sudesh and a point to Kiyomi turned the trend of the bout. Sudesh had to take the offensive, which gave ample chance to Kiyomi to play safe ... Sudesh trailed behind by three points to one in the seventh minute. He tried a beautiful nikaal, which was countered and Kiyomi got another point.'[20]

In the dying minutes of the contest, Sudesh almost floored Kiyomi, but time robbed him of a victory. Soon after the bout, the secretary general of the Wrestling Federation of India, Dewan Pratapchand, raised an objection about bad refereeing but for some reason did not lodge a formal protest. Had India filed a formal complaint against the referee, it might have been a different story.[21]

Premnath, competing in the Olympics for the first time, had raised medal hopes by defeating the Argentine Naggiolio in the 57 kg class. He applied the 'multani' on his opponent and floored him in four minutes and seventeen seconds. Had he defeated Richard Sandero of the US in the fifth round, he would have been certain of either gold or silver. However, he failed to stand up to Sandero and was trailing 2–14 when he was finally floored. In his semi-final, which followed his defeat against Sandero, Premnath, a seventeen-year-old teenager, was injured and carried off on a stretcher. Both Sudesh and Premnath finished fourth.

Sushil Jain ended his report on India's wrestling challenge in Munich with an interesting observation:

> This was the first time I saw an Indian visitor to the wrestling arena and he was Milkha Singh, who has been encouraging our wrestlers. Besides WFI officials none from the Indian camp including the Chef De Mission and the Government of India observers have ever cared to visit the wrestling matches.[22]

The third Singh who made an Olympic final after Milkha and Gurbachan was Sriram, who finished seventh in the final of the 800 metres race in Montreal in 1976. A protégé of the dynamic Ilyas Babar, one of the best Indian athletics coaches of all time, Sriram moved to middle-distance running at Babar's insistence. He won silver at the Asian Games of 1970 in Bangkok and followed it up with a gold in Tehran in 1974. However, Montreal was surely his finest hour, though he failed to win a medal.

That Sriram was a medal prospect was evident when he won at a practice meet in Montreal days before the start of the Games.[23] Most leading runners had participated in this meet and Sriram gained valuable confidence from his performance. Running in the first lane of the opening heat in Montreal, Sriram set a scorching pace to lead the field at the end of the first lap with a timing of 51.35 seconds. He continued with the good run for the next 300 metres before the American Richard Wohlhuntr, the favourite to win gold in Montreal, overtook him. While the American finished first in this heat with a timing of one minute and 45.7 seconds, Sriram with a career best of one minute 45.80 seconds finished second.[24]

He ran a strategically bad semi-final and was in fact very close to missing out on a final berth, allowing competitors from America, Britain and Cuba to stay ahead of him.

> Allowing himself to be boxed, which a front runner like him never relishes, Sriram had to stay content in the fourth position, but with only five meters for the finish, James Robinson from the United States put in a tremendous burst all but overtaking the Indian...Indian observers waited with bated breath for the result for to the naked eye it seemed the American, a world class runner, had just about made it but the wonderful world of electronics which leaves nothing to chance put the Indian a hundredth of a second or so ahead. There was a burst of cheering in the Indian camp when the result was flashed on the giant board. None looked more delighted than Sriram's mentor Ilyas Babar ...[25]

In the final, as in the heat, Sriram set a blistering pace and led the field in the first 400 metres with an amazing time of 50.85 seconds, faster than the eventual gold medal winner Alberto Juantorena of Cuba. It was in the home stretch that he faded away and ultimately finished seventh with a timing of one minute and 45.77 seconds. Juantorena, who won a gold medal with a world record timing of one minute 43.50 seconds, attributed his success to the pace set by Sriram Singh.

INDIA'S FIRST CHAK DE! GIRLS

Twenty-seven years before the 2007 Sharukh Khan starrer *Chak De! India* was released, the first Indian women hockey players made it to the Olympics. Those early pioneers would perhaps be able to empathize with the trials and tribulations of the fictional players in the film. When women's hockey was first introduced at the Moscow Olympiad in 1980 as a medal sport, India was one of the six teams that contested for honours. The other nations in the fray were Zimbabwe, USSR, Czechoslovakia, Poland and Austria. India began its campaign by defeating the Austrians 2–0 at the Young Pioneers stadium in Moscow.

Despite the victory, coach Kartar Singh was dissatisfied. Speaking to the media, he declared, 'I would say what you saw was 50 per cent of the true capabilities of the team'.[26] Interestingly, the Indian girls began with the battle cry 'Sat Sri Aakaal' as their male compatriots had done in Moscow. A fairly large contingent of Indian women, some of them Moscow residents, were seen in the stands supporting their team.

In their second match, the Indians beat the Poles 4–0. Yet again, their performance was below par, a claim supported by their coach. 'Frankly, they played worse today than against Austria. They are not clicking the way they should, not combining well at all.'[27] Despite their unconvincing performances, they had won a large number of fans, evident from the following observation by K. Datta in the *Times of India*: 'The Indian girls' performance might not have satisfied the team officials or a few other critics. But it cannot be denied that their two wins so far have won them increasing respect of many a visitor to Moscow's hockey stadiums'.[28]

India's campaign was derailed in round three when, in an unexpected result, the Indians lost a close contest to Czechoslovakia 1–2. The defeat, more than the performance of the Czechs, was a result of some atrocious umpiring errors. The Indians were shocked at the two penalty corners given to the Czechs, one of which resulted in the winning goal nine minutes before the game ended. Antonina Tsetlina, a Soviet lady umpire, awarded the penalty corner. Kartar Singh was enraged by this decision and complained that an umpire from a country very much in the race for honours had been assigned for the match although there were several umpires from 'neutral' countries available. However, in a show of sportsmanship, the Indians did not lodge a formal complaint with the organizers.[29]

Following this defeat, the Indians rallied brilliantly and put up a fighting performance against eventual winners Zimbabwe, drawing the contest 1–1. This left the Indians in second place, with just one match to be played. Despite what they felt were bad umpiring decisions yet again against Zimbabwe, the Indians, the *Times of India* reported, 'fought gallantly all the way against a very fit looking Zimbabwe side ... It was a creditable performance under the added strain of unpredictable whistling'.[30]

In their last encounter against the Russians, the Indian girls frittered away all the good work against Zimbabwe and their loss meant that they were out of medal contention. Eventually, they finished fourth in the competition. The next time the hockey girls qualified for an Olympics was at the Rio Games in 2016 when they finished twelfth.

The Disappointment of P.T. Usha: The Second National Heartbreak

In Los Angeles, history was made when the IOA picked five women in a contingent of eight athletes. Of the five, P.T. Usha been the most impressive, having won the 400 metre hurdles in a pre-Olympic meet by defeating some of the world's best, including Debbie Flint of Australia and L. Mazie of the US. Her timing of 55.8 seconds may have been slightly higher than her best but it was certainly enough to make her a sure finalist for the Los Angeles Games.[31]

Usha sailed through to the semi-final without trouble, finishing second behind Judy Brown from the US. She ran a good race in the second lane, cleared the hurdles without trouble and finished off strongly to bring cheer to the faces of the Indians in stadium.[32]

The semi-final saw Usha at her best. In the second semi- final, she won convincingly with a timing of 55.54 seconds, beating Judy Brown, who finished second with 55.97 seconds. K. Datta reported in the *Times of India* that the afternoon timing of the semi-final suited Usha, who changed her tactics and preferred not to surge ahead from the start. It was only on the home stretch that Usha put in a last-ditch effort, leaving the others behind. Her timing was the third best among all the finalists and she had emerged a strong medal prospect by the time of the final.

The story of how P.T. Usha missed out on a bronze in the final is now part of Indian sporting folklore. Her loss ushered India into a state of mourning and the race was reported in the press as folows:

> P T Usha came as close as one hundredth of a second to breaking India's medal drought in the Olympic Games. The finish had to be replayed again and again on the giant screen at the Los Angeles memorial Coliseum before the results were declared ... For the third place Usha was beaten by the last desperate lunge by Romania's Cristina Cojecaru who was credited with a timing of 55.41 seconds. Usha's timing was officially shown as 55.42.[33]

In fact, to make sure nothing was left to chance, the Indians lodged a formal protest claiming third place for Usha. However, the jury, justly, did not agree. The medal ceremony was delayed to make sure every doubt had been cleared. After the event, Usha retreated to her room in the Olympic Village without speaking a word to anyone. Her silence said it all. It was a tragedy that continues to haunt her even today. As she later recounted, for the first few minutes she didn't even realize that her dream had ended. It was only when reality dawned on her that she felt an emptiness that she had never felt before in her life. Her Olympic dream had been shattered, as it appeared, due to her own inexperience.

There's little doubt, however, that P.T. Usha had done herself and her country proud. She was only the fourth athlete and the first woman from India to have figured in an Olympic track and field final. One contemporary report noted:

> Coming to think of it, for all the disappointment of not winning a medal, it was a most creditable performance by a girl of her limited experience. Usha took up the event six months earlier and this was her first taste of international competition. Before taking the plane to Los Angeles she had competed in only two big hurdles races in India, the Bombay Open meet and the pre-Olympic trials. Her own state,

Kerala, had objected to her entry when she first wished to try her hand
at the event in the Inter-State meet in New Delhi ... An Olympic
medal would have been a great reward for a girl who has dominated
Indian athletics for half a decade ... When coach Nambiar introduced
her to hurdling he had predicted a place in the final for her. Perhaps
Usha herself had not expected to win a medal.[34]

She may not have won the Olympic medal but she inspired an
extraordinary rise of women athletes from Kerala – Shiny Wilson, M.D.
Valsamma, Molly Chacko and Mercy Kuttan. The trend coincided with a
concentrated focus on athletics by the Kerala Sports Council during that
period.

BEING LEANDER PAES

No history of Indian sports can be complete without an elegy to the grit
and determination of Leander Paes. In an age of instant stardom for even
the worst performers in the national cricket team, Leander soldiered on,
relatively unsung. Never very high on the tennis singles rankings, he won
Grand Slam after Grand Slam (in doubles), beating far higher ranked
opponents while representing the country in the Asian Games, the Olympics
and the Davis Cup. When he won his Olympic medal in 1996, he ended a
forty-four-year individual medal drought for India.

In Atlanta, as a rank outsider and hardly a medal contender at the start
of the tournament, he finished in third place because of his never-say-die
attitude and unparalleled patriotism, which helped him raise his game to
a level he never matched again. Rohit Brijnath, one of India's finest sport
writers, beautifully captured the magic of the player:

> Everyone who has watched Leander Paes play has a story. Mine is
> corny. In 20 years of sports writing, no player has done what he did
> to me. On the day in Atlanta at the 1996 Olympics, as he battled
> stuttering form to win bronze, the strangest thing happened. I cried.
>
> It wasn't just because a nation of a billion had been tired of
> mediocrity, had been waiting so long, 44 years at that point, for one
> more individual Olympic medal, just to show we belonged, to feel
> briefly empowered.

It was more than that. You cared because he cared. Because he was technically defective, and too short, and his game too high risk, but he'd fight every flaw, he'd front every challenge, he'd tilt wildly at windmills.

This was not a great player by any stretch…But somehow he'd manage to transcend his averageness when his nation's flag flew.

He'd move you because when he played for India he did that simplest of things. He tried.[35]

It has often been suggested that Leander is an average tennis player who reached another level when he donned Indian colours. This is meant as praise but it also dwarfs all his other achievements: eighteen Grand Slam titles in doubles and mixed doubles, which helped place India on the world tennis map again.

When Leander beat Fernando Melligeni of Brazil in the battle for third place in Atlanta, the country was too stunned at first to react. Finally, the medal drought had ended. But the true sportsman in Leander did not want to ride high on this achievement by coming back to India to bask in Olympic glory. Rather, he stayed back in the US for a while to improve on his rankings, allowing the craze to die down a little. His reaction after winning the bronze is proof of his sportsmanship: 'It's just amazing how things can happen with a little bit of effort. And that's really been my story at the Olympics. I've just been putting in effort match after match, point after point … Even on Saturday I was down a set. I was really nervous this morning. I guess the 44 years and 16 years that we have not won a medal was getting to me. It took a while to get over my nerves out there. The effort paid off in the end.'[36]

Interestingly, Paes, who had entered the Atlanta Olympics as a wildcard, praised the role played by his coach, Jaideep Mukherjea, and then doubles partner Mahesh Bhupathi in propelling him to Olympic glory: 'Bhupathi skipped one week of ATP tour play to stay with me and give me encouragement. I am very grateful for the gesture.'[37]

THE FIRST WOMAN OLYMPIC MEDALLIST

For Karnam Malleswari, the Sydney Olympic Games of 2000 will always be a reverie that came true. It was in Sydney that she rewrote the history books by becoming the first Indian woman to win an Olympic medal. For the record, Malleswari won a bronze medal in the 69 kg weightlifting category. This was her first international meet in the 69 kg division after moving up from her usual 63 kg class. In Sydney, she lifted a total of 240 kg – 110 kg in snatch and 130 kg in clean and jerk – to end up behind China's Lin Weining and Hungary's Erzsebet Markus, who won gold and silver respectively. Soon after her victory, Prime Minister Atal Behari Vajpayee hailed her performance as 'a tribute to Indian womanhood'.

As is typical with Indian sports, her trip to Sydney was in jeopardy until the very last minute. The choice of the women's weightlifting team had been mired in controversy and Malleswari even ran the risk of missing out on participation altogether. On her return from Sydney, she made this stunning revelation in an interview:

> I was even blackmailed (on the eve of the Games). Coach Mr Sandhu told me if there was a choice between Malli or Kunjarani (Devi) then I would be the one who would be forced out of the team, because *Chanu* was an automatic choice. We were all tense till the last minute. We had no idea as to what might happen the next moment. I did not know that the choice was between Sonamacha and Kunjarani. I believed what I was told … I had won two world medals, but it did not seem to count for those who were involved in the selection process. I was hurt when someone came and told me that Sonamacha was better than me. Of course, the whole thing was being orchestrated. I felt bad about it. This misinformation campaign was being carried on by one of the coaches.[38]

Trained by the Belarussian, Leonid Taranenkohe, Malleswari was only the third individual Indian medal winner.

For a lifter moving up from the 63 kg to 69 kg class and taking part in her first competition in the category, Malleswari far exceeded expectations. Her effort was all the more commendable because a leading magazine had dismissed her chances of a medal on the eve of the Games saying that she was overweight, drank beer and ate 'too much' chicken and cheese.

THE RIFLE SHOOTER: NARANG IN LONDON

With Abhinav Bindra winning gold in the 10 m air rifle event at the Beijing Games in 2008, Gagan Narang had somewhat gone under the radar in India. An Olympic gold, that too the first ever individual one for an Indian, meant Bindra was the toast of the nation. Narang, on the other hand, was like Karna to Bindra's Arjun.

For the record, Narang, who also shot in the 10 m air rifle event, had done extremely well at the 2006 Commonwealth Games in Melbourne. He was very much into reckoning in Beijing before he lost out on countback. He came back strong after a period of depression to win multiple gold medals at the 2010 Commonwealth Games in Delhi. Despite these heroics, however, Narang needed an Olympic medal to elevate himself to the status of a legend. The London Games of 2012 was when he finally arrived, for many Indians .

Anyone who had followed Narang closely was aware that he was in prime form leading into London. He was in good shape physically and felt he was in that special zone that athletes want to be in ahead of a big competition. Having watched Gagan shoot in London while standing right behind him, it was apparent that he was focused and committed. Looking at him then, it would have been be a real surprise to find out that he'd miss out on a medal. He was in such form that making the final wasn't a big deal for him. Soon after the qualifiers were done, all he did was pump his fist as if to say the first hurdle had been crossed. And as the athletes entered the final hall, all of India was praying for Gagan.

Then-sports minister Ajay Maken was in the seat next to us waving the tricolour and after every shot was anxious to know if Narang was in contention. To everyone's satisfaction, Narang was consistent throughout. Even before the last shot, it was apparent that the medal had been sealed. It was India's first one in London 2012. Coming as it did in the early part of the Games, this was the best possible start for the country.

The television cameras caught the winning moments. Behind the scenes, an abiding memory for us is the awfully long time Narang took to finish the mandatory dope test immediately after! Every Indian journalist was eagerly waiting for Narang and it was only after two and a half hours that he emerged from the medical room, having given his dope sample. We even joked that all the tension had made it impossible to pee! Each of us was up against a deadline and it was a relief when Narang finally emerged from the medical room to speak to the cameras.

SNAPSHOTS OF INDIAN SPORTS

Along with more recent sporting triumphs, this chapter has been a tribute to some exceptional figures who have given India a voice in the greatest sporting realm of all. We remember watching Leander Paes play Andre Agassi in Atlanta in 1996 and the pride we felt each time Paes stunned the crowd with one of his fancy drop shots, too many of which may have ultimately cost him the match.

Leander, then ranked 127 in the world, was an average tennis player who raised the bar when he donned the national colours at the Olympics. In qualifying for the semi-final, Leander upset four competitors ranked higher than him in the ATP rankings. This was a player who, by sheer force of his passion, transcended 'his averageness when his nation's flag flew'. He was a rare non-cricketing hero who moved India like no other and went on to be hailed as the 'spiritual leader' of a new movement of 'the art of the possible'.[39]

We also remember the elation in the voice of the All India Radio newsreader when she revealed to the nation Karnam Malleswari's feat, finally getting Indian women into the Olympic medal winner's list. And we remember watching Rajyavardhan Rathore shoot around 4 p.m. in the afternoon in India, becoming the first Indian to win a silver medal in an individual event.

We remember, as children, the heart-wrenching gloom at school and in our localities when inexperience cost P.T. Usha the bronze in Los Angeles. Having won her semi-final, Usha, someone we had never seen or heard of before, was truly at the centre of our nationalist imagination in 1984. When the serious-looking Doordarshan newsreader on the black and white television set made the announcement, a sense of loss and sympathy extended far beyond the sporting realm. Everyone, including our grandmothers, could empathize with the poor Indian girl who was believed to have been let down by the lack of modern training. If only she had bent her body forward as she crossed the finishing line. If only someone had told her... and so the conversations went on for days after the competition was over.

In a country where sporting achievements were few and far between and where pathos is an enduring theme in popular culture, the misfortune of P.T. Usha struck a chord and turned her into a legend. Despite having failed to win a medal, Usha became a national icon and a symbol of women's empowerment at the same time.

Finally, we remember Abhinav Bindra shooting a miraculous 10.7 in his final shot in Beijing, giving India her first individual Olympic gold.

Moments like these have defined Indian sports: its highs, its lows and its multiple tragedies. They are as much a part of the catalogue of the individual trials, triumphs and heartbreaks of India's athletes as they are a cultural snapshot of our wider journey as a nation.

TOKYO AND BEYOND

Epilogue

High Stakes for the Tricolour in Tokyo

Wrestler Vinesh Phogat's father was shot dead by a relative when she was eight. When her mother was asked to marry her late husband's brother as per custom, she refused. The decision triggered such uproar in her conservative Haryana village of Balali, as Sonia Faleiro has documented, that family members from far and wide were called in to counsel her. She remained resolute in her refusal, started a micro-finance business and her daughter, while growing up in the same conservative village, went on to become a world medal-winning wrestler.

Her story is the measure of the distance India has travelled.

Four years after she was carried off screaming and writhing from the wrestling quarter-final in Rio after a horrible knee injury and her career was written off by many, Vinesh Phogat has ensured that she will be back in Tokyo in 2020 – this time as a strong medal contender. Will she add to India's medals tally? Will she redeem herself like Abhinav Bindra did in Beijing 2008 after Athens 2004?

Will badminton world champion P.V. Sindhu, looking to change the colour of her Rio silver medal, make us proud? Will Saina, looking for her own Olympic salvation, find her holy grail a second time in Tokyo? Will India's World Championship medal-winning wrestlers – Bajrang Punia, Ravi Dahiya and Deepak Punia – manage to replicate their successes from Nur Sultan in 2019? Will the phalanx of shooters, who have benefitted

299

from a complete overhaul of the base structures of Indian shooting over the past four years, find their mark? Will the constantly improving hockey team rise to the challenge three decades after the Indian team stood on an Olympic podium?

These are the questions swirling in the wind as India's athletes prepare for their Tokyo test. What does India realistically hope for at the 2020 Olympics? Three years after the Olympic Task Force submitted its report and five years after the TOPS was launched, what is India's best-case scenario? After three medals in Beijing 2008, six in London 2012 and two in Rio 2016, will the graph curve move up again for India?

Narendra Batra, IOA president and one of the two Indian members of the IOC, announced in July 2019 that the target for India is 'double figure medals'. Speaking at a function in Agra, Batra outlined the ambitions of India's sport administrators saying, 'We must start winning medals in double digits. We can target ten to twelve medals in Tokyo, twenty-five in 2024 and around forty in the 2028 Olympics. Unless we set targets, we will not achieve anything. I feel these are achievable targets.'

Tokyo 2020 will be a crucial reality check for Indian sports. India's Tokyo contingent has a number of medal hopefuls and a lot will be riding on the outcome of these Games beyond the individual fortunes of these athletes. Nothing is predictable in sports, but if the sporting gods smile, it could mean a new phase of growth.

In an age where sporting success is also a barometer for chest-thumping nationalism, Tokyo will determine whether India's sporting administrators will make the bid to host the Olympics in India. For a while now, the IOA has been considering a potential bid for the 2032 Olympics. Such bids are put in years before the event. The bidding process for the 2032 Games will start in 2022 and the decision will hinge a great deal on India's medal performance in Tokyo.

Medal targets are closely tied to this ambition. Batra told a press conference in Bengaluru in June 2019, 'If we have to bid for the 2032 Olympics, the target should be twenty medals in 2024 and thirty-five to forty medals by 2028. Otherwise they won't even allow you to bid. You have to make sure the performance is such.'

Beijing used the 2008 Olympics to showcase its status as a new superpower. As India's clout rises, it too has similar ambitions but it won't stand a good chance to host the Olympics without being at least a middling sporting nation. Greece won sixteen medals (and ranked fifteenth on the medals tally) when it hosted the Athens Games in 2004, Britain as sporting powerhouse won sixty-five in London in 2012 (third on the tally) and Brazil won nineteen in 2016 (standing thirteenth on the tally). Apart from economic and strategic clout, a possible Indian bid would need a strong sporting base as well to be successful.

Can India make such a bid? India has hosted big sporting events before, like the Commonwealth Games in 2010 or the Asian Games in 1982 and 1951. It has also hosted single sports tournaments like the ICC Cricket World Cup (2011), the FIFA U-17 World Cup (2017) and men's Hockey World Cup (2018). Yet, these pale in comparison to the size of an Olympics which requires facilities for over 10,000 athletes, 30,000 members of the media and over 300 events. In anticipation of a possible bid, Olympic administrators have been planning to host several big global events after Tokyo. Batra announced,'India will be a country which will host many events. We are looking at the 2026 Youth Olympic Games and the IOC Congress in 2021. We have also expressed our interest to host the 2030 Asian Games so that the infrastructure will be ready early with just a two-year gap to the Olympics.'

Which Indian city would host a possible Indian Olympics? The IOA says it could be Delhi, Bengaluru or Mumbai, or all three. 'The only pre-condition is that a city should have an international airport,' said Batra. 'Bhubaneswar too may be considered, as we are calling it the sports capital of India. That (decision) we will leave for later.' IOA General Secretary Rajeev Mehta told reporters in mid-2019 that 'At the moment, Mumbai and Delhi are frontrunners. But we can surely consider other cities like Bengaluru and Bhubaneswar.'

This is not a pipe dream. In 2018, the IOA submitted a formal expression of interest to the IOC. Earlier that year, its president informed the visiting IOC Chief Thomas Bach that India would consider bidding for the 2032 Games. This is how IOA Secretary General Rajeev Mehta described his meeting with the three-member bid committee to the Press Trust of India: 'We are dead serious about this bid for the 2032 Olympics. So, we have already submitted to the IOC the letter expressing our interest in hosting the 2032 Olympic Games. I had a meeting with the bid committee of the IOC. They welcomed the move and said that India should have hosted an Olympic Games much earlier.'

The idea of hosting an Olympics hasn't had any formal sanction from the government yet. In fact, the sports ministry in 2018 was lukewarm to the IOA's expression of interest. Yet, this is an ambition that could take wind if India does well in Tokyo. Paris will host the 2024 Olympics and Los Angeles has already received the nod for 2028. Others who have expressed an interest for 2032 include Indonesia, China, Australia, Germany and possibly a joint bid by North and South Korea.

Would it be a good idea for India to host the Olympics? The annals of Olympic history are full of cities that wanted to host the Games to project their soft power globally, only to end up with humungous cost overruns and deficits that lasted years thereafter. Only Barcelona (1992) and London (2012) in recent times gained economically with long-lasting positive legacies. Historically, the famous example of a financial disaster at the Olympics was Montreal in 1976, which left the Canadian city with a C$1.6 billion debt that took it forty years to recover from. Rio 2016 is said to have used up over $13 billion and left in its wake a swathe of empty apartments and corruption scandals that engulfed a host of Brazilian politicians. This included then-President Luiz Inacio Lula da Silva, who wept when the games were awarded to Rio but was later convicted for twelve years on corruption charges.

Apart from memories of the Commonwealth Games in 2010 that landed Suresh Kalmadi in jail, there is of course the bigger question of whether India should invest in a mega event when the same money could be used to train athletes or invest in infrastructure.

It is an open question. At one level, there is no point in building modern Potemkin villages for a global show when our own systems don't work. One mustn't forget when officials at the Delhi 2010 Commonwealth Games publicly talked about using giant bamboo curtains to shield visitors from the sight of poor bastis (slums). Of course, such ideas involve building a beautiful façade only for the benefit of visitors without actually fixing anything, and hence do nothing to actually help our situation.

Yet, if done the right way with the right sustainable investments – like Barcelona in 1992 or Seoul in 1988 – an Olympic Games can also be a major economic booster for India. Barcelona, for example, transformed forever from an industrial backwater into one of Europe's most popular and visited cities. City unemployment, according to one study, dropped dramatically from an all-time high of 127,774 in November 1986 to 60,885 in July

1992. Olympic infrastructure created for the Games is believed to have provided over 20,000 permanent jobs for the city. 'Crucially the games seemed to change the way people thought of Barcelona,' said Adam Taylor in a profile for Business Insider.

If it does come to that, India would be better off hosting a multi-city Olympics. Hyderabad, for example, could host badminton and rowing, Delhi's Karni Singh ranges for shooting, Kolkata for football, Bhubaneswar for hockey and so on. There is no point creating new artificial islands. India could leverage its existing strengths, build on them and create a truly pan-Indian festival.

All of this, however, is just speculation. Whether India should host an Olympics or not is a debatable question. Its pros and cons must be put under speculation, but whether this remains an academic debate or a genuine public policy issue will depend a great deal on what happens in Tokyo 2020. A good medal haul will reignite this subject while a bad one may well bury it.

Such questions shouldn't concern the athletes, of course, who will be travelling to Japan in search of glory. In the end, it is their stories, their triumphs and their struggles that will matter. Yet, as the Olympic-hosting debate illustrates, the stakes on their journey will be greater than ever before.

INDIA AND THE OLYMPICS: A VISUAL HISTORY

INDIA AND THE OLYMPIC GAMES

COMPETITION OPEN TO EVERY ELIGIBLE YOUTH IN THE INDIAN EMPIRE

ALL INDIA ATHLETIC MEET
DELHI, FEBRUARY 9, 1924

VIII OLYMPIAD, PARIS, JULY, 1924

HEADQUARTERS OF
ALL INDIA OLYMPIC COMMITTEE:
Y.M.C.A., QUEEN'S GARDENS,
DELHI.

A. G. NOEHREN, M.D.,
SECRETARY.

Y.M.C.A. Wodehouse Road,
Bombay, 1st April 1924.

Dear Sir Dorabji,

I have delayed sending you a detailed report of the great Olympic Games contest at Delhi until I could enclose you a reprint of the account I wrote for "The Young Men of India". You might perhaps think me biased in my judgment of the unique contribution made to the country at large through these games, but I think it is fair to state that these have been far more successful, have created a wider interest throughout the country and have produced more permanent results, than any of us dared to hope for. The sportsmanship displayed by the athletes on the part of the losers as well as the winner was magnificent. Just the other day I received a cheque from the Treasurer of The Punjab Olympic Committee for Rs.1114-5-6 which represents contributions made by the Punjab schoolboys through 47 schools. Altogether the Punjab has contributed Rs.2500. The U.P., Bihar & Orissa and Madras have contributed Rs.2000 each, the C.P. Rs.1500.

Word has just reached me from Calcutta that Bengal will most probably raise Rs.4000 and possibly Rs.5000. I am now touring to certain Provinces where the response has not been so encouraging in an effort to raise the remainder necessary to send our 8 men to France. I shall for instance try to get the Maharajah of Patiala subscribe enough to support Dalip Singh, the magnificent long jumper, who hails from Patiala. We hope to get the Military to do the same for their representative and we shall expect a minimum of Rs.5000 from the Government of India. If these plans succeed we shall have enough money in hand to finance the team by the exercise of strict economy.

The most hopeful outcome of the whole Olympic programme is the fact that a permanent All India Olympic Association has now been formed along the lines suggested in the enclosed reprints and it only remains for me, on behalf of the All India Olympic Committee, to extend you a most earnest invitation to consent to be the President of this permanent organisation, in view of the enthusiastic and unanimous conviction of all the Members of the Committee and those interested in the

INDIA AND THE OLYMPIC GAMES

COMPETITION OPEN TO EVERY ELIGIBLE YOUTH IN THE INDIAN EMPIRE

ALL INDIA ATHLETIC MEET
DELHI, FEBRUARY 9, 1924

VIII OLYMPIAD, PARIS, JULY, 1924

HEADQUARTERS OF
ALL INDIA OLYMPIC COMMITTEE:
Y.M.C.A., QUEEN'S GARDENS,
DELHI.

A. G. NOEHREN, M.D.,
SECRETA

-2-

Olympic Programme, that you are emphatically the one
logical person to undertake this office. I do trust
that you may be pleased to accept this position.

In conclusion I wish to express to you my warm
appreciation, not only for your own invaluable help in
making the Olympic enterprise a success, but also for
the great services rendered to me personally, and to the
Olympic project in general, by your Private Secretary,
Mr. Naoroji, who is even now helping me to raise money
in Bombay.

With renewed thanks for all that you have done
for us,

Yours very sincerely,

Sir Dorabji J. Tata, Kt.,
Capel House, New Broad Street,
London, E. C. 2.

AGN/SK.

1924: All India Olympic Committee letter to Sir Dorabji Tata

TATA LIMITED.

TELEGRAMS.
FOREIGN: "TATALO LONDON"
INLAND: "TATALO AVE LONDON".

TELEPHONE NUMBER.
LONDON WALL 3030 (3 LINES)

CODES USED.
WESTERN UNION.
A B C 5TH EDITION.
BENTLEYS.
ALL COMMUNICATIONS TO BE
ADDRESSED TO THE FIRM.

J/FBS.

Jude

15

Reference No.

C.I.O. Capel House,
N°. 2003 New Broad Street,
Reçu: 15.9.27 London. E.C.2
Transmis: 19.9.27
Répondu:
12/3

13th September, 1927

Dear Count Baillet Latour,

     Sir Dorabji Tata thanks you for your
letter of the 8th inst., and for the sheet of Parchment
Paper which he has signed and which I return to you under
separate cover by registered post.

     Sir Dorab regrets that the Maharajah of
Kapurthala has declined the Presidentship of the I.O.C.
At the moment he cannot suggest anyone for that honour, as
in India it is very difficult to find people of high standing
who are interested in that kind of sport and who at the same
time would be able to devote their time to it and come to
Europe frequently.

     I am writing to Dr. Noehren, the Secretary
of the I.O.C. to ask if he could possibly suggest anyone and
I will let you know directly I have a reply from him.

     I am glad to say that Sir Dorab is slightly
improved in health.

     He is leaving on the 24th of this month to
go to America to take a course of treatment in a wellknown

Sanitarium there.

With best respects,

Yours sincerely,

[signature]

Comte de Baillet Latour,
Comite International Olympique,
Mon Repos,
Lausanne,
SIUSSE.

1927: Letter to Count Baillet-Latour

1928: Amsterdam Olympics

1932: The Indian hockey team in action, Los Angeles Games

1932: The Indian Olympic team, Los Angeles Games

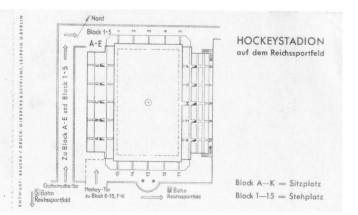

1936: Hockey tickets, Berlin Games

1936: The Indian hockey team, Berlin Games

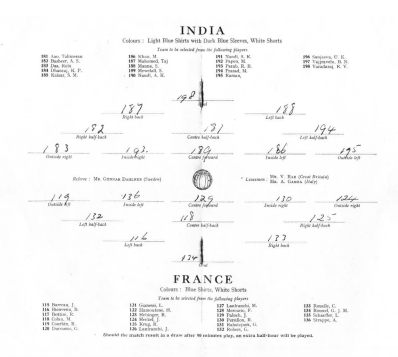

1948: India vs France Football Programme, London Games

1952: Indian Olympic team marchpast, Helsinki Games

Khashaba Dadasaheb Jadhav

1952: K.D. Jadhav (right) after winning bronze, Helsinki Games

1956: Hockey ticket, Melbourne Games

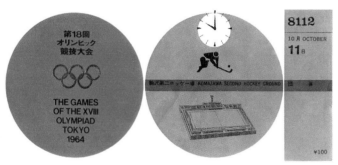

1964: Hockey ticket, Tokyo Games

1980: Hockey ticket, Moscow Games

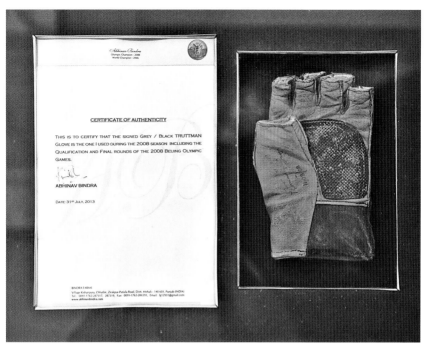

2008: Abhinav Bindra's gloves, Beijing Games

2008: Sushil Kumar (right) after winning bronze, Beijing Games

2012: Gagan Narang after winning bronze, London Games

2012: Mary Kom with her bronze medal, London Games

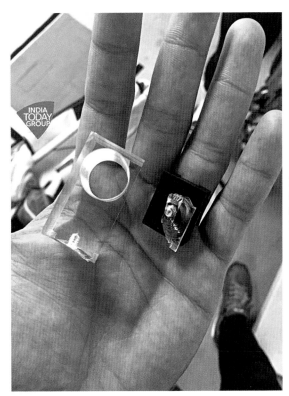

2016: Abhinav Bindra's sighter that broke half an hour before his event, Rio Games

2016: Deepa Malik, Rio Games

2016: P.V. Sindhu & Pullela Gopichand after winning silver, Rio Games

2016: Jersey signed by P.V. Sindhu & Pullela Gopichand, Rio Games

2016: Sakshi Malik after winning bronze, Rio Games

2018: Devendra Jhajharia with Sachin Tendulkar and Sourav Ganguly

2018: P.V. Sindhu, Pullela Gopichand, Pinky Reddy & Saina Nehwal at a FICCI FLO event (left to right)

Notes

INTRODUCTION

1. Norman Pritchard's two medals in 1900 were claimed for years by both Britain and India. There is considerable debate over Pritchard's identity and we thought it best to leave out his medals from India's tally. The IOC archives and contemporary records that we could access do not shed light on his antecedents – whether he was an Anglo Indian (being of mixed race) or an Anglo-Indian (a Britisher who simply lived in India). Be that as it may, his medals are now listed under India's name by the IOC, as the then-sports minister proudly told Parliament in March 2018 after an intervention by the International Society of Olympic Historians. While this may be a technical win for India, he was not part of any official Indian entry into the Olympics and his status remains a mystery. Answer to Rajan Vachare. Lok Sabha Unstarred Questions No. 3289, answered on 15.03.2018.
    http://164.100.24.220/loksabhaquestions/annex/14/AU3289.pdf

2. Ministry of Youth Affairs and Sports Annual Reports, 2012-13 to 2018-19.

3. Minister of State for Sports (Independent. Charge) Rajyavardhan Singh Rathore in response to Dr P.K. Raju, Unstarred Question No. 2158, Lok

Sabha, 8.3.2018. http://164.100.24.220/loksabhaquestions/annex/14/ AU2158.pdf

4. According to a CNBC comparison, the bonus awards were: US - $37,500 for gold, $22,500 for silver and $15,000 for bronze; France - $55,00 for gold, $22,000 for silver or $14,000 for bronze; and Germany - $22,000 for gold, $17,000 for silver or $11,00 for bronze. https://www.cnbc.com/2018/02/23/heres-how-much-olympic-athletes-earn-in-12-different-countries.html

CHAPTER 8

1. Personal letter from Dorabji Tata to the IOC president, Count Baillet Latour, 21 May 1929. Housed at the International Olympic Museum, Lausanne, ID Chemise 7334 CIO 3535 MBR-TATA-CORR, Correspondence de Dorabji Tata 1926–1930.

2. See Cecil Headlam, *Ten Thousand Miles through India and Burma: An Account of the Oxford University Cricket Tour with Mr K. J. Kay in the Year of the Coronation Durbar* (London, 1903).

3. Personal letter from Dorabji Tata to the IOC president, Count Baillet Latour, 21 May 1929. Housed at the International Olympic Museum, Lausanne, ID Chemise 7334 CIO 3535 MBR-TATA-CORR, Correspondence de Dorabji Tata 1926–1930.

4. Ibid.

5. See the letters in ID Chemise 7334 CIO 3535 MBR-TATA-CORR, Correspondence de Dorabji Tata 1926–1930, International Olympic Museum, Lausanne.

6. Personal letter from Dorabji Tata to the IOC president, Count Baillet Latour, 21 May 1929. Housed at the International Olympic Museum, Lausanne, ID Chemise 7334 CIO 3535 MBR-TATA-CORR, Correspondence de Dorabji Tata 1926–1930.

7. *The Statesman*, 3 June 1920, 'Indian Athletes at the Olympic Games: Team of Six from Bombay'.

8. Letter from A.G. Noehren to Dorabji Tata on 1 April 1924 housed at the International Olympic Museum, Lausanne. File OU MO 01 14 36, CIO CNO IND CORR, Olympic Studies Center, IOC Museum, Lausanne. This file deals primarily with correspondence exchanged between the Indian Olympic Association and the International Olympic Committee.

Also, all documents sent from India to the IOC—letters, pamphlets, constitutions etc have been retained in this file. Also see IDD Chemise 9404 CIO CNO INDE CORR, Correspondence India 1924-1963. All factual details in this section are from this file, unless otherwise indicated.

9. *Amrita Bazar Patrika*, 18 January 1924.

10. Saradindu Sanyal, 'India and the Olympics', in *XVIII Olympiad Tokyo 1964: Official Souvenir of the Indian Olympic Association*: (Mumbai: Sportswriters Publishers, 1964), pp. 25–26.

11. Personal letter from Dorabji Tata to the IOC president, Count Baillet Latour, 21 May 1929. Housed at the International Olympic Museum, Lausanne, ID Chemise 7334 CIO 3535 MBR-TATA-CORR, Correspondence de Dorabji Tata 1926–1930.

12. Personal letter from Dorabji Tata to the IOC president Count Baillet Latour, 21 Feb 1927. Housed at the International Olympic Museum, Lausanne, ID Chemise 7334 CIO 3535 MBR-TATA-CORR, Correspondence de Dorabji Tata 1926–1930.

13. For details on the stadium controversy see; Boria Majumdar, *Twenty Two Yards to Freedom: A Social History of Indian Cricket* (New Delhi: Penguin Viking, 2004), pp. 171–99.

14. For most of his letters see IOC Archives, ID Chemise 7334 CIO 3535 MBR-TATA-CORR, Correspondence de Dorabji Tata 1926–1930.

15. Personal letter from Sir Dorabji Tata to Count Baillet Latour, Geneva, 16 June 1927. IOC Archives, ID Chemise 7334 CIO 3535 MBR-TATA-CORR, Correspondence de Dorabji Tata 1926-1930. Also see; File OU MO 01 14 36, CIO CNO IND CORR, Olympic Studies Center, IOC Museum, Lausanne.

16. IOC Archives, ID Chemise 7334 CIO 3535 MBR-TATA-CORR, Correspondence de Dorabji Tata 1926–1930.

17. For details see; Boria Majumdar, *Twenty Two Yards to Freedom: A Social History of Indian Cricket* (New Delhi: Penguin Viking, 2004), Chapter 1.

18. Personal letter from Sir Dorabji Tata to Count Baillet Latour on 13 September 1927. File OU MO 01 14 36, CIO CNO IND CORR, Olympic Studies Center.

19. Personal letter from Sir Dorabji Tata to to Count Baillet Latour on 17 Jan. 1928. File OU MO 01 14 36, CIO CNO IND CORR, Olympic Studies Center.

20. Anthony S. De Mello, 'A Wardrobe of Coloured Blazers', in *Portrait of Indian Sport*, (New Delhi: Macmillan 1959), pp. 48–49.
21. File OU MO 01 14 36, CIO CNO IND CORR, Olympic Studies Center. All quotes in this paragraph are from a personal letter from Henry Gray to Count Baillet Latour, 28 December 1928. IOC Archives, ID Chemise 7334 CIO 3535 MBR-TATA-CORR, Correspondence de Dorabji Tata 1926–1930.
22. Personal letter from IOC president to Sir Dorabji Tata, 22 April 1927. The IOC chief thanked Tata for his wonderful work in promoting the Olympic cause in India and indicated that the IOC was aware of the difficulties involved in replacing Sir Dorab with someone equally capable and equal to the task of assuming effective control of the Olympic movement in India. IOC Archives, ID Chemise 7334 CIO 3535 MBR-TATA-CORR, Correspondence de Dorabji Tata 1926–1930.
23. John J. MacAloon, 'Introduction', Revised and Updated edition of *This Great Symbol: Pierre De Coubertin and the Origins of the Modern Olympic Games*, Special Issue, *The International Journal of the History of Sport*, 23 (3–4), 2006, p. 344.
      This chapter is mostly constructed from archival details in three files at the International Olympics Museum, Lausanne, Switzerland: File OU MO 01 14 36, CIO CNO IND CORR, Olympic Studies Center; IOC Archives, ID Chemise 7334 CIO 3535 MBR-TATA-CORR, Correspondence de Dorabji Tata 1926–1930; IOC Archives, IDD Chemise 9404 CIO CNO INDE CORR, Correspondence India 1924–1963.

CHAPTER 9

We have extensively used *The Statesman* reportage for this chapter for the relevant time periods.

1. Review of the 1932 Olympic expedition by the president of the IHF, A.M. Hayman housed at the International Olympic Museum, Lausanne. File OU MO 01 14 36, CIO CNO IND CORR, Olympic Studies Center.
2. For details see; 'We Climb the Victory Stand: Hockey in *Excelsis*', in Anthony S. De Mello, *Portrait of Indian Sport*, (New Delhi: Macmillan, 1959).
3. Dhyan Chand, *Goal*, published in *Sport and Pastime*, 1952. The book has been digitized and is available in http://www.bharatiyahockey.org/granthalaya/goal/, accessed 10 September 2007.

All subsequent Dhyan Chand quotes in this chapter are from this source, unless otherwise specified.

4. Details in this section from; 'We Climb the Victory Stand: Hockey in *Excelsis*', op. cit., pp. 82-83.

5. For details see C.D. Parthasarathy, 'Indian Hockey: Rise and Fall', in *Sport and Pastime*, 16 February 1963.

6. 'We Climb the Victory Stand...', op. cit., p. 85.

7. Ramachandra Guha, *India After Gandhi: The History of the World's Largest Democracy* (New Delhi: Picador, 2007), pp. 115–16

8. Subroto Sirkar, 'They came...they played...they conquered', *World Hockey*, 13 March 1995, p.8.

9. Notes from Jaipal's Singh's memoirs passed on to us by Amar Singh, Jaipal Singh's son, then secretary of the CC Morris Cricket Library, Pennsylvania in 2001. The memoirs were later edited by Rashmi Katyayan and published by Prabhat Khabar Publications, Ranchi, 2004.

10. Rashmi Katyayan (ed.), *Lo Bir Sendra* (Ranchi: Prabhat Khabar Publications, 2004), p. 35.

11. *Lo Bir Sendra*, op. cit., pp. 35–37.

12. Personal interview with Amar Singh, 2001, Jaipal Singh's life has quite a few unsolved mysteries. For example, Jaipal's real name was Pramod Pahan. Later, his name was changed to Jaipal and even he isn't sure why this happened. On Jaipal not playing in the final of the 1928 Olympiad, Dhyan Chand writes in his memoirs, 'Jaipal Singh, I believe, used to fly from London to Amsterdam most of the time, returning after the match was over. It is still a mystery to me why Jaipal Singh, after ably captaining us in England, and in two of the three matches in the Olympic Games, suddenly left us. I have heard many stories, but so far I have not had the truth.' He later hints that 'communal and racial issues' might have been involved in Jaipal's sudden absence. According to Dhyan Chand, the only person who could clear the mystery was Jaipal himself. But Jaipal merely says in his autobiography that on his return to London from the Olympics, Lord Irwin, Viceroy of India, congratulated him personally.

13. Dhyan Chand, *Goal*, published in *Sport and Pastime*, 1952, Section on the 1928 Amsterdam Olympiad.

14. Quoted in C.D. Parthasarathy, 'That Golden Age', in *Sport and Pastime*, 23 February 1963.

15. Rashmi Katyayan (ed.), *Lo Bir Sendra* (Ranchi: Prabhat Khabar Publications, 2004), p. 37.

16. Ibid. p. 38.

17. Ramachandra Guha, *India After Gandhi: The History of the World's Largest Democracy* (New Delhi: Picador, 2007), pp. 115–16.

18. Review of the 1932 Olympic expedition by the president of the IHF, A.M. Hayman housed at the International Olympic Museum, Lausanne. File OU MO 01 14 36, CIO CNO IND CORR, Olympic Studies Center.

19. Pankaj Gupta, 'India's Hockey Supremacy', in *Sport and Pastime*, 10 May 1958, pp. 37–38.

20. Details from Review of the 1932 Olympic expedition by the president of the IHF, A.M. Hayman housed at the International Olympic Museum, Lausanne. File OU MO 01 14 36, CIO CNO IND CORR, Olympic Studies Center.

21. Quoted in *The Statesman*, 2 August 1932, p. 11.

22. Details from *The Statesman*, 4-13 August 1932.

23. Details from Hayman's review *The Statesman* 4-13 August, 1932.

24. All match details from the pages of *The Statesman*, 4-14 August, 1932, and Review of the 1932 Olympic expedition by the president of the IHF, A.M. Hayman housed at the International Olympic Museum, Lausanne. File OU MO 01 14 36, CIO CNO IND CORR, Olympic Studies Center

25. Review of the 1932 Olympic expedition by the president of the IHF, A.M. Hayman housed at the International Olympic Museum, Lausanne. File OU MO 01 14 36, CIO CNO IND CORR, Olympic Studies Center.

26. Quoted in C.D. Parthasarathy, 'That Golden Age', in *Sport and Pastime*, 23 February 1963. The original report is housed in the International Olympic Museum, Lausanne. File OU MO 01 14 36, CIO CNO IND CORR, Olympic Studies Center.

27. Quoted in, 'We Climb the Victory Stand: Hockey in *Excelsis*', in Anthony S. De Mello, *Portrait of Indian Sport* (New Delhi: Mcmillan 1959), pp. 93–95.

28. C.D. Parthasarathy, 'That Golden Age', in *Sport and Pastime*, 23 February 1963.

29. Same as Reference 1.

30. Boria Majumdar, *Twenty Two Yards to Freedom: A Social History of Indian Cricket*, (New Delhi: Penguin Viking, 2004), pp. 44.

31. Mihir Bose, *History of Indian Cricket* (London: Andre Deutsch, revised and updated 2002), p. 80.

32. For details see Boria Majumdar and Kausik Bandyopadhyay, *Goalless: The Story of a Unique Footballing Nation* (New Delhi: Penguin Viking, 2006), Ch. 4.

33. For Indian cricket and the nationalist imagination, particularly in colonial India, see for instance, Ramachandra Guha, *Corner of a Foreign Field: The Indian History of a British Sport* (New Delhi: Pan Macmillan, 2002) and Boria Majumdar, *Twenty Two Yards to Freedom: A Social History of Indian Cricket* (New Delhi: Penguin, 2004).

34. See for instance, Kausik Bandopadhyaya, '1911 in Retrospect: A Revisionist Perspective on a Famous Indian Sporting Victory', pp. 27–47.

35. Boria Majumdar and Kausik Bandopadyay, Introduction to *A Social History of Indian Football: Striving to Score* (London: Routledge, 2006), p. 122.

CHAPTER 10

We have extensively used *The Statesman* reportage for this chapter because the memoirs/travel diaries of the Indian team members were published in this newspaper. Also, the paper documented in considerable detail India's gold medal-winning tryst and thus served as a valuable contemporary source. Other papers like *The Times of India* were also consulted. However, with the match reports being of a similar nature, we preferred *The Statesman* for this chapter.

Some facts mentioned in this chapter do not square up with the details in Dhyan Chand's autobiography. Where there is a dispute over facts, we have decided on balance to favour the considered evidence from other contemporary sources and press reportage on the Berlin Olympiad because Dhyan Chand's autobiography was only published a decade and a half later in 1952 and it is likely that he may have forgotten some details.

1. Dhyan Chand, *Goal*, published in *Sport and Pastime*, 1952. Section on the 1936 Berlin Olympiad. The book has been digitized and is available in http://www.bharatiyahockey.org/granthalaya/goal/ accessed 29 September 2007.

2. Ibid.

3.   *The Statesman*, 20 July 1936, p. 11.

4.   *The Statesman*, 22 July 1936, p. 11.

5.   *The Statesman*, 22 July 1936, p. 11.

6.   Dhyan Chand, *Goal*, op. cit.

7.   Details in this section are from *The Statesman*, 23 July-20 August 1936.

8.   M.N. Masood, *The World's Hockey Champions 1936*, The book has been digitized and is available in http://www.bharatiyahockey.org/granthalaya/champions/, accessed 4 October 2007.

9.   Ibid.

10.   M.N. Masood, *The World's Hockey Champions 1936*, op. cit.

11.   Ibid.

12.   Ibid.

13.   *The Statesman*, 2 August 1936, p.9

14.   *The Statesman*, 30-31 July 1936.

15.   Details in this section from *The Statesman*, 4-13 August 1936.

16.   Details in this section from *The Statesman*,10 Juhly-31 August 1936.

17.   Ibid. and Dhyan Chand, Goal.

18.   M.N. Masood, *The World's Hockey Champions 1936*, op. cit.

CHAPTER 11

1.   Balbir Singh, *The Golden Hattrick*, The book has been digitized and is available in http://www.bharatiyahockey.org/granthalaya/hattrick/, accessed 12 December 2007. Section on 1956 Melbourne Olympiad.

2.   Dhyan Chand, *Goal*, published in *Sport and Pastime*, 1952. The book has been digitized and is available in http://www.bharatiyahockey.org/granthalaya/goal/, accessed 10 November 2007.

3.   All further references to Balbir Singh are, unless specified otherwise, from *The Golden Hattrick*, op. cit.

4.   'Indian Hockey Team in London', in the *Times of India*, 16 July 1948.

5.   Details in this section from *The Times of India*, 2-28 July 1948.

6.   All details in this section *The Times of India*, July-August 1948

7.   For details see 'We Climb the Victory Stand: Hockey in *Excelsis*', in Anthony S. De Mello, *Portrait of Indian Sport* (New Delhi: Macmillan, 1959).

8.   All factual details in these sections from *The Times of India*, June--August 1952.

9. Balbir Singh, *The Golden Hattrick*, op. cit.
10. *The Times of India*, June--August 1952.
11. Balbir Singh, *The Golden Hattrick*, op. cit.
12. Ibid.
13. For details see; Pankaj Gupta, 'India's Hockey Supremacy', in *Sport and Pastime*, 10 May 1958, pp. 37–38.
14. The *Hindu*, 27-29 November 1956.
15. *The Hindu*, 1 Dec. 1956
16. For details see Pankaj Gupta, 'India's Hockey Supremacy', in *Sport and Pastime*, 10 May 1958, pp. 37–38.
17. The *Hindu*, 4 December 1956.
18. Balbir Singh, *The Golden Hattrick*, op cite
19. Pankaj Gupta, 'Past Matches Recalled', the *Hindu*, 26 August 1960.
20. Emphasis is ours. For details see; Pankaj Gupta, 'India's Hockey Supremacy', in *Sport and Pastime*, 10 May 1958, pp. 37–38.
21. For details see the *Hindu* 28 August-10 September 1960.
22. S.M. Sait, 'Rome Debacle and Its Lessons', *Indian Olympic News* Vol. 1, no. 4, July 1962. The writer was honorary secretary, Indian Hockey Federation, NA
23. See for instance, S.M. Sait, 'Robust Hockey Vs. Skilful Hockey', *Indian Olympic News* Vol. 2, no. 2, May 1963 pp. 35–36.
24. S.M. Sait, 'Rome Debacle and Its Lessons', *Indian Olympic News* Vol 1, no. 4, July 1962., NA
25. Charanjit Rai, 'How to Regain World Hockey Title', *Indian Olympic News* Vol. 1, no. 4, July 1962, p. 35.
26. T.D. Parthasarathy, 'India's Chances in Hockey', the *Hindu*, 10 October 1964
27. For details on this match see the *Hindu* 12 October 1964.
28. All details from The Hindu, 13-22 October 1964.
29. Rene G. Frank, 'Sayonara Tokyo—Au Revoir Tokyo: The Olympic Tournament in Retrospect', *FIH Official Bulletin*, No. 13, Dec. 1964, pp. 10–11.
30. Match details from The *Hindu*, 24 October 1964.
31. For details see the *Times of India*, 21 July 1980.
32. Match details from *Times of India*, 22-30 July 1980
33. Match details from *Times of India*, 22 July-3 August 1980

CHAPTER 12

1. Pankaj Gupta quoted in *IOA Annual Report*, 1962, p. 2 CIO CNO IND GENER OU MO 01 14 36 INDE Correspondance Generale 1950– 1981

2. For details see; Steve Ruskin, 'Reign on the Wane', *Sports Illustrated*, 85 (4), 22 July 1996, pp. 170–74.

3. 'Milestones Along the Olympic Road', See section 'The Fall of Rome', *World Hockey: The Magazine of the International Hockey Federation*, No. 26, June 1976, p. 6.

4. This is point made forcefully by Shekhar Gupta in 'The HMT Advantage', *The Indian Express*, Feb 15, 2003. Shekhar Gupta defines 'HMT' as 'Hindi- medium types' who are increasingly breaking the barriers of elitism in various sectors of the economy and also in Indian cricket.

5. 'Germany First Champions on Artificial Turf', *World Hockey*, October 1975, No 24, p. 8.

6. File OU MO01 14 36, CIO CNO IND CORR, Olympic Studies Centre, IOC Museum, Lausanne. This file deals primarily with correspondence exchanged between the Indian Olympic Association and the Indian Olympic Committee. Also, any document sent from India to the IOC— letters, pamphlets, constitutions etc have been retained in this file.

7. Ibid.

8. 'Hockey on an Artificial Pitch', *World Hockey*, October 1975, No. 24, p. 10.

9. Ibid.

10. For details see; Steve Ruskin, 'Reign on the Wane', *Sports Illustrated*, 85 (4), 22 July 1996, pp. 170-174.

11. Ibid.

12. See file OU MO01 14 36, CIO CNO IND CORR, Olympic Studies Centre, IOC Museum, Lausanne.

13. Rene Frank, president, FIH, to Lord Killanin, president, IOC, Feb 27, 1978, OU MO01 14 36, CIO CNO IND CORR 1977–78, Olympic Studies Centre.

14. See File IDD CHEMISE 9404 CIO CNOINDE CORR, Olympic Studies Centre. Correspondence between the IOC and the Indian Olympic Association is chronologically arranged. This file mostly contains material on issues relating to Indian hockey.

15. Letter from Raja Bhalindra Singh to IOC president, 11 October 1974, ID Chemise 6826 CIO MBR SINGH CORR OU MO 01 41 07 SINGH, Bhalindra Raja Correspondance 1947–1985, Olympic Studies Centre.

16. Rene Frank, president, FIH, to Lord Killanin, president, IOC, 27 February 1978, OU MO01 14 36, CIO CNO IND CORR 1977–78, Olympic Studies Centre. Also see Raja Bhalindra Singh to Lord Killanin, March 10, 1978 ID Chemise 6826 CIO MBR SINGH CORR OU MO 01 41 07 SINGH, Bhalindra Raja Correspondance 1947–1985, Olympic Studies Centre.

17. Balbir Singh, 'Kuala Lumpur Has Always Been Lucky', available online at http://www.indianhockey.com/mcol3/1.php, accessed 15 December 2005.

18. The release reported verbatim by UNI is available in OU MO01 14 36, CIO CNO IND CORR, Olympic Studies Centre.

19. Letter sent on 25 January 1976 by the Pakistan Olympic Association to Lord Killanin, available in file CIO FI FIH CORR OU MO 01 1433, Olympic Studies Centre, IOC Museum, Lausanne.

20. Raja Bhalindra Singh to Lord Killanin, March 10, 1978 ID Chemise 6826 CIO MBR SINGH CORR OU MO 01 41 07 SINGH, Bhalindra Raja Correspondance 1947-1985, Olympic Studies Centre.

21. Extracts from the minutes of the IOA General Assembly Meeting held on 2 July 1977, OU MO01 14 36, CIO CNO IND CORR, Olympic Studies Centre.

22. The *Hindustan Times*, 10 January 1978.

23. Raja Bhalindra Singh, letter to Lord Killanin, 15 Jan. 1978, OU MO01 14 36, CIO CNO IND CORR, Olympic Studies Centre.

24. Injunction issued by the Madras Court on 18 Jan. 1978, OU MO01 14 36, CIO CNO IND CORR, Olympic Studies Centre.

25. Letter from Ramaswamy to Rene Frank, 21 Jan. 1978, OU MO01 14 36, CIO CNO IND CORR, Olympic Studies Centre.

26. Ibid.

27. OU MO01 14 36, CIO CNO IND CORR 1977–78, Olympic Studies Centre.

28. Bobby Talyarkhan, 'When Rene gets too Frank', OU MO01 14 36, CIO CNO IND CORR 1977–78, Olympic Studies Centre.

29. Air Chief Marshall O.P. Mehra, president, IOA, to Rene G. Frank, president, IHF, 24 June 1978. OU MO01 14 36, CIO CNO IND CORR 1977–78, Olympic Studies Centre.

30. OU MO01 14 36, CIO CNO IND CORR 1977–78, Olympic Studies Centre.

31. Lord Killanin, president, IOC to Rene Frank, president, IHF, OU MO01 14 36, CIO CNO IND CORR 1977–78, Olympic Studies Centre.

32. 'They Don't Give a Damn', Dhanraj Pillay interview with Shantanu Guha Ray, 16 June 2007, http://www.tehelka.com/story_main31.asp? filename= hub160607They_dont.asp.

CHAPTER 13

1. Shekhar Gupta, 'Hockey Isn't just Cricket', the *Indian Express*, 7 September 2002.

2. The players were S.V. Sunil, Vickram Kanth, Ignace Turkey and V. Raghunath. They were accompanied by Ramesh Parameshwaram, assistant coach of the national team and R.K. Shetty, Karnataka State Hockey Association President. Report telecast on Times Now, 26 September 2007.

3. Live phone interview with Nalin Mehta on Times Now, 26 September 2007. The Indian Hockey Federation acted fast to nip the hunger strike but the point had been made.

4. Quoted in T.N. Raghu, 'Starved Hockey Ready to Fast', the *Asian Age*, 27 September 2007.

5. *Amrit Bazar Patrika*, 31 July 1911.

6. Quoted in *Mohun Bagan Platinum Jubilee Souvenir* , (Calcutta: Mohun Bagan Club, 1964), p. 25

7. *Nayak*, 4 August 1911.

8. Swami Vivekanand, quoted in Boria Majumdar, Kausik Bandpadhyay, 'From Recreation to Competition: Early History of Indian Football', in 'A Social History of Indian Football: Striving to Score', *Soccer & Society*, Special Issue, Vol. 6, No. 2/3, June–September 2005, p. 135

9. Boria Majumdar, Kausik Bandopadyay, Introduction to 'A Social History of Indian Football: Striving to Score', *Soccer & Society*, Vol. 6, No. 2/3, June/ September 2005, p. 122.

10. Mihir Bose, *A History of Indian Cricket* (London: Andre Deutsch Ltd., 1990), pp. 16–17.

11. Boria Majumdar, Kausik Bandopadhyay, Introduction to 'A Social History of Indian Football: Striving to Score', *Soccer & Society*, Vol. 6, No. 2/3, June/ September 2005, p. 288.

12. Alarm bells rang in India when Helsinki, in 1949, expressed its unwillingness to host all hockey teams for 1952 because of a lack of accommodation. The Indian Hockey Federation immediately proposed to the IOC to host the hockey event separately in Delhi. Eventually, Helsinki did host the event but the Indian offer was indicative of how important hockey was to Indian sports. Letter from Dr. A.C. Chatterji, honorary secretary, Indian Hockey Federation, to Demaurex, honorary secretary, Switzerland Hockey Federation, May 10, 1949, CIO FI FIH PROGR OU MO 0114 33 FIH- Hockey Programe 1946–1949.

13. Anthony De Mello, *Portrait of Indian Sport* (London: P.R. Macmillan, 1959), p. 3.

14. Ibid.

15. See Ramachandra Guha, *Corner of a Foreign Field: The Indian History of a British Sport* (New Delhi: Pan Macmillan, 2002). Mihir Bose, *History of Indian Cricket* (London: Andre Deutsch, 2002).

16. See Boria Majumdar, *Twenty Two Yards to Freedom: A Social History of Indian Cricket* (New Delhi: Penguin, 2004).

17. Anthony De Mello, *Portrait of Indian Sport* (London: P.R. Macmillan, 1959), pp. 9-10.

18. Eastern Railways advertisement, published in *Indian Olympic News*, Vol. 1, No. 3, June 1962.

19. South Eastern Railways advertisement, published in *Indian Olympic News*, Vol. 1, No. 2, May 1962.

20. Air India advertisement, published in *Indian Olympic News*, Vol. 1, No. 4, July 1962.

21. J. Butalia, Jwalamukhi— the Olympia of India, *Indian Olympic Association Official Bulletin*, Vol. 2, January–March 1960, pp. 35-38. All details in this section from here.

22. Mir Ranjan Negi's Interview with Shekhar Gupta, the *Indian Express*, 17 September 2007.

23. Shekhar Gupta, 'Hockey Just Isn't Cricket', the *Indian Express*, 7 September 2002.

24. Ramachandra Guha, *India After Gandhi: The History of the World's Largest Democracy* (India: 2007), pp. 736–37.

25. Sevanti Ninan, *Through the Magic Window: Television and Change in India* (New Delhi: Penguin, 1995), p. 30.

26. David Page and William Crawley, *Satellites Over South Asia: Broadcasting, Culture and the Public Interest* (New Delhi: Sage, 2001). p. 56.

27. William Mazzarella, *Shoveling Smoke: Advertising and Globalization in Contemporary India* (Durham: Duke University Press, 2003), p. 98.

28. 28. Audience Research Unit, Directorate General Doordarshan, Cited in Joshi, *Asia Speaks Out*, pp. 5–8; NRS 2006.

29. Quoted in William Mazzarella, *Shoveling Smoke: Advertising and Globalization in Contemporary India* (Durham: Duke University Press, 2003), pp. 74–75.

30. Audience Research Unit, Directorate General Doordarshan, 1995.Cited in Joshi & Trivedi, *Mass Media and Cross-Cultural Communication*, p. 16.

31. Vir Sanghvi, 'A New Middle Class Fidelity?' the *Hindustan Times,* New Delhi, 20 May 2006, http://www.hindustantimes.com/news/181_1702508, 00300001. htm, accessed 21 May 2006.

32. Shalimar Mary, letter to editor, the *Indian Express*, 5 October 1986. Quoted in Nandy, *The Tao of Cricket*, pp. 1–2.

33. Harsha Bhogle, 'India Needs to Rediscover Another Sport', the *Week*, 27 July 2003.

34. Rohit Brijnath, 'The Lopsidedness in Indian Sports', *Sportstar*, 5–11 June, 2004.

35. Rupert Murdoch's News Corporation bought a controlling stake in Sky in 1983 and re-launched as Sky Television in 1989 but it made heavy losses until 1992 when BSkyB (Sky and BSB merged in 1990) acquired the rights to broadcast Premier League Soccer games for $465 million. Almost a million subscribers signed up immediately and by 1993 it reached financial stability. Bharat Anand & Kate Attea, 'News Corporation', Harvard Business School Case No. 9-702-425 (Boston: Harvard Business School Publishing, rev. 27 June 2003), p. 8. For a concise history of Sky Television and News Corporation's television operations see also, Pankaj Ghemawat, 'British Satellite Broadcasting Versus Sky Television,' Harvard Business School Case No. 9-794-031 (Boston: Harvard Business School Publishing, rev. ed. 22 August 1994).

36. Emphasis is ours. Rupert Murdoch to his shareholders in Adelaide, 15 October 1996. Quoted in S. Millar, 'Courtship Ends as Soccer and TV are United', the Guardian, 7 September 1998.

37. In 1999, for instance, News Corporation owned the Los Angeles Dodgers baseball club and had shares in the New York Knicks and Los Angeles Lakers basketball clubs, and the New York Rangers. In September 1998, BSkyB launched a takeover bid for Manchester United, the world's richest football club, which was blocked by the British Mergers and Monopolies Commission on grounds that it was 'anti-competitive' in broadcasting. David Rowe, 'To Serve and To Sell: Media Sport and Cultural Citizenship', Paper at How you Play the Game: First International Conference on Sports and Human Rights, Sydney, 1–3 September 1999, p. 186, http:// www. ausport. gov.au/fulltext/1999/nsw/p182-191.pdf, accessed 27 August 2006.

38. Supreme Court Case 161 before Justices, P.B. Sawant, S Mohan and B.P. Jeevan Reddy, Civil Appeals Nos. 1429-30 of 1995, The Secretary Information & Broadcasting, Government of India & Others vs. Cricket Association of Bengal & Others, with Writ Petition (Civil) No. 836 of 1993, Cricket Association of Bengal vs. Union of India and Others (decided on 9 February 1995). See details in Nalin Mehta, *India on Television: How Satellite Television Channels Changed the Way We Think and Act* (New Delhi: HarperCollins, 2008)

39. All details in this section from Nalin Mehta, *India on Television: How Satellite Television Channels Changed the Way We Think and Act* (New Delhi: HarperCollins, 2008), chapter 3.

40. C.R. Irani, 'Someone is Remembering Sanjay Gandhi', *The Statesman,* 13 November 1993.

41. Supreme Court Case 161 before Justices, P.B. Sawant, S Mohan and B.P. Jeevan Reddy, Civil Appeals Nos. 1429–30 of 1995.

42. B.P.J. Reddy concurring, Supreme Court Case 161 before Justices, P.B. Sawant, S Mohan and B.P. Jeevan Reddy, Civil Appeals Nos. 1429–30 of 1995.

43. Ministry of Information and Broadcasting, Policy Guidelines for Downlinking of Television Channels, 11 November 2005.

44. 'Don't Interfere with Ten Sports' Rights: Court', the *Hindu,* 5 August 2006.

45. UNI, 'SC allows ESPN-STAR to Approach it if coerced by the Centre', 8 January 2007, http://www.indlawnews.com/2C829C337F2DBD858EAC 77A542 63988C, accessed 8 January 2007.

46. The government contended that about 9–10% of Doordarshan's 25% share would pay for its expenditure in the broadcast while the remaining revenue would be ploughed back into national sports. Rajya Sabha, Synopsis of Debates (Proceedings other than Questions and Answers), Statutory Resolution Seeking Disapproval of the Sports Broadcasting Signals (Mandatory Sharing with Prasar Bharati) Ordinance, 2007 and the Sports Broadcasting Signals (Mandatory Sharing with Prasar Bharati) Bill, 2007 (9 March 2007),

47. http://www.rajyasabha.nic.in/rsdebate/synopsis/ 210/09032007.htm, accessed 11 March 2007.

48. Ibid.

49. Ibid.

50. In the Rajya Sabha, for instance, only two speakers dissented. http://www.rajyasabha.nic.in/rsdebate/synopsis/210/09032007.htm, accessed 11 March 2007. See Nalin Mehta, *India on Television: How TV News Changed the Ways We Think and Act* (New Delhi: HarperCollins, 2008).

51. Appadurai, *Modernity at Large: Cultural Dimensions of Globalization*, (Minneapolis: University of Minnesota Press, 1996), p. 101.

52. Atul Phadnis, 'New TAM-ADEX Analysis: Greater Opportunities for In-Program or On-Ground Promotions During Cricket than Soccer!' (Mumbai: TAM ADEX, 24 January 2002, http://www.indiantelevision. com /tamadex/y2k3/tamadex.htmm, accessed 29 August 2006.

53. Appadurai, *Modernity at Large*, p. 111.

54. Interview with Uday Shankar, CEO and editor, Star News, 2003–07, Shanghai, 22 August 2005.

55. Kunal Dasgupta, CEO, Sony Entertainment Television, interview on http://www.indiantelevision.com/interviews/y2k2/executive/kunal.htm, 3 June 2002, accessed 1 August 2006.

56. Sheela Reddy, 'Hooked,' *Outlook*, 24 March 2003, http://www.outlookindia. com/archivecontents.asp?fnt=20030324, accessed 1 August 2006.

57. Atul Phadnis, 'Adex World Cup Barometer: 2nd Week of Cricket World Cup Rakes in 36.5 Million Female Viewers,' TAM India Report, 3 March

2003, http://www.indiantelevision.com/tamadex/y2k3/mar/cricbra5.
htm, accessed 31 July 2006.

58. Purnendu Bose, COO, SaharaOne, quoted in Latha Venkatraman, Ajita
Shashidhar, 'Taking Refuge in Cricket', *BusinessLine*, 9 March 2006.

59. Ashis Nandy, *The Tao of Cricket: On Games of Destiny and the Destiny of the
Games* (New York: Viking, 1989), p. 1.

CHAPTER 14

1. Sanjay Sharma, 'President APJ Abdul Kalam Looks to Indian Army &
Govt Support to Produce Indian Olympic Medallists', 15 September
2004. www.indian olympic.com/story/2004/9/15/205540/587, accessed
15 August 2005.

2. http://mod.nic.in/rec&training/body.htm, accessed 15 August, 2005.
Also see *Ministry of Defence Annual Report*, 2001–2002, p. 32.

3. Gopal Sharma, 'Army Out to Salvage Pride in Olympics', The *Tribune*,
14 August 2004.

4. Ibid.

5. Krishna Bobji, 3 February 2005.
http://mboard.rediff.com/board/board.php?action=m&boardid
=sports2003sep04spec&messageid= 1598131597#1598131597

6. Anthony De Mello, *Portrait of Indian Sport* (London: P.R. Macmillan,
1959), pp. 3, 8.

7. The entire collection of this magazine is available in the Rare Section of
the Regenstein Library, University of Chicago.

8. *Sporting Intelligence Magazine*, March 1845, p. 450.

9. Boria Majumdar, 'When the Sepoys Batted: 1830–1850 on the Playing
Field', in Sharmistha Gooptu and Boria Majumdar (eds.), *Revisiting 1857:
Myth, Memory, History*, (New Delhi: Roli Books, 2007), p. 77.

10. Chris Moore, 'A History of Hockey', *6th FIH World Hockey Cup for Men:
National Hockey Centre, London, England, 4th–19th October, 1986, Official
Souvenir Programme* (London: World Hockey Cup), pp. 33–34.

11. Dhyan Chand, *Goal*, published in *Sport and Pastime*, 1952. http://www.
bharatiyahockey.org/granthalaya/goal/, accessed 29 September 2007.

12. Chris Moore, 'A History of Hockey', *6th FIH World Hockey Cup for Men:
National Hockey Centre, London, England, 4th–19th October, 1986, Official
Souvenir Programme* (London: World Hockey Cup), p. 34.

13. Dhyan Chand, *Goal*, published in *Sport and Pastime*, 1952. http://www. bharatiya hockey.org/granthalaya/goal/, accessed 29 September 2007.

14. 'Olympians Dot Sansarpur Plains', the *Tribune*, 8 November 2003

15. Steve Ruskin, 'Reign on the Wane', *Sports Illustrated*, 85 (4), 22 July 1996, p. 172.

16. Boria Majumdar and Kausik Bandyopadhyay, *Striving to Score: A Social History of Indian Football*, (London: Routledge, 2006), p. 124.

17. The Calcutta Football Club (1872) devoted to playing rugby football initially, predated the Dalhousie Club by over a decade and is technically the oldest Indian football club. See Boria Majumdar, Nalin Mehta, *Olympics: The India Story* (New Delhi: HarperCollins, 2008, 2nd ed. 2012)

18. 'Services Lead the Way', *Indian Olympic News*, July 1962, Vol. 1, No. 4, p. 5.

19. Raju G.C. Thomas, 'The Armed Forces and the Indian Defence Budget', *Asian Survey*, Vol. XX, No. 3, March 1980, pp. 280–82.

20. 'Services Lead the Way', *Indian Olympic News*, July 1962, Vol. 1, No. 4, pp. 5-7

21. Ibid.; *Indian Olympic News*, Aug 1963, Vol 2, No. 5, p. 6–7; *Indian Olympic News*, Nov. 1962, Vol. 1, No, 8, p. 3.

22. 'Sportsmen Come Forward', editorial in *Indian Olympic News*, Dec. 1962, Vol. 1, No. 8, p. 3.

23. 'To the National Defence Fund', *Indian Olympic News*, Dec. 1962, Vol. 1, No. 9, p. 37.

24. Others who donated were Behala Athletics Sports Association, Rs 151 (as a first installment); Obaid Al, retired cricketer of Mohammedan Sporting Club, one gold ring; Fani Mitra, one time well known footballer and boxer, three gold medals and a gold souvenir; Bimal Mukherjee, for his father the late Moni Mukherjee, member of the 1911 Mohun Bagan team, one gold medal. Ibid., pp. 37–38.

25. The volumes of *Indian Olympic News* for late 1962 carry lovely pictures of film stars holding cricket bats as they gather for the game.

26. 'Sportsmen Come Forward', editorial in *Indian Olympic News*, November 1962, Vol. 1, No, 8, p. 3.

27. Quoted in 'To the National Defence Fund', *Indian Olympic News*, December 1962, Vol. 1, No. 9, p. 37.

28. See Stephen Cohen, *The Indian Army: Its Contribution to the Development of a Nation* (Berkeley: University of California Press, 1971).

29. Ramachandra Guha, *India After Gandhi: The History of the World's Largest Democracy* (New Delhi: Picador, 2007).

30. 'Services Lead the Way', *Indian Olympic News*, July 1962, Vol. 1, No. 4, pp. 6–7.

31. Interview with Brig (retd.) Rakesh Mehta, former commander, Territorial Army, Western Command; former DDG Training and Logistics, National Cadet Corps, 25 January 2008. (Full disclosure: Brigadier Mehta is Nalin Mehta's father)

32. 'Services Lead the Way', *Indian Olympic News*, July 1962, Vol. 1, No. 4, p. 7.

33. Major General A.A. Rudra in the foreword of Dhyan Chand's biography, *Goal*, published in *Sport and Pastime*, 1952. The book has been digitized and is available in http://www.bharatiyahockey.org/granthalaya/goal/, accessed 29 September 2007.

34. Steven W. Pope, 'An Army of Athletes: Playing Fields, Battlefields, and the American Military Sporting Experience, 1890–1920', *Journal of Military History*, Vol. 59, No. 3., July 1995, p. 435.

35. Ibid., p. 436.

36. Ibid.

37. Ibid.

38. Dan Allen Willey, 'The Spirit of Sport in the Army', *Harper's Weekly*, 50, 1906, pp. 1,100–01.

39. Maj. Gen. (Retd) D. Bannerjee, 'Manpower Reduction in the Army', Article No.53, Jan 27, 1998, Institute of Peace and Conflict Studies. http://www. ipcs.org/printArticle.jsp? kValue=53, accessed 30 January 2008.

40. Ibid. In this context also see Lt Gen. Vijay Oberoi, *Army 2020* (New Delhi: Knowledge World, 2005).

41. In a clear reflection of the Army's social base, 60% of the officers commissioned from 2001–2 004 came from families with an income of less than Rs 10,000 a month. The figures are from Indian Military Academy, Dehradun. News reports compiled by the author for New Delhi Television. Broadcast on 17/12/200 and 14/6/2004 respectively.

42. Data on Data on Army's manpower shortage in 2019 is from Indian Defence News, 'Indian Army Short of 7,399 Officers and 38, 235 Soldiers: Defence Minister', 25 June 2019, http://www.indiandefensenews.in/2019/06/indian-army-short-of-7399-officers-and.html.

43. The information on 31 Armoured Division is gleaned from a senior officer who was serving in the division at the time but does not want to be named for obvious reasons.

44. AFP, 'Olympic history for India, UAE', 18 August 2004, http://www.abc. net.au/sport/content/200408/s1178859.htm.

45. He was the cadet sergeant major of the Echo squadron at the NDA. Vibhay Sharma, 'A Sure Shot', *The Tribune*, 21 August 2004, http://www. tribuneindia. com/2004/20040821/saturday/main1.htm.

46. AFP, 'Olympic history for India, UAE', 18 August 2004, http://www.abc. net.au/sport/content/200408/s1178859.htm.

47. 'A Sure Shot', the Tribune, 21 August 2004, http://www.tribuneindia. com/2004/20040821/saturday/main1.htm.

48. Prabhjot Singh, 'At Last a Silver Lining', the Tribune, 21 August 2004, http://www.tribuneindia.com/2004/20040821/saturday/main1.htm.

49. Emphasis is ours. Quoted in 'A Sure Shot', the Tribune, 21 August 2004, http://www.tribuneindia.com/2004/20040821/saturday/main1.htm.

50. Rathore interview with Harish Kotian, 25 August 2005, http://www. rediff.com/sports/2005/aug/26sinter.htm.

51. Rajesh Mishra, 'Officer and a Gentleman', Swagat, October 2005, pp. 88–89.

52. Rajvardhan Singh Rathore, quoted in Rajesh Mishra, 'Officer and a Gentleman', Swagat, Oct. 2005, pp. 88–89.

53. Emphasis is ours. Rathore interview with Harish Kotian, 25 August 2005, http://www.rediff.com/sports/2005/aug/26sinter.htm.

54. Rajesh Mishra, 'Officer and a Gentleman', *Swagat*, October 2005, pp. 89.

55. PTI, 'Vijay Kumar Wants to Quit Indian Army', *The Economic Times*, 6 August 2012.

56. Faisal Sharif, 'Indian Army Launches Operation Olympic Medal', 4 September 2003, http://www.rediff.com/sports/2003/sep/04spec.htm.

57. Faisal Sharif, 'Indian Army Launches Operation Olympic Medal', 4 September 2003, http://www.rediff.com/sports/2003/sep/04spec.htm.

58. Col. Ajay Das, SC, Dir ALC, ADGPI. Email correspondence on 21 February 2008. We are thankful for Srinjoy Chowdhary for facilitating this data from the Army.

59. Figures from directorate general, NCC, ministry of defence, 2008.

CHAPTER 15

1. The *Times of India*, 23 July 1952.
2. Gulu Ezekiel, 'K D Jadhav- A man of bronze' in http://sify.com/sports/olympics/fullstory.php?id=13538760&page=2, accessed 12 January 2008.
3. The *Times of India*, 24 July 1952.
4. The gold medal-winning jump at London measured 50 ft 6 inches.
5. For details see, Gulu Ezekiel, 'Oh Henry', *Sportstar*, 17–23 December 2005.
6. Ibid.
7. For details on Pinto's performance see the *Times of India*, 21 July 1952.
8. The *Hindu*, 2 December 1956.
9. Ibid., 5 December 1956.
10. Interview with P.K. Banerjee, 10 January 2007.
11. The *Hindu*, 30 August
12. Ibid., 7 September 1960.
13. Interview with Milkha Singh, 28 November 2007.
14. Ibid.
15. Interview with Bruce Kidd at the University of Toronto, 25 May 2007.
16. For details see Gulu Ezekiel, 'Gurbachan Randhawa—A rare Breed' in *The Sportstar*, 8 April 2006.
17. Ibid.
18. Ibid.
19. The *Times of India*, 31 August 1972.
20. Ibid., 1 September 1972.
21. Ibid.
22. Ibid.
23. He won this race with a timing of 1.48.9 seconds. For details on this race see the *Times of India*, 16 July 1976.
24. Ibid., 25 July 1976.
25. Ibid., 26 July 1976.
26. Ibid., 26 July 1980.
27. Ibid., 28 July 1980
28. Ibid.
29. For details see The *Times of India*, 29 July 1980.
30. Ibid., 2 August 1980.

31. *The Times of India*, 29 July 1984.
32. Ibid., 6-8 August 1984.
33. Ibid., 6-10 August 1984.
34. Usha Sujit Nair, 'Government and Sport in Kerala, India', *Journal of Sport Management*, September 1993, Vol. 7, No. 3, pp. 256–62.
35. Rohit Brijnath, 'Leander—leading the way', 23 April 2006 http://news. bbc.co.uk/2/hi/south_asia/4929784.stm, accessed 10 February 2008.
36. The *Times of India*, 5 August 1996.
37. Ibid.
38. Karnam Malleswari interview published in www.rediff.com, http:// 202.54.124.133/sports/2000/oct/05malles.htm, accessed 10 February 2007.
39. Rohit Brijnath, 'He Doesn't Surrender', Sportstar, Vol 28, No. 20, 14–20 May 2005, http://www.hinduonnet.com/tss/tss2820/stories/200505140058 00900. htm.

Index

Acknowledgements

This book is the result of conversations on Indian sports over the past two decades. But it is born out of the passions of our childhoods, waking up at odd hours to catch Team India in action, cheering for the men and women who wore Indian colours and, inevitably, dealing with the heartbreaks that came with it. As children, we remember waking up at 4 am to catch the first broadcasts of the Seoul Olympics in 1988 – the first ones to be broadcast into India in colour. It is unimaginable now, in the age of smartphones, but it opened up new worlds for us, setting us off on multiple journeys that have culminated in this book.

This book is also a tribute to the sportsmen and women who have enriched Indian lives, opened up their worlds to us and squeezed in time between their schedules to talk to us about their craft, their highs, their lows and their struggles. The space here is too little to thank all of them by name, but it is necessary to mention at least a few.

In badminton, we thank Pullela Gopichand for opening his academy to us as well as for his delicious egg curry. We spent close to 100 hours talking to Gopi and trying to understand things better. And for the record, the conversations were held between 4 am and 5.30 am. That's when Gopi could make time, for the rest of his day is dedicated to training his athletes! P.V. Sindhu, Saina Nehwal, Parupalli Kashyap, H.S. Prannoy and Sai Praneeth have always been generous with their time. In shooting, the

341

thoughtful and gentlemanly Abhinav Bindra opened up his treasure trove of stories and personal experiments with excellence, as did Gagan Narang. Raninder Singh was open to taking hard questions and never hesitated in giving us the important information we needed. Vijay Kumar took time out of his police training in Palampur to speak to us on his journey as a sporting soldier. The Paralympians Deepa Malik and Devendra Jhajharia opened not only their lives to us but also their hearts and their personal turmoils. In boxing, Mary Kom always picks up the phone with warmth and never minces her words. In gymnastics, Deepa Karmakar has always been candid. In wrestling, we benefited from long conversations with Saskshi Malik, Sushil Kumar and many others.

Among sport administrators, Indian Olympic Association (IOA) President and International Hockey Federation (FIH) Chief Narendra Batra and IOA Secretary General Rajeev Mehta candidly provided us emails on the issues faced by India's hockey players at the Rio Games in 2016. Hemanta Biswa Sarma, president of the Badminton Federation of India, has been extremely supportive as was Adille J. Sumariwalla, who heads the Athletics Federation of India. Viren Rasquinha at Olympics Gold Quest set up our first conversation with Mary Kom. Deepthi Bopaiah and Nandan Kamath have been friends of ours for years and it was no surprise that both helped us with valuable information. Parth Jindal and Mustafa Ghouse invited us to Bellary and allowed us detailed insights into JSW's vision for sports. We also thank Vivek and Anil Singh of Procam for their inputs.

Uday Shankar, chairman of Star India and the president of Disney Asia-Pacific, has been a dear friend and a great source of information and perspective on sports, television and nationalism. The chapter on sporting nationalism owes a great deal to wide-ranging conversations with him over the years. Sanjay Gupta (now at Google) and Sanjog Gupta at Star have always been there to answer queries and we are grateful to both of them. Ashok Namboodri at Star is a long-time friend who has given us insights into what is going on at the regional level and how regional sports broadcast is shaping up going forward. N.P. Singh and Rajesh Kaul at Sony have explained to us how they are looking at the Tokyo Games and how interest in the Olympics has grown manifold.

Raghav Gupta of Fanatic Sports, ATR for India for Rio and Tokyo, tells us he is taking 6,000–8,000 Indians to Tokyo – a testimony to the growing viability of Olympic sports among Indian corporate houses. That corporate leaders like Sanjeev Goenka are planning on setting up an Olympic sports foundation is another indication of the changing trend.

Anthony Edgar, head of media operations at the International Olympic Committee (IOC) has always been supportive. The staff of the IOC Olympic Studies Center at Lausanne, Switzerland, helped with unlimited access to the IOC archives when we were both research fellows at the museum. We are grateful especially to current and former members of the IOC staff, Nuria Puig, Maria Bogner, Philleppe Blanchard, Ruth Beck Perrenoud and Patricia Eckert, for accommodating our requests on extremely short notice. Randhir Singh, life member of the IOC, has been a treasure of information as well.

We are also indebted to the staff of the International Olympic Academy in Olympia, Greece; Wayne Wilson, Director of the Amateur Athletic Federation, Los Angeles; the National Library in Kolkata; the National Archives and Teen Murti Library in Delhi.

We would also like to thank several senior Army officers who provided inputs to piece together the story of its role in sports. Jasprit Sahni helped us with updated numbers from the Army's Mission Olympics Wing and Rajiv Pundir with consolidating data on sports funding.

Milkha Singh, Leander Paes, P.T. Usha, Manavjit Singh, Rajyavardhan Rathore and Gulu Ezekiel were always willing to share their experiences and tell us more. Olympic journalists Digvijay Singh Deo and Vimal Mohan, who have both covered multiple Olympic Games, have always been a call away and have shared their stories and anecdotes. A special thanks to Prof. John MacAloon, Colleague at the University of Chicago, for pointing us to the IOC archive in Lausanne.

When you work on a book as critical as this, you need a good lawyer. Rajneesh Chopra does the job smilingly for us, and always pro bono.

Rajesh Kalra, member of the Olympics Task Force and chief editor of Times Internet provided insights and encouragement. Trisha Ghosal, Boria's research associate, added value because being involved with sports for years, she understands what we both wanted to say all through the book. We greatly appreciate the support of our publishers. We would also like to thank Udayan Mitra and Ananth Padmanabhan, as well as Karan Singh, for painstakingly copy-editing the manuscript. HarperCollins published our first book on this subject in 2008, then a revised edition in 2012. When we approached them about writing a new book ahead of Tokyo 2020, not only did they agree immediately but their enthusiasm to get it done fast spurred us on. We appreciate their support at every step.

Finally, we are most grateful to our families for enduring the time taken off for this book: Aisha Gooptu Majumdar, who kept saying, 'Babba, can you stop looking at your computer?', Arjun Mehta, who kept saying, 'You are always writing your chapters' and Raghav Mehta, who kept asking, 'Is this necessary?', but remained forever cheerful. Brigadier Rakesh Mehta provided invaluable inputs on the Army and read every chapter as minutely as we did.

Nitika and Sharmistha remain our biggest inspirations and also our most severe critics. To them – the rocks of our lives – we will always remain indebted.

Boria Majumdar   Nalin Mehta